Everything to Gain

BARBARA TAYLOR BRADFORD

Everything to Gain

HarperCollins*Publishers*

HarperCollins books may be purchased for educational, business, or sales promotional use. For information please write: Special Markets Department, HarperCollins Publishers, Inc., 10 East 53rd Street, New York, NY 10022.

FIRST EDITION

Designed by Nancy Singer

Library of Congress Cataloging-in-Publication Data

Bradford, Barbara Taylor, 1933–
   Everthing to gain / Barbara Taylor Bradford. — 1st ed.
     p. cm.
   ISBN 0-06-017723-3
   1. Man-woman relationships—United States—Fiction. 2. Widows—United States—Fiction. I. Title.
PS3552.R2147E94 1994
813'.54—dc20   94-13795

94 95 96 97 98 ❖/RRD 10 9 8 7 6 5

For Bob, ever true-blue, with my love

CONTENTS

PROLOGUE

Connecticut, August 1993

I have been alone for so long now, it is almost impossible for me to think in terms of living with another person again. But that is what Richard wants me to do. To live with him.

When he asked me last night to marry him, I told him I could not. Undaunted by my answer, and bravely, as is his way, he suggested we move in together. A sort of trial marriage, he said, with no strings, no commitment necessary on my part. "I'll take my chances, Mal," he said with a small, wry smile, his dark eyes anxiously holding mine.

Yet even this idea seems as out of the question to me now, this morning, as it did last night. I suppose, if I am scrupulously honest with myself, I fear the intimacy living with another human being entails. It is not so much the sexual intimacy that appalls me but the physical closeness on a day-to-day basis, the emotional bonding that weaves two people together and makes them part of each other. I am convinced I cannot handle this, and the more I think about it the more I am coming to understand truly my reaction to Richard's suggestion.

I am afraid. Afraid to make a commitment . . . afraid of caring for him too deeply . . . afraid of becoming too attached to him . . . perhaps even of falling in love with him, if, indeed, I am capable of such a strong emotion.

Fear has paralyzed me emotionally for a number of years. I am well aware of that, and so I have created a life for myself, a life alone; this has always seemed so much safer. Brick by brick by brick I have erected a wall around myself, a wall built on the foundations of my business, my work, and my career. I have done this in order to protect myself, to insulate myself from life; work has been my strong citadel for such a long time now, and it has given me exactly what I have needed these few years.

Once I had so much. I had everything a woman could possibly want. And I lost it all.

For the past five years, since that fateful winter of 1988, I have lived with pain and heartache and grief on a continuing basis. I have lived with a sorrow that has been, and still is, unendurable. And yet I have endured. I have gone on; I have fought my way up out of a terrible darkness and despair when I had hardly any strength left and when I had lost even the will to live. I have managed, somehow, to survive.

And I taught myself to live alone, have grown used to doing so, and I'm not sure that I can ever share myself again, as I once did, certainly not in the way I did in the past, in that other life which I once had.

But this is exactly what Richard is asking of me. He wants me to share my life with him and therefore to share myself. He is a good man. I don't think there is one better anywhere on this earth, and any woman would be lucky to have him. But I am not any woman. I have gone through far too much, have been scarred forever, my soul damaged irretrievably, beyond repair, so I believe. And I'm fully aware that I can never be the kind of woman he deserves, a woman who can give him her all, a woman without a past, with no heavy baggage, no burdens or sorrows weighing her down, such as I have.

The easiest thing for me, emotional cripple that I have become, would be to send Richard Markson away, to tell him *no* much more firmly than I did last night, and never see him again. Yet I cannot . . . something holds me back, prevents me from saying those words. It is Richard himself, of course, I realize that. In my own way, I do have certain feelings for him, and have come to rely on him lately, perhaps more than I care to admit.

Richard came into my life quite by accident about a year ago, not long after he rented a house near mine in this pastoral corner of northwestern Connecticut, just above Sharon near Wononpakook Lake and Mudge Pond, close to the Massachusetts border. I have always called these western highlands of Connecticut God's own country, and so I was somewhat startled when he used exactly those words to describe his appreciation of this magnificently beautiful part of the world.

I liked Richard the moment he walked into my house. On that winter's evening, over supper in my kitchen, I was convinced it was my friend Sarah Thomas with whom Richard was taken. It was not until a few weeks later that he made it perfectly clear to me *I* was the object of his interest, the one he wished to know better.

Wary, I held him at bay for a long time; then, slowly, cautiously, I allowed him to enter a small corner of my life. Yet in many ways I've withheld much of myself. So it's not without reason that I was stunned last night when he proposed to me. I promised to give him an answer today.

My eye caught the top of *The New York Times* which lay on my desk, and I read the date: Monday, August 9, 1993. I wondered if he would remember this date later, recall it as the day I rejected him, just as I remembered so many dates myself . . . markers along the path of my life that brought back so many memories when they rolled around every year.

On the spur of the moment, I reached for the phone, wanting to get it over with, and then almost instantly my hand fell away. There was no point dialing his apartment in Manhattan, since I was not sure how to couch the words I knew must be said. I didn't want to hurt him unduly; I must be diplomatic.

Suddenly irritated with myself, I sighed under my breath, impatiently pushed back my chair, and went to turn on the air conditioner. It was unusually humid this morning, the air heavy and oppressive in my office here at the back of the house. My skin was clammy, and I felt stifled, claustrophobic all of a sudden.

Returning to my desk, I sat down and stared into space, my thoughts continuing to focus on Richard. Last night he'd said I was too young to lead such a solitary existence. There's truth in this, I suppose. After all, I *am* only thirty-eight years old. Still, there are days when I feel like an old woman of eighty, older than that, even. I realize this is because of the things which have happened to me, as well as my newfound knowledge about life and people. Certainly I've learned a lot about their insensitivity and selfishness, their callousness and indifference. I've learned about evil too, firsthand; yes, and even about good. There *are* some good people in this world, those who are kind and concerned and compassionate, but not many, not really. I have come to understand only too well that for the most part we are entirely alone with our troubles and pain. I suspect I've become something of a cynic these days, as well as much wiser, more self-protective, and self-reliant than I ever was before.

A few weeks ago I railed on about the doers of evil who inhabit this planet, and Richard listened attentively, as he always does. When I finished and discovered I was on the verge of unexpected tears, he joined me on the sofa, simply took my hand in his and held it tightly. We sat together like that for a long time, surrounded by the silence, until he said finally, ever so quietly, "Don't try to understand the nature of evil, or analyze it, Mal. It's a mystery, one nobody has ever been able to fathom. Evil has touched your life, more so than it's touched most people's. You've been through hell, and I certainly have no proper words with which to console you. Anyway, words are empty, cold comfort at best. I just want you to know that I'm always there for you whenever you need me. I'm your friend, Mal."

I know I will always be grateful to him, not only for expressing those lovely sentiments that particular day, but because he did not attempt to placate me with platitudes, those meaningless words the well-meaning tend to offer when confronted with another person's pain or anger or despair. Also, I must admit, I admire Richard Markson. He is a decent human being, a man of integrity and compassion, qualities that mean a great deal to me. Although he has never been married, he has not passed through this life totally unscathed—that I know. He is thirty-nine, a year older than I, and now it strikes me, and quite forcibly, how ready he is to make a commitment, to embark on a long-term relationship. He is willing to accept everything this means. But am I? Ambivalent, uncertain, wary, scared, caught on an eddying tide of fears and deep-rooted problems, I feel completely helpless this morning, unable to think with clarity.

I snapped my eyes shut, leaned forward, and dropped my head onto the desk, realizing, as I did, that I was spiraling down into a cold funk. There was no way I could make that call to Richard, as I had promised I would. Very simply, I had nothing to say to him, no answer to give him.

The shrill ring of the telephone a few moments later brought me upright in my chair with a start, and I reached for the receiver and said, "Hello?"

"Mallory?"

"Yes."

"It's me. Richard."

"I know."

"Mal, I have to go out of town. On an assignment."

"Oh," I said, surprised by his announcement. "This is very sudden, isn't it?"

"Yes. It just came up a short while ago. The magazine's sending me to Bosnia. I'm leaving immediately. This United Nations-NATO situation is turning out to be something of a fiasco. So off I'm going to—"

"But you don't usually cover things like this, do you?" I cut in. "I mean, you don't cover *wars.*"

"Nor am I doing so now. Not really. I'm going to be writing one of my special think pieces, based on the kind of things we've all been saying about the wholesale carnage going on over there, the dithering of the Western leaders and the terrible indifference the world is showing to such human suffering." He paused, then murmured, "It's a replay of everything that happened in Nazi Germany sixty years ago . . . " His quiet, concerned voice trailed off into silence.

"It's the most hideous situation!" I exclaimed, my voice rising. "We're no more civilized now than we were in the tenth century! Nothing's changed, we've learned nothing. Man *is* rotten. *Evil.*"

"I know that, Mal," he answered, sighing imperceptibly.

Striving to adopt a more normal tone, I said, "And so you're leaving today?"

"I'll be heading for Kennedy in a couple of hours." There was a little pause, and then he said, "Mal."

"Yes, Richard?"

"Do you have an answer for me?"

I was silent for a moment or two. Eventually, clearing my throat, I said, "No, I'm afraid I don't. I'm sorry, Richard, I need time. I told you that . . . " Now it was my turn to let my voice fade away.

Richard did not say a word.

I held the phone tightly, waiting, wondering how he was going to take my negative attitude.

Suddenly, he spoke. "Perhaps when I get back from Bosnia," he said in a firm, strong voice, "you'll have good news for me, tell me what I want to hear. You will, won't you?"

"When will you be back?" I asked, not rising to the bait.

"In a week to ten days."

"Be careful, Richard. It's dangerous where you're going."

That light, careless laugh I had grown to know echoed down the wire. "I don't aim to catch a stray bullet, if that's what you're getting at. That's not part of my destiny."

"Nevertheless, just be careful."

"I will. And take care of yourself, Mal. So long."

He hung up before I could say good-bye.

After a moment or two I walked out of my office, across the back hall, and out into the garden.

I took the stone-paved path that led across the vast lawns at the back of the house, walking rapidly until I came to the ridge overlooking part of my property and the valley far beyond. Hills darkly green with lush and splendorous trees soared high above this valley, giving it some shelter from the elements in the harsh winter months. The two small houses nestled in the bed of the valley, always so forlorn in bad weather, now looked cool and inviting with their white-painted shingles and dark rooftops, their gardens bright with vivid color.

Presently I shifted my gaze, let it rest just below me. Here, at the bottom of verdant lawns sloping away from the ridge where I stood, the horses grazed contentedly in the long meadow. To the left of them, and adding to this bucolic scene, were the old barns, freshly painted dark red with white trim. To the right of the long meadow, the pond, calm and glassy as a mirror, shimmered in the sun; a family of Canada geese swam, one after the other, in a straight line across its dark surface, where water lilies, waxy and pale pink, floated in profusion.

After a short while, my eyes wandered, my glance sweeping over the resplendent rosebushes, luxuriant in full flower, then moved on to survey my vegetable garden behind its white picket fence, the cutting garden bursting with perennials in a galaxy of the gayest hues. Everything blooms so well here; how beautiful the land is, so rich, so ripe with life.

I lifted my head and looked up at the sky. It was the brightest, most piercing of blues, banked high with pure-white flossy clouds, and dazzling. I blinked several times against the coruscating light, and then I realized, suddenly, that I was crying.

As the tears ran down my cheeks unchecked, I thought of Richard's words a short while before: "I don't aim to catch a stray bullet," he had said, almost dismissively.

I shivered in the sunlight, unexpectedly cold in the sultry air. No one ever knows what life holds, I thought, what destiny has in store. I understand that better than anyone.

Five years fell away.

I stepped back into the past, into the summer of 1988, a summer which would be etched on my heart forever.

PART ONE

INDIAN MEADOWS

1

I awakened with a sudden start, as though someone had touched my shoulder, and I half expected to see Andrew standing over me as I blinked in the dim room. But he was not there. How could he be? He was in Chicago on business, and I was here in Connecticut.

Pulling the covers over me more securely, I slid farther down into the bed, hoping to fall asleep again. I soon realized there was no chance of that, since my mind had already started to race. Andrew and I had quarreled earlier in the week, and that silly little row, over something so petty I could scarcely bear to think about it now, still hovered between us.

I should have swallowed my pride and called him last night, I admonished myself. I *had* thought about it, but I had not done so. He hadn't phoned me either, as was his custom normally when he was away, and I was worried things would get blown out of all proportion; then our weekend together, which I had been so looking forward to, would be spoiled.

I'll make it right when he gets here tomorrow, I resolved. I'll apologize, even though it really wasn't my fault. I hated to have rifts with anyone I loved; it has always been that way with me.

Restlessly, I slipped out of bed and went to the window. Raising the shade, I peered out, wondering what kind of day it was going to be.

A band of clear, crystalline light was edging its way along the rim of the distant horizon. The sky above it was still ashy, cold and remote, tinged slightly with green at this early hour just before dawn broke. I shivered and reached for my cotton robe. It was cool in the bedroom, almost frosty, with the air conditioner set at sixty degrees, where I'd positioned it last night in an effort to counteract the intense July heat. I flicked it off as I left the bedroom and headed along the upstairs hallway toward the staircase.

It was dim and shadowy downstairs and smelled faintly of apples and cinnamon and beeswax and full-blown summer roses, smells which I loved and invariably associated with the country. I turned on several lamps as I moved through the silent, slumbering house and went into the kitchen; once I had put on the coffee, I swung around and made my way to the sunroom.

Unlocking the French doors, I stepped outside onto the wide, paved terrace which surrounded the house and saw that the sky had already undergone a vast change. I caught my breath, marveling as I always did at the extraordinary morning light, a light peculiar to these northern Connecticut climes. It was luminous, eerily beautiful, and it appeared to emanate from some secret source far, far below the horizon.

There were no skies like this anywhere in the world, as far as I knew, except, of course, for Yorkshire; I have come across some truly spectacular skies there, most especially on the moors.

Light has always fascinated me, perhaps because I am a painter by avocation and have a tendency to look at nature through an artist's eyes. I remember the first time I ever saw a painting by Turner, one of his masterpieces hanging in the Tate Gallery in London. I stood in front of it for a full hour, totally riveted, marveling at the incandescent light that gave the picture its breathtaking beauty. But then, capturing light on canvas so brilliantly and with such uncanny precision was part of Turner's great genius.

I don't have that kind of gift, I'm afraid; I'm merely a talented amateur who paints for pleasure. Nonetheless, there are times when I wish I could re-create a Connecticut sky in one of my paintings, get it just *right,* just *once,* and this morning was one of those times. But I knew, deep down, that I would never be capable of doing it.

After lingering for a few minutes longer on the terrace outside the sunroom, I turned and walked around the house, heading for the back. Heavy dew clung to the grass, and I lifted my nightgown and robe as I walked across the lawns, not wishing to get them drenched.

The light was changing yet again. By the time I reached the ridge overlooking the valley, the sky above me was suffused with a pale, silvery radiance; the bleak, gray remnants of the night were finally obliterated.

Sitting down on the wrought-iron seat under the apple tree, I leaned back and relaxed. I love this time of day, just before the world awakens, when everything is so quiet, so still I might be the only person alive on this planet.

I closed my eyes momentarily, listening.

There was no sound of any kind; nothing stirred, not a leaf nor a blade of grass moved. The birds were silent, sleeping soundly in the trees, and the stillness around me was like a balm. As I sat there, drifting, thinking of nothing in particular, my anxiety about Andrew began slowly to slip away.

I knew with absolute certainty that everything would be all right once he arrived and we made up; it always was whenever there had been a bit of friction between us. There was no reason why this time should be different. One of the marvelous things about Andrew is his ability to put events of today and yesterday behind him, to look forward to tomorrow. It was not in his nature to harbor a grudge. He was far too big a man for that. Consequently, he quickly forgot our small, frequently silly quarrels and differences of opinion. We are much alike in that, he and I. Fortunately, we both have the ability to move forward optimistically.

I have been married to Andrew Keswick for ten years now. In fact, next week, on the twelfth of July, we will be celebrating our wedding anniversary.

We met in 1978, when I was twenty-three years old and he was thirty-one. It was one of those proverbial whirlwind romances, except that ours, fortunately, did not fizzle out as so many do. Our relationship just grew better and better as time went on. That he swept me off my feet is a gross understatement. I fell blindly, madly, irrevocably in love with him. And he with me, as I was eventually to discover.

Andrew, who is English, had been living in New York for seven years when we met. He was considered to be one of the boy wonders of Madison Avenue, one of those naturals in the advertising business who can make an agency not only fabulously successful but incredibly famous as well, attracting a flock of prestigious multinational clients. I worked in the copy department of the same agency, Blau, Ames, Braddock and Suskind, and at the time, despite my lowly position, I rather fancied myself a writer of slick but convincing advertising copy.

Andrew Keswick seemed to agree.

If his compliments about my work went to my head, then he himself went straight to my heart. Of course, I was very young then, and even though I was a graduate of Radcliffe, I think I was most probably rather naïve for my educational background, age, and upbringing. I was a slow starter, I suppose.

In any event, Andrew captivated me entirely. Despite his brilliance and his standing on Madison Avenue, I soon came to realize that he was not in the least bit egotistical. Quite the opposite, in fact. He was unassuming, even modest for a man of his considerable talents; also, he had a great sense of fun and a dry humor which was often rather self-deprecating.

To me he was a dashing and sophisticated figure, and his very Englishness, as well as his mellifluous, cultivated voice set him apart. Medium of height and build, he had pleasant, clean-cut looks, dark brown hair, and candid eyes set wide apart. In fact, his eyes were his most arresting feature, of the brightest blue and thickly lashed. I don't think I've ever before seen eyes so vividly blue, nor would I ever again, except years later, in Clarissa and Jamie, our six-year-old twins.

Every young woman in the advertising agency found Andrew immensely attractive, but it was I whom he eventually singled out for special attention. We began to go out together, and at once I discovered that I was completely at ease with him; I felt comfortable, very natural in his presence. It was as though I had known him forever, yet there was so much that intrigued me about him and his life before we met, so much to learn about him.

Andrew and I had been seeing each other for only two months when he whisked me off to London for a long weekend to meet his mother. Diana Keswick and I became friends instantly, actually within the first hour of knowing each other. You could say we fell in love, and that is the way it has been between us ever since.

To some people, the term "mother-in-law" inevitably conjures up the image of an enemy, a woman who is overly possessive of her son and in competition with his wife for his attention and affection. But not Diana. She was lovely to me from the moment we met—a female Andrew. Or rather, I should say, Andrew is a male version of his mother. In a variety of different ways, she has proved to be loyal and devoted to me; I truly love, respect, and admire her. Many qualities make her unique in my eyes, not the least of which is her warm and understanding heart.

That weekend in London, which was actually my first trip to England, remains vivid in my mind to this very day. We had only been there for twenty-four hours when Andrew asked me to marry him. "I love you very much," he'd said, and taking hold of me, he had pulled me close and continued in that beautiful voice of his, "I can't imagine my life without you, Mal. Say you'll marry me, that you'll spend the rest of your life with me."

Naturally I said I would. I told him that I loved him as much as he loved me, and we celebrated our engagement by taking his mother to dinner at Claridge's on Sunday night before flying back to New York on Monday morning.

On the return journey, I kept glancing surreptitiously at the third finger of my left hand, admiring the antique sapphire ring gleaming on it. Andrew had given me the ring just before we had gone out to our celebration dinner, explaining that it had belonged first to his grandmother and then to Diana. "My mother wants you to have it now," he said, "and so do I. You'll be the third Keswick wife to wear it, Mal." He smiled in that special, very loving way of his as he slipped it on my finger. And in the next few days, every time I looked at it, an old-fashioned phrase sprang into my mind: "With this ring we pledge our troth." And indeed we had.

Twelve weeks after our first dinner date, Andrew Keswick and I were married at Saint Bartholomew's Church on Park Avenue. The only person who was not entirely overjoyed by this sudden union was my mother. Liking Andrew very much though she did and approving of him, she was nonetheless filled with disappointment about the extreme hastiness of the nuptials. "Everyone is going to think it's a shotgun wedding," she kept muttering, throwing me piercing glances as she rushed to have the invitations engraved and hurriedly planned a reception to be held at the Pierre Hotel on Fifth Avenue.

My glaring eyes and stern, obstinate mouth must have warned her off, warned her not to ask if I *was* pregnant, which I wasn't, by the way. But my mother deems me impractical, has for years characterized me as an artistic dreamer, a lover of poetry, books, music, and painting, with my head forever in the clouds.

Some of what she says was true. Yet I am also much more pragmatic than she could ever imagine; my feet have always been firmly planted on the ground, despite what she thinks. We married quickly simply because we wanted to be together, and we saw no reason to wait, to drag out a long engagement.

Not all brides enjoy their weddings. I loved mine. I was euphoric throughout the church ceremony and the reception. After all, it *was* the most important day of my life; but furthermore, I had also managed to outwit my mother and get my own way in everything. This was no mean feat, I might add, when it came to social situations.

By my own choice, and with Andrew's acquiescence, the whole affair was tiny. Both our mothers were present, of course, as well as a few relatives and friends. Andrew's father was dead. Mine wasn't, although my mother behaved as though he was, inasmuch as he had left her some years before and gone to live in the Middle East. In consequence, she thought of him as nonexistent.

But exist for me he did, and very much so. We corresponded on a regular basis and spent as much time together as we could, whenever he came to the States. And he flew to New York to give away his only daughter. Much to my astonishment, my mother was pleased he had made this paternal gesture. And so was I, although I had expected nothing less. The thought of getting married without him by my side as I walked down the aisle had appalled me. Once Andrew and I became engaged, I had called him in Saudi Arabia, where he was at the time, to tell him my good news. He had been overjoyed for me.

Even though my mother barely spoke to my father the entire time he was in Manhattan, she at least behaved in a civilized manner when they were together in public. But, not unnaturally, he departed as soon as it was decent to do so, once the reception at the Pierre was drawing to a close. My father, an archaeologist, seems to prefer the past to the present, so he had rushed back to his current dig.

He had fled my mother permanently when I was eighteen. I had gone off to Cambridge, Massachusetts, and my new life at Radcliffe College, and it was as though there was no longer a good reason for him to stay in the relationship, which had become extremely difficult for him to sustain. That they have never divorced I've always found odd; it is something of a mystery to me, given the circumstances.

We left the wedding reception together, my father and I and my bridegroom, and rode out to Kennedy Airport in one of the grand stretch limousines my mother had hired. Just before we headed in different directions to catch our planes to different parts of the world, he had hugged me tightly, and as we said our good-byes, he had whispered against my hair, "I'm glad you did it your way, Mal, had the kind of wedding *you* wanted, not the big, splashy bash your mother would have preferred. You're a maverick like me. But then, that's not half bad, is it? Always be yourself, Mal, always be true to yourself."

It had pleased me that he'd said that, about being a maverick like he was. We had been very close since my childhood, an emotional fact that I suspect has been a constant irritant to my mother. I don't believe she understood my father, not ever in their entire life together. Sometimes I've wondered why they married in the first place; they are such opposites, have come from worlds that are completely different. My father is from an intellectual family of academics and writers, my mother from a family of affluent real estate developers of some social standing, and they have never shared the same interests.

Yet something must have attracted Edward Jordan to Jessica Sloane and vice versa, and they must have been in love, or thought they were, for marry they did in 1953. They brought me into the world in May of 1955, and they stayed together until 1973, struggling through twenty years of bickering and quarreling, punctuated by stony silences that lasted for months on end. And there were long absences on the part of my father, who was always off to the Middle East or South America, seeking the remains of ancient civilizations lost in the mists of antiquity.

My father aside, my mother has never understood me, either. She is not remotely conscious of what I'm about, what makes me tick. But then, my mother, charming and sweet though she can be, has not been blessed with very much insight into people.

I love my mother, and I know she loves me. But for years now, ever since I was a teenager, I've found her rather trying to be with. Unquestionably, there is a certain shallowness to her, and this is something which dismays me. She is forever concerned with her social standing, her social life, and her appearance. Not much else interests her, really. Her days revolve around her dressmaker, hair and manicure appointments, and the luncheons, dinners, and cocktail parties to which she has been invited.

To me it seems such an empty, meaningless life for any woman to lead, especially in this day and age. I am more like my father, inasmuch as I am somewhat introspective and serious-minded; I'm concerned, just as he is, about this planet we inhabit and all that is happening on it and to it.

In many ways, the man I married greatly resembles my father in character. Like Daddy, Andrew *cares,* and he is honorable, strong, straightforward, and dependable. *True-blue* is the way I categorize them both.

Andrew is my first love, my only love. There will never be anyone else for me. We will be with each other for the rest of our lives, he and I. This is the one great constant in my life, one which sustains me. Our children will grow up, leave us to strike out on their own as adults, have families of their own one day. But Andrew and I will go on into our twilight years together, and this knowledge comforts me.

Suddenly, I felt the warmth of the sun on my face as its rays came filtering through the branches of the big apple tree, and I pushed myself up from the wrought-iron seat where I sat. Realizing that it was time for the day to begin, I walked back to the house.

It was Friday, the first of July, and I had no time to waste today. I had planned a special weekend for Andrew, Jamie, and Lissa, and my mother-in-law, who was visiting us from England, as she did every year. Monday, the Fourth of July, was to be our big summer celebration.

2

As I approached the house, I could not help thinking how beautiful it looked this morning, gleaming white in the bright sunlight, set against a backdrop of mixed green foliage under a sky of periwinkle blue.

Andrew and I had fallen in love with Indian Meadows the minute we set eyes on it, although it wasn't called Indian Meadows then. It didn't have a name at all.

Once we had bought it, the first thing I did was to christen it with a bottle of good French champagne, much to Andrew's amusement. Jamie and Lissa, on the other hand, were baffled by my actions, not understanding at all until I explained about ships and how *they* were christened in exactly the same way. "And so why not a house," I had said, and they had laughed gleefully, tickled by the whole idea of it. So much so that they had wanted their own bottle of Veuve Clicquot to break against the drainpipe as I had done, but Andrew put a stop to that immediately. "One bottle of good champagne going down the drain is enough for one day," he quipped, laughing hilariously at his own joke. I'd rolled my eyes to the ceiling but couldn't resist flashing a smile at him as I appeased the twins, promising them some cooking wine with which to do their own house christening the following day.

As for the name, I culled it from local lore, which had it that centuries ago Indians had lived in the meadows below the hill upon which our house was built. And frequently, when I am standing on the ridge looking down at the meadows, I half close my eyes and, squinting against the light, I can picture Pequot squaws, their braves, and their children sitting outside their wigwams, with horses tethered nearby and pots cooking over open fires. I can almost smell the pungent wood smoke, hear their voices and laughter, the neighing of the horses, the beat of their drums.

Highly imaginative of me, perhaps, but it *is* a potent image and one which continues to persist. Also, it pleases me greatly to think that I and my family live on land favored centuries ago by Native Americans, who no doubt appreciated its astonishing beauty then as we do today.

We found the house quite by accident. No, that's not exactly true, when I look back. The house found us. That is what *I* believe, anyway, and I don't suppose I will ever change my mind. It reached out to us like a living thing, and when for the first time we stepped over the threshold into that lovely, low-ceilinged entrance hall, I knew at once that it would be ours. It was as though it had been waiting for us to make it whole, waiting for us to make it happy again. And this we have done. Everyone who visits us is struck by the feeling of tranquility and happiness here, the warm and welcoming atmosphere that pervades throughout, and which envelopes everyone the moment they come through the front door.

But in June of 1986 I had no idea that we would finally find the house of our dreams, or any house, for that matter. We had looked for such a long time for a weekend retreat in the country, and without success. And so we had almost given up hope of ever finding a suitable place to escape to from New York. The houses we had viewed in various parts of Connecticut had been either too small and pokey, or too large, too grand, and far too expensive. Or so threadbare it would have cost a fortune to make them habitable.

That particular weekend, Andrew and I were staying with friends in Sharon, an area we did not know very well. We had taken Jamie and Lissa to Mudge Pond, the town beach, for a picnic lunch on the grassy bank that ran in front of the narrow strip of sand and vast body of calm, silver-streaked water beyond.

Later, as we set out to return to Sharon, we inadvertently took a wrong turn and, completely lost, drove endlessly around the hills above the pond. As we circled the countryside, trying to get back to the main highway, we unexpectedly found ourselves at a dead end in front of a house.

By mistake, we had gone up a wide, winding driveway, believing it to be a side road which would lead us back, we hoped, to Route 41. Startled, Andrew brought the car to a standstill. Intrigued by the house, we stared at it and then at each other, exchanging knowing looks. And in unison we exclaimed about its charm, which was evident despite the sorry signs of neglect and disuse which surrounded it.

Made of white clapboard, it had graceful, fluid lines and was rather picturesque, rambling along the way it did on top of the hill, set in front of a copse of dark green pines and very old, gnarled maples with great spreading branches. It was one of those classic colonial houses for which Connecticut is renowned, and it had a feeling of such mellowness about it that it truly captured our attention.

"What a shame nobody cares enough about this lovely old place to look after it properly, to give it a fresh coat of paint," Andrew murmured, and opening the door, he got out of the car. Instructing Jenny, our English au pair, to stay inside with the children, I quickly followed my husband.

In a way I cannot explain, certainly not in any rational sense, the house seemed to beckon us, pull us toward it, and we found ourselves hurrying over to the front door, noticing the peeling paint and tarnished brass knocker as we did. Andrew banged the latter, whilst I peeked in through one of the grimy windows.

Murky though the light was inside, I managed to make out pieces of furniture draped in dust cloths and walls covered with faded, rose-patterned wallpaper. There were no signs of life, and naturally no one answered Andrew's insistent knocking. "It looks totally deserted, Mal, as if it hasn't been lived in for years," he said, and after a moment, he wondered out loud, "Could it be for sale, do you think?"

As he put his arm around my shoulders and walked me back to the car, I found myself saying, "I hope it is," and I still remember the way my heart had missed a beat at the thought that it may very well be on the market.

A few seconds later, driving away down the winding road, I suddenly spotted the broken wooden sign, old and weather-worn and fallen over in the long grass. When I pointed it out to Andrew, he brought the car to a standstill instantly. I opened the door, leaped out, and sprinted across to the grass verge to look at it.

Even before I reached the dilapidated sign, I knew, deep within myself, that it would say that the house *was* for sale. And I was right.

During the next few hours we managed to find our way back to Sharon, hunted out the real estate broker's office, talked to her at length, then followed her out of town to return to the old white house on the hill, almost too excited to speak to each other, hardly daring to hope that the house would be right for us.

"It doesn't have a name," Kathy Sands, the real estate broker, remarked as she fitted the key into the lock and opened the front door. "It's always been known as the Vane place. Well, for about seventy years, anyway."

We all trooped inside.

Jamie and Lissa were carefully shepherded by Jenny; I carried Trixy, our little Bichon Frise, listening to Kathy's commentary as we followed her along the gallerylike entrance, which, Andrew pointed out, was somewhat Elizabethan in style. "Reminds me of Tudor interior architecture," he explained, glancing around admiringly. "In fact, it's rather like the gallery at Parham," he added, shooting a look at me. "You remember Parham, don't you, Mal? That lovely old Tudor house in Sussex?"

I nodded in response, smiling at the remembrance of the wonderful two-week holiday we had had in England the year before. It had been like a second honeymoon for us. After a week with Diana in Yorkshire we had left the twins with her and gone off alone together for a few days.

Kathy Sands was a local woman born and bred and a font of information about everything, including the previous owners— over the last couple of centuries at that. According to her, only three families had owned the house from the time it had been built in 1790 to the present. These were the Dodds, the Hobsons, and the Vanes. Old Mrs. Vane, who was formerly a Hobson, had been born in the house and had continued to live there after her marriage to Samuel Vane. Eighty-eight, widowed, and growing rather frail, she had finally had to give up her independence and go to live with her daughter in Sharon. And so she had put the house, which had been her home for an entire lifetime, on the market two years earlier.

"Why hasn't it been sold? Is there something wrong with it?" I asked worriedly, giving the broker one of those sharp, penetrating looks I had learned so perfectly from my mother years before.

"No, there's nothing wrong with it," Kathy Sands replied. "Nothing at all. It's just a bit off the beaten track, too far from Manhattan for most people who are looking for a weekend place. And it *is* rather big."

It did not take Andrew and me long to understand why the real estate broker had said the house was big. In actuality it was huge. And yet it had a compactness about it, was not as sprawling and spread out as it appeared to be from the outside. Although it did have more rooms than we really needed, it was a tidy house, to my way of thinking, and there was a natural flow to the layout. Downstairs the rooms opened off the long gallery, upstairs from a central landing. Because its core was very old, it had a genuine quaintness to it, with floors that dipped, ceilings that sloped, beams that were lopsided. Some of the windows had panes made of antique blown glass dating back to the previous century, and there were ten fireplaces, eight of which were in working order, Kathy told us that afternoon.

All in all, the house was something of a find, and Andrew and I knew it. Never mind that it was farther from New York than we had ever planned to have a weekend home. Somehow we would manage the drive, we reassured each other that afternoon. Andrew and I had fallen in love with the place, and by the end of the summer it was ours, as was a rather large mortgage.

We spent the rest of 1986 sprucing up our new possession, camping out in it as we did, and loving every moment. For the remainder of that summer and fall our children became true country sprites, practically living outdoors, and Trixy reveled in chasing squirrels, rabbits, and birds. As for Andrew and myself, we felt a great release escaping the tensions of the city and the many pressures of his high-powered job.

Finally, in the spring of 1987, we were able to move in properly, and then we set out taming the grounds and planting the various gardens around the house. This was some task in itself, as challenging as getting the house in order. Andrew and I enjoyed working with Anna, the gardener we had found, and Andrew discovered he had green fingers, something he had never known. Everything seemed to sprout under his hands, and in no time at all he had a rose garden, vegetable patch, and herb garden under way.

It did not take either of us long to understand how much we looked forward to leaving the city, and as the weeks and months passed we became more and more enamored of this breathtaking corner of Connecticut.

Now, as I walked through the sunroom and into the long gallery, I paused for a moment, admiring the gentle serenity of our home.

Sunlight was spilling into the hall from the various rooms, and in the liquid rafts of brilliant light thousands of dust motes rose up, trembled in the warm July air. Suddenly, a butterfly, delicately wrought, jewel-tinted, floated past me to hover over a bowl of cut flowers on the table in the middle of the gallery.

I caught my breath, wishing I had a paintbrush and canvas at hand so that I could capture the innocent beauty of this scene. But they were in my studio, and by the time I went to get them and returned, the butterfly surely would have flown away, I was quite certain of that. So I just continued to stand there, looking.

As I basked in the peacefulness of the early morning, thinking what a lucky woman I was to have all that I had, there was no possible way for me to know that my life was going to change so profoundly, irrevocably.

Nor did I know then that it was this house which would rescue me from the destructiveness within myself. It would become my haven, my refuge from the world. And in the end it would save my life.

But because I knew none of this at that moment, I walked blithely on down the gallery and into the kitchen, happy at the prospect of the holiday weekend ahead, lighthearted and full of optimism about my life and the future.

Automatically, I turned on the radio and listened to the morning news while I stood toasting a slice of bread and drinking a cup of coffee I had made earlier. I studied a long list of chores I had made the night before and mentally planned my day. Then, once I had eaten the toast, I ran upstairs to take a shower and get dressed.

3

I have red hair, green eyes, and approximately two thousand freckles. I don't think I'm all that pretty, but Andrew does not agree with me. He is forever telling me that I'm beautiful. But, of course, beauty lies in the eye of the beholder, so I've been told, and anyway, Andrew is prejudiced, I have to admit that.

All I know is that I wish I didn't have these irritating freckles. If only my skin were lily-white and clear, I could live with my vivid coloring. My unruly mop of auburn curls has earned me various nicknames over the years, the most popular being Ginger, Carrot Top, and Red, none of which I have ever cherished. Quite the opposite, in fact.

Since I have always been somewhat disdainful of my mother's preoccupation with self, I have schooled myself not to be vain. But I suspect that secretly I am, and just as much as she is, if the truth be known. But then I think that most people *are* vain, care a lot about the way they look and dress and the impression they make on others.

Now, having showered and dressed in a cotton T-shirt and white shorts, I stood in front of the mirror, peering at myself and grimacing at my image. I realized that I had spent far too long in the garden unprotected yesterday afternoon; my freckles seemed to have multiplied by the dozen.

A few fronds of hair frizzled around my temples and ears, and I sighed to myself as I slicked them back with water, wishing, as I so frequently did, that I were a pale, ethereal blonde. As far as I'm concerned, my coloring is much too vibrant, my eyes almost unnaturally green. I have inherited my coloring from my father; certainly there is no mistaking whose daughter I am. My eyes mirror his, as does my hair. Mind you, his is a sandy tone now, although it was once as fiery as mine, and his eyes are not quite as brightly green as they once were.

That's one of the better things about getting older, I think—everything starts to fade. I keep telling myself that I'm going to look like the inestimable Katharine Hepburn when I'm in my seventies. "Let's only hope so," Andrew usually remarks when I mention this little conceit of mine. And it *is* wishful thinking on my part; what woman, redheaded or not, doesn't want those lean, thoroughbred looks of hers?

Brushing back my hair, I secured it with a rubber band, then tied a piece of white ribbon around my ponytail and ran down the stairs.

My little office, where I did paperwork and household accounts, was situated at the back of the house, looking out toward the vegetable garden. Seating myself at the large, old-fashioned desk, which we had found at Cricket Hill, a local antique shop, I picked up the phone and dialed our apartment in New York.

On the third ring my mother-in-law answered with a cheery, very British "Hello?"

"It's me, Diana," I said, "and the top of the morning to you."

"Good morning, darling, and how is it out there?" she asked. Not waiting for my response, she went on, "It's frightfully hot here in the city, I'm afraid."

"I thought it would be," I answered. "And we're having the same heat wave in Connecticut. All I can say is, thank God for air-conditioning. Anyway, how are my holy terrors today?"

She laughed. "*Divine.* And I can't tell you how much I relish having them to myself for a couple of days. Thanks for that, Mal, it's so very sweet and considerate of you, letting me get to know my grandchildren in this way."

"They love you, Diana, and they enjoy being with you," I said, meaning every word. "And what are you planning to do with them?"

"I'm taking them to the Museum of Natural History, after breakfast. You know how they are about animals, and especially dinosaurs. Then I thought I'd bring them home for a light lunch, since it's so nice and cool in the flat. I promised to take them to F.A.O. Schwarz after their nap. We're going shopping for toys."

"Don't spoil them," I warned. "Doting grandmothers have been known to spend far too much money at certain times. Like when they're on holiday visits."

Diana laughed, and over her laughter I heard my daughter wailing in the background. Then Lissa said in a shrill voice, "Nanna! Nanna! Jamie's broken my bowl, and the goldfish is on the carpet. *Dying!*" The wailing grew louder, more dramatic.

"I didn't do it on purpose!" Jamie shouted.

My mother-in-law had not spoken for a moment, no doubt distracted by this sudden racket exploding around her. Now she exclaimed, "Oh, God, hang on a minute, Mallory, the fish *is* gasping. I think I'd better grab a glass of water and pop the fish in it. Won't be a tick." So saying she put the phone down, I strained to hear my children.

Jamie cried plaintively, "I'm sorry, Lissa."

"Pick up the phone and speak to your mother," I heard Diana instruct from a distance, sounding very brisk and businesslike. "She's waiting to say hello to you, darling. Go on, Lissa, speak to your mummy," my mother-in-law commanded in a tone that forbade argument.

After a moment, a small, tearful voice trickled down the wire. "Mommy, Jamie's killed my goldfish. *Poor* little fish."

"No, I haven't!" Jamie shrieked at the top of his lungs.

"Don't cry, honey," I said to Lissa, then added in a reassuring voice, "And I'm sure your goldfish isn't dead. I bet Nanna has it safely in water already. How did the bowl break?"

"It was Jamie that broke it! He banged on it with a spoon, and all the water fell out and my little fish."

"He must have been banging awfully hard to break the glass," I said. "Perhaps it was already cracked. I'm sure it was an accident, and that he didn't do it on purpose."

In the background, Jamie cried again, "I'm sorry."

Lissa said, "He *was* banging hard, Mommy. He's mean, he was trying to frighten Swellen."

"Swellen?" I repeated, my voice rising slightly. "What kind of name is that?"

"She means Sue Ellen," Diana said to me, having relieved my daughter of the phone. "And I suspect the fishbowl was defective, Mal. In any case, the goldfish is alive and kicking, or should I say *swimming,* in one of your Pyrex dishes. I'll get a goldfish bowl later, at the pet shop where I bought the goldfish yesterday. That'll make her happy."

"You don't have to bother buying a new one," I said. "There's a bowl from the florist's in the cupboard where I keep the vases. It's perfectly adequate."

"Thanks for the tip, Mal. Jamie wants to speak to you."

My son took the phone. "Mom, I didn't do it on purpose, honestly I didn't. *I didn't!*" he protested.

"Yes, you *did!*" Lissa yelled.

She must have been standing directly behind Jamie, I heard her so clearly. "I'm sure you didn't mean to break it, honey," I murmured. "But tell Lissa you're sorry again and give her a kiss. Then everything will be fine."

"Yes, Mom," he mumbled.

Because he still sounded tearful, I tried to reassure him. "I love you, Jamie,"

"I love you, too, Mom," he answered a bit more cheerfully, and then he dropped the receiver down with a clatter.

"Jamie, ask Nanna to come to the phone!" I exclaimed, then

repeated this several times to no avail. I was about to hang up when Diana finally came back on the line.

"I think peace reigns once more," she said, chuckling. "Oh, dear, I do believe I speak too soon, Mal."

A door banged; there was the sound of Trixy barking. "I guess Jenny just came back from walking the pooch," I said.

"Exactly. And I'd better prepare breakfast for my little troop here, then get the twins ready for their outing. And seriously, Mal, everything seems to be all right between them. They've kissed and made up, and Sue Ellen is happily contained in the bowl, swimming her heart out." She chuckled again. "I'd forgotten what a handful six-year-olds can be. Either that or I'm getting too old to cope."

"You, old! *Never*. And if you remember, their little spats never last long. Basically, they're very close, like most twins are."

"Yes, I do know that."

"I've loads of chores, Diana, so I must get on. I'll talk to you tonight. Have a lovely day."

"We will, and don't work too hard, Mallory dear. Bye-bye now."

"Bye," I said and hung up.

My hand rested on the receiver for a few moments, my thoughts lingering with my mother-in-law.

Diana was a sweet and caring woman, truly loving, and I've always thought it was such a shame she never remarried after Andrew's father died in 1968, when he was very young, only forty-seven. Michael Keswick, who had never been sick a day in his life, had suffered a sudden heart attack that proved fatal.

Michael and Diana, who originally hailed from Yorkshire and went to live in London after university, had been childhood sweethearts. They had married young, and Andrew had been born two years after their wedding; it had been an idyllic marriage until the day of Michael's untimely death.

Diana once told me that she had met quite a few men over the years since then, but that none of them had ever really measured up to Michael. "Why settle for second best?" she had said to me during one of our treasured moments of genuine intimacy. On another occasion, she had confided that she much preferred to be on her own, rather than having to cope with a man who didn't meet her standards, did not compare favorably with Michael.

"I'd always be making mental notes about him, passing private judgments, and it wouldn't be fair to the poor man," she had said. "Being on my own means I'm independent, my own boss, and I can therefore do what I want, when I want. I can come to New York to see all of you when the mood strikes me. I can work late every night of the week, if I so wish, and I can go up to Yorkshire whenever I feel like it. Or dash over to France on a buying trip, on the spur of the moment. I don't have to answer to anyone, I'm a free agent, and believe me, Mal, it's better this way, it really is."

I had asked her that day whether Michael had been her only love, or if she had ever fallen in love again. And she had muttered something and glanced away. Intrigued by the way she had flushed, albeit ever so slightly, and averted her head with sudden swiftness, I had been unable to resist repeating my question. After a moment's hesitation and an unexpected stiffening of her shoulders, she had finally turned her face back to mine. Her gaze had been direct, her eyes filled with the honesty I'd come to appreciate and rely on. I always knew where I stood with her, and that was important to me.

Slowly, she had said in the softest of voices, "The only man I've ever been remotely interested in on a serious level, and very strongly attracted to is . . . not free. Separated for the longest time, but not actually divorced, God knows why. And that's not good. I mean, it would be impossible for me to have a relationship with a man who was *legally* tied to another woman, even if not actually living with her. Untenable, really, and certainly no future in it."

Her shoulders had relaxed again, and she had shaken her head. "I came to the conclusion a very long time ago that I'm much better off living on my own, Mal. And I *am* happy, whatever you think. I'm at peace with myself."

Yet it has often struck me since that Diana must have moments of great sadness, of acute loneliness. But Andrew doesn't agree with me.

"Not Ma!" he had exclaimed when I first voiced this opinion. "She's busier than a one-legged toe dancer doing *Swan Lake* alone and in its entirety. She's up at the crack, behind her desk at the antique shop by six, cataloguing her stock of antiques, bossing her staff around, and floating over to Paris to buy furniture and paintings and *objets* at the drop of a hat. Not to mention wining and dining her posh clients, and fussing over us, her dearest darlings. Then there's her life in Yorkshire. She's forever racing up there to make sure the old homestead hasn't tumbled down."

Shaking his head emphatically, he had finished, "Ma, *lonely*? Never. She's the least lonely person I know."

At that time I had thought that perhaps she keeps herself so frantically busy in order not to notice her loneliness, perhaps even to assuage it. But I hadn't mentioned this to Andrew. After all, he was her son, her only child, and he ought to know her well, if anybody did. And yet there have been times over the years when I have noticed a wistful expression on Diana's face, a sadness in her eyes, a look of longing, almost. A yearning, maybe, for Michael? Or for that love who was not entirely available? I wasn't sure, and I have never had the nerve to broach the subject.

Nora startled me, and I jumped in my chair as she came crashing into my office. I sat bolt upright, gaping at her.

"Sorry I'm late, Mal," she exclaimed, striding forward and flopping down in the chair opposite my desk.

For a dainty, petite person she could certainly make a lot of noise.

"Phew! It's hot today! A real scorcher!" She fanned herself energetically with her hand and gave me a smile. Then her face dropped as she took in my expression.

"Oh, sorry, did I give you a start when I came in?"

I nodded. "You did. But then, I was miles away, I must admit. Daydreaming."

A look of incredulity swept across Nora's face. Narrowing her eyes, she uttered a dry little laugh. "Daydreaming! Not you, Mallory Keswick! That's the last thing you'd be doing. You're a human dynamo. I've never seen *you* waste a minute."

Her words amused me, but I made no comment.

Rising, I said to her, "How about a glass of iced tea, before we get down to the task of putting this house in order for the weekend?"

"Sounds good," she answered, immediately jumping up and leading the way out of the office. "I didn't stop at the market stand on the way here. It's better I buy your vegetables and fruit tomorrow, Mal. They'll be fresher for Monday's barbecue."

"That's true. Listen, are you and Eric coming? You haven't really given me a proper answer."

She swung her head, looked over her shoulder at me, gave a quick nod. "We'd love to, and thanks, Mal, for including us. It's good of you."

"Don't be so silly, you and Eric are like part of the family."

She didn't say anything, just moved on into the kitchen, but there was a small, pleased smile on her face, and I knew she was happy that I'd asked her again, that I had not taken no for an answer.

Nora, who was about forty, was a slender pixie of a woman, with unusual, prematurely silver hair, an intelligent but merry face, and silvery-gray eyes. She had been my helper for the past year and a half, almost since we had moved in, and her husband, Eric, who worked at the local lumberyard, did carpentry and outdoor chores for us on weekends. Married for nearly twenty years, they were childless, and both of them doted on the terrible twins, as I jokingly called Jamie and Lissa at times.

Nora was a practical, down-to-earth, no-nonsense woman, a real Connecticut Yankee with her feet on the ground, which made us totally compatible, since I tend to be pragmatic and plain-speaking myself.

Utterly without pretension, she refused to be called a housekeeper. "Too fancy for me," she had said the day I had hired her.

"Let's just say I'm your helper, Mal. All right if I call you Mal, isn't it?"

I had nodded, and she had continued, "It's friendlier. Anyway, that's the way it is in the country. First-name basis." She had laughed then. "*Housekeeper* sounds a bit formidable to me. Makes me think of a woman in a black dress with a grim expression and a bunch of keys tied to her belt." The silvery-colored eyes had twinkled. "Maybe I've read too many gothic novels."

As far as I'm concerned, Nora Matthews can call herself anything she wants. She is invaluable to me; I couldn't manage without her.

Pouring two glasses of iced tea, Nora remarked in her clipped way, "Fourth's going to be a lot hotter than today. Weather forecast says we're in for it. Better think about dressing cool on Monday. Lightweight all the way." She eyed my T-shirt and shorts. "You've got the right idea. Stick to that outfit for the barbecue."

"Aw, shucks, Nora, there goes my plan to wear my new cocktail dress!" I exclaimed, arranging a suitably disappointed expression on my face.

Swiftly, she glanced at me. Her brow furrowed. Nora was never absolutely certain about my humor, never knew whether I was teasing her or not.

I burst out laughing. "This is *exactly* what I intended to wear. Shorts and a T-shirt. You know very well they constitute my summer uniform."

"I guess so," she muttered.

For a split second I thought that I had offended her, teasing her in this way, but then I saw a glint of hidden laughter in her eyes, and I relaxed.

"Come on, let's get this show on the road," I said, adopting a bustling manner.

"Beds first?"

"You bet," I answered, and gulping down the last of my iced tea, I followed her out of the kitchen.

4

Four hours later I carried a turkey sandwich and a Diet Coke out to the low wall which surrounds the terrace in front of the sunroom.

Selecting a corner which was well-shaded by one of the large old maples, I sat down and took a bite of the sandwich, enjoying it. I was starving, having been up since before dawn. Also, besides changing all the bed linens, Nora and I had done a marathon job of cleaning the bathrooms and the bedrooms. The hard work had helped to give me an appetite. Not only that, I wanted to fortify myself for the rest of the day; there was still the entire downstairs to clean.

I take great pride in Indian Meadows.

I love it most of all when everything sparkles and gleams and looks perfect. Diana has always said I should have been an interior decorator. She thinks I have great talent for putting furniture and things together to create unique and attractive settings. The idea doesn't appeal to me; I don't think I would enjoy doing this kind of work for clients in the way that Diana buys antiques, paintings, and beautiful objects for the customers who patronize her prestigious antique shop in London. I am sure it would be far too frustrating, trying to please other people, not to mention convincing them that my taste is superior to theirs.

I prefer to be an amateur decorator creating a home which pleases Andrew and me, just as I paint for my own pleasure, for the satisfaction and gratification it gives me.

Nora never joins me on this wall for a picnic. Invariably, she eats her lunch inside, preferring the cool, air-conditioned interior. Certainly it is much more comfortable inside the house today; it is positively grueling out here. A great yellow orb of a sun seems to be burning a hole in the fabric of the sky, which is of such a sharp and brilliant blue it almost hurt my eyes to look at it.

The wall where I'm sitting is wide, with big flat stones along the top, and it is very old, built by hand by a local stonemason many years ago.

In Yorkshire, drystone walling, as it is called, is an ancient craft. All of the stones have to be perfectly balanced, one on top of the other, so that they can remain tightly wedged together without the benefit of cement. It is done by the crofters on the Yorkshire moors and in the lush green dales, but it is a dying craft, Diana says, almost a lost art. I'm sure it is here, too, and more's the pity, since these ancient walls are beautiful, have such great character.

I am extremely partial to this particular wall on our property, mostly because it is home to a number of small creatures. I know for a fact that two chipmunks live inside its precincts, as well as a baby rabbit and a black snake. Although I know the chipmunks well and have spotted the bunny from time to time, I have never actually seen the snake. But our gardener, Anna, has, and so have the twins. At least, that is what they claim, most vociferously.

Ever since my childhood, I have loved nature and the wild creatures who inhabit the countryside, and I have encouraged Jamie and Lissa to respect all living things, to treasure the animals, birds, and insects that frequent Indian Meadows.

Unconsciously, and very often without understanding what they are doing, some children can be terribly cruel, and it always makes me furious when I see them hurting small, defenseless animals, pulling wings off butterflies, grinding their heels into earthworms and snails, throwing stones at birds. I made my mind up long before the twins were born that no child of mine would ever inflict pain on any living thing.

To make nature more personal, to bring it closer to them, I invented stories about our little friends who inhabit the garden wall. I tell Jamie and Lissa tales about Algernon, the friendly black snake, who has a weakness for chocolate-covered cherries and wishes he owned a candy store; about Tabitha and Henry, the two chipmunks, married with no children, who want to adopt; and about Angelica, the baby bunny rabbit, who harbors an ambition to be in the Fifth Avenue Easter Parade.

Jamie and Lissa had come to love these stories of mine; they can't get enough of them, in fact, and I have to repeat them constantly. In order to satisfy my children, I'm forever inventing new adventures, which entails quite a stretch of the imagination on my part.

It's struck me several times lately that perhaps I should write down the stories and draw pictures to illustrate them. Perhaps I will, but only for Jamie and Lissa. This idea suddenly took hold of me. What a wonderful surprise it would be for the twins if I created a picture book for each of them, and put the books in their Christmas stockings.

I groaned inside; how ridiculous to be thinking of Christmas on this suffocatingly hot summer's day. But the summer will soon be drawing to an end; it always does disappear very quickly after July Fourth weekend. Then Thanksgiving will be upon us before I can blink, with Christmas not far behind.

This year we are planning to spend Christmas in England. We will be staying with Diana at her house in West Tanfield in the Yorkshire dales. Andrew and I are really looking forward to it, and the children are excited. They are hoping it will snow so that they can go sledding with their father. He's promised to take them on the runs he favored when he was a child; and he is planning to teach them to skate, providing Diana's pond has frozen solid.

I was ruminating on our winter vacation ten minutes later when Nora poked her head around the sunroom door. "It's Sarah on the phone," she called.

"Thanks," I called back, but she had already disappeared.

I slid off the wall and went inside. Flopping down on a chair, I picked up the phone, which sat on a nearby end table. "Hi, Sarah. When are you coming out here?"

"I don't think I will be coming," she replied.

I thought she sounded woeful, a little glum for her; she was normally so cheerful.

"What's wrong?" I asked, gripping the phone a bit tighter, instinctively aware that all was not right.

We had been best friends all of our lives, ever since we were babies in prams being walked on Park Avenue by our mothers, who were also friends. We had attended the same kindergarten and then Miss Hewitt's. Later on we had gone off to Radcliffe together, and we have always been extremely close, inseparable. I know Sarah Elizabeth Thomas as well as I know myself, and so I understood that she was upset about something.

Since she had remained totally silent, I asked again, more insistently, "What's the matter?"

"It's Tommy. We had a foul row last night, the worst we've ever had, and he's just informed me, by phone no less, that it's over between us. Finished, terminated, kaput. He doesn't want to see me . . . ever again. And he says he's going to L.A. this afternoon. To be succinct, Mal, I've been dumped. *Dumped! Me!* Can you imagine that! It's never happened to me before."

"I know. You've always done the dumping. And I'm sorry you're upset. I realize you cared about Tommy. On the other hand, I've always felt—"

"You don't have to say it," she cut in softly. "I know you never liked him. You were always a bit wary of him. I guess you were right. As usual. How come you know men better than I do? Don't bother to answer that. Listen, recognizing that Tommy's a bit of a louse doesn't make it any easier for me. I sort of—liked him."

Her voice had grown tiny, and I knew she was on the verge of tears.

"Don't cry, it'll be all right, Sash," I soothed, using the nickname I had given her when we were children. "Admittedly it's cold comfort, but it *is* better this way. Honestly. Tommy Preston the third isn't worth weeping over. The break was bound to happen sooner or later. And preferably now than later. Think how awful it would be if you married him and then this kind of thing happened—"

"He did ask me," Sarah interrupted. "Half a dozen times, to be exact."

There was a sniffling sound, and then I heard her blowing her nose.

"I know he proposed. You've told me about it—numerous times, actually," I muttered. "And I'm glad you were cautious and didn't plunge. But why aren't you coming for the weekend? I don't understand."

"I can't come by myself, Mal. I'll feel like a spare wheel."

"That's ridiculous! You'll be with me, your very, *very* best friend, and Andrew, who loves you like a sister. And your godchildren, who adore you. And Diana, who thinks you're the greatest thing since Typhoo tea."

"Flattery will get you everywhere, but then, you know that," she said, and I heard the laughter surfacing in her voice. "However, I think I'll stay in Manhattan and lick my wounds."

"You can't do that!" I protested, my voice rising. "You'll only pig out on ice cream and all those fattening things you love to eat when you're upset. And just think of the hard work you've put in, losing ten pounds. Besides, it's going to be hotter than hell in Manhattan. Nora told me they predict a hundred and twenty degrees in the shade."

"I'm afraid *I* take Miss Nora's weather forecasts with a grain of salt, Mal."

"Honestly, it *is* going to be hot in the city. I heard it on television myself. Last night. Just think how much cooler it will be out here in Sharon. And then there's the swimming pool, some shady corners in the garden. You know how much you love it here. This is your second home, for heaven's sake."

"Nevertheless, at the moment I think I prefer the blistering sidewalks of Manhattan, the lonely confines of my stifling apartment. At least I can wallow unashamedly in my memories of Tommy," she intoned dramatically. "My lost love, my greatest love."

Her theatricality, such an integral part of her personality, was coming through all of a sudden, and I was relieved. It told me she wasn't quite so heartsick as she had first made herself out to be at the outset of our conversation. I began to chuckle.

"Don't you dare laugh at me, Mallory Christina Jordan Keswick. Stop laughing, I tell you!" she cried indignantly. "I'm heartbroken. *Heartbroken.*"

Still laughing, I whooped, "That's a load of cod's wallop!" This was one of Andrew's favorite expressions, and I had made it my own over the years. "You're no more heartbroken about him than I am. Your pride's injured, that's all it is. I'll tell you something else, I bet if the truth be known, that . . . that . . . that little creep was always intending to go off to the West Coast for the July Fourth weekend. To see his family. You've always said he dotes on his mother and adores his sisters and constantly complains about their recent move to California."

"Oh." She said nothing more for a moment, then she murmured thoughtfully, "I must admit, I hadn't thought of that." There was another brief pause. I could visualize her digesting my point. "But we *did* have a terrible row, Mal."

"No doubt one he manufactured," I replied sharply. I had never liked Thomas Preston III. An Eastern seaboard uptight WASP, he was tight with a buck as well as his emotions, high on snobbery and low on brains. He was employed by a famous private merchant bank as a vice president only because the bank bore his family name and was run by his uncle. My beautiful, generous, talented, loving Sarah deserved much better; she deserved the best. Personally, I thought Tommy Preston was the worst, a poor excuse for a man. He wasn't even all that good-looking; at least I could've understood it if she'd fallen for a pretty face.

I took a deep breath. "So, when are you coming out to Connecticut? Tonight or tomorrow?"

"I've just arranged to take one of my buyers to dinner tonight. I'll come sometime tomorrow, is that okay?"

"It sure is, Sashy darling. July Fourth wouldn't be quite the same without you."

5

After Nora had left for the day, I toured the house as I generally do on Fridays, checking that everything was in order in all of the rooms.

I was happy with the way things looked, and even though I say so myself, the house *is* beautiful; I stood in the doorway of each room, admiring what I saw, taking the most intense pleasure and gratification from our home.

In the sitting room, the antiques I had so lovingly waxed and polished that morning gleamed in the soft, early-evening light, the smooth wood surfaces darkly ripe and mellow with age. The pieces of old silver on display in the small dining room glittered brightly on the sideboard, and everywhere there was the sparkle of mirrors, the shine of newly cleaned windows. The many flowering plants and vases of cut flowers, which I had placed in various strategic spots throughout the house, added splashes of intense color against the cool, pale backgrounds, and their mingled fragrances filled the air with sweetness.

There was a lovely feeling of well-being about the house tonight. It was completely ready for the holiday weekend, comfortable, warm, and welcoming, truly a home. All that was missing was my family. But they would be with me tomorrow morning, to enjoy the house and everything in it and to fill it with their happy voices and laughter. I could hardly wait for Andrew, the twins,

Diana, and Jenny to arrive. Andrew was going to drive them out very early, at least so he had said before leaving for Chicago at the beginning of the week.

After a few more moments of wandering around scrutinizing everything, I ran upstairs to our bedroom. Stripping off my clothes, I took a quick shower, toweled myself dry, put on a pair of white cotton trousers and a clean white T-shirt, then tied my hair in a ponytail with a red ribbon.

Later I would make myself a bowl of spaghetti and a green salad, but right now I wanted to relax after my hard day's work. I would call Diana to check on her and the twins and then settle down with a book.

There is a long, low room opening off one end of our bedroom, and I went into it now. I had made it mine right from the beginning when we first bought the house. It is such a peculiar shape and size, I can't imagine what it was ever used for before, but I have turned it into a comfortable sitting room, my private inner sanctum, where I sit and think, listen to music, watch television, or read.

Because of its odd shape and size, I painted it white with just the merest hint of green in the paint mix. The pale, apple-green carpeting I chose matches the green-and-white plaid I found for floor-length draperies, the sofa, and armchairs. There are floor-to-ceiling bookshelves along one wall; pretty porcelain lamps grace two tables, skirted in pale-green silk, which stand on either side of the sofa. Some of my watercolors line the walls, and above the sofa hangs the portrait in oils of the twins I painted two years ago. Another oil, this one of Andrew, takes pride of place above the mantelpiece, and so my husband and children keep me company here the entire time, smiling out at me from their gilded frames.

All in all, it's a charming room, pleasant and inviting, with its wash of white and pale greens, a room which benefits from a great deal of sunshine in the afternoons because of its southern exposure. Yet it has a restful feeling to it, especially at this hour of the day when the sun has set and twilight begins to descend. It is one of my favorite corners of Indian Meadows, and as with the rest of the house, decorating it was a labor of love on my part.

Sitting down at the country French *bureau plat,* I pulled the phone toward me and dialed our apartment in New York. After speaking briefly to Diana, I wished my children a loving good night, told them I would see them tomorrow morning, and hung up.

Rising, I crossed to the sofa, stretched out on it, and picked up the book I was reading. This was two novels in one volume, *Cheri* and *The Last of Cheri* by Colette; I had always had a love of her books, and lately I had begun to read her again. And so quickly I found my place, looking forward to becoming a captive of this author's imagination once more.

I had read only a couple of pages when I heard the sound of a car in the driveway. Putting the book down, I got up and hurried to the window, glancing at the carriage clock on the mantelpiece as I did, asking myself who it could be. Very few people came calling on me unannounced, especially at night.

Although the bright summer sky had dimmed considerably, it was still light, and much to my surprise, I saw Andrew alighting from the back of the car, his briefcase in his hand. I dropped the lace curtain, flew out of the room, and tore down the staircase at breakneck speed.

We met, he and I, in the long entrance gallery and stood staring at each other.

He had his luggage with him, and I exclaimed, "You came straight from the airport!" My surprise at his sudden unexpected arrival was quite evident.

"That's right, I did," he answered, eyeing me carefully.

I gazed back at him, searching his face, trying to determine his frame of mind; I wondered if he was still angry with me. I saw nothing but love and warmth reflected there, and I knew instantly that everything was all right between us.

My eyes remained fixed on his face as I asked, "But what about

Jamie and Lissa, and your mother and Jenny? How are they going to get out here?"

"I've arranged for a car and driver to pick them up tomorrow morning, very early," he explained, and moving toward me, he took hold of me, drew me into his arms, and embraced me tightly. "You see, I fancied an evening alone with my wife."

"Oh, I'm so glad you did," I exclaimed, clinging to him harder.

We stood holding each other like this without speaking for a second or two. Eventually I said quietly, "I'm sorry for being petty about Jack Underwood, or rather, about his girlfriend. I don't mind if they come for the Fourth, really I don't, Andrew."

"I was petty too, Mal. Anyway, as it turns out, Jack can't come after all. He has to fly to Paris on business, and Gina wouldn't dream of coming alone. Listen, I'm sorry we quarreled. It was my fault entirely."

"No, it was mine," I protested, genuinely meaning this.

"Mine," he insisted.

We pulled apart, looked at each other knowingly, and burst out laughing.

Bending toward me, Andrew kissed me lightly on the mouth, then taking hold of my arm, he said, "Let's have a drink, shall we?" And so saying he propelled me in the direction of the kitchen.

"What a good idea," I agreed and looked up at him, smiling broadly, happy that all was as it should be between my husband and me and that he and I were about to spend an evening alone together for once.

When we got to the kitchen, Andrew slipped off his jacket, undid his tie, and threw both on a chair. I took ice out of the refrigerator and made two tall glasses of vodka and tonic with wedges of lime, and handed one to him.

"Cheers, darling," he said, clinking his drink against mine.

"Cheers," I answered, and I couldn't resist ogling him over the rim of my glass. Then I winked.

He laughed, gave me a quick peck on the cheek, and said, "Shall we sit on the terrace?"

"It's a bit hot out there," I answered, then seeing his face drop in disappointment, I added, "Oh, but why not, the garden's so pretty at this time of day."

"My grandmother used to call this hour the gloaming," he remarked as we walked through the sunroom heading for the terrace beyond the French doors. "It's an old north-country word, I think. Or perhaps it's a Scottish term. You know my mother's mother was originally from Glasgow, before she went to live in Yorkshire, after her marriage to Grandfather Howard. That's why she dressed my mother in so much tartan when she was little, and then me." He chuckled. "She loved me to wear a kilt and a sporan and a little black velvet jacket. She always chose the Seaforth Highlander's dress tartan. Her father, my great-grandfather, had been in the Seaforths, you see."

"Yes, you've told me all about your Scottish ancestry before," I said, glancing at him over my shoulder.

He grinned at me. "Oh, sorry. I do seem to have a bad habit of repeating family history."

"It's not a *bad* habit," I said, "just a habit, and I don't mind."

Once outside we settled down at the circular table with the big white canvas market umbrella, where we usually ate meals in the summer months. We sipped our drinks and were silent for a while, comfortable in this silence, as happily married people frequently are, content simply to be together. Words were not necessary. We communicated without them, as we always had. Andrew and I usually seemed to be on the same wavelength, and often he would say something I had been thinking only a few seconds before, or vice versa. I found that uncanny.

It was not as stiflingly hot outside as I'd expected it to be, now that the sun had gone down. Although the air was balmy, there was a soft breeze moving through the trees, rustling the leaves. Otherwise everything was absolutely quiet, as tranquil as it always was up here atop our lovely Connecticut hill.

The lawn which flowed away from the terrace wall on this side of the house sloped down to a copse of trees; beyond were protected wetlands and a beaver dam. Soaring above the copse and the stretch of water were the foothills of the Berkshires covered with trees densely massed and of a green so dark they were almost black tonight under that midsummer sky now completely faded. Its periwinkle blue had turned to smoky gray edging into anthracite, with wisps of pink and lilac, saffron and scarlet bleeding into one another along the rim of those distant hills.

Andrew lolled back in the chair and breathed deeply, letting out a long, contented sigh. "God, it's so great here, Mallory. I couldn't get back fast enough . . . to you and this place."

"I know." I looked at him through the corner of my eye and said in the quietest of voices, "I thought you'd call me from Chicago . . . " I let my voice trail off, feeling suddenly rather silly for even mentioning it.

A half smile flitted across Andrew's mouth. He looked somewhat amused as he said, "And *I* thought you'd call *me.*"

"Aren't we a couple of stubborn idiots," I laughed, and lifting my glass, I took a sip of my drink.

He said, "I don't know how my stubborn idiot feels about me, but I adore her."

"And I adore mine," I responded swiftly, smiling warmly at him.

He smiled back.

There was another small silence. After a short interval, I said suddenly, "Sarah's broken up with the Eastern seaboard's greatest snob."

Andrew chuckled. "Yes, he is that. And I know about it, be—"

"How?" I cut in peremptorily.

"Sarah told me."

"She did! *When?*"

"Today. I called her this afternoon, just before I left Chicago. I asked her not to come out here tonight, if that was what she was planning to do. I explained that I wanted to get you alone, to have you all to myself for a change, that I was a bit sick of sharing you with the world at large."

Leering at me wickedly, he continued, "That's when she said

she wasn't coming at all, because she had just finished with Tommy Preston that very morning. I'm afraid I couldn't persuade her otherwise. She was quite adamant about staying in New York for the weekend."

"I got her to change her mind. She's going to drive out tomorrow sometime."

"That's good to hear, and I'm glad you had more success than I did. To tell you the honest truth, I'm not surprised in the least that she's finished with Tommy. He never measured up, in my opinion."

"I wish . . . "

"Wish what, darling?" Andrew leaned closer to me, searching my face, no doubt picking up on my wistfulness as he observed my sad expression.

"I wish that Sarah could find a really nice guy to fall in love with, so that she could get married and have babies, just as she wants to. I really do wish *we* knew somebody for her."

"So do I, Mal, but we don't. In the meantime, I think she's quite happy in her own way. She does love her job, you know, and that's quite a career she's carved out for herself as fashion director of Bergman's."

"That's true. Still, I do think she'd like to be married."

"I suppose she would." Andrew fell quiet. A thoughtful expression settled on his face; he finished his drink in a fast little gulp, put his glass on the table, and turned to me. "Talking of careers and jobs, I've just had another offer."

"From the Gordon Agency again?" I asked eagerly, knowing how much he admired this advertising group.

He shook his head. "No, from Marcus and Williamson."

I sat up a bit straighter, staring at him. "That's a fantastic agency. What's the offer?"

"A great one, as far as the money's concerned. But they didn't offer me a partnership. Unfortunately."

"Well, they should have, you're the best in the business," I shot back. "And I guess you didn't take it, did you?"

"No. I didn't want to move just for the money. In all honesty, it would have been worth considering only if Marcus and Williamson had offered me a slice of the pie. Also, to tell you the truth, I did have rather a pang at the thought of leaving Babs."

This was the name everyone on Madison Avenue used for Blau, Ames, Braddock and Suskind, and I did understand how Andrew felt. He had been with them for a number of years, and he was sentimentally attached. He also earned a big salary and had many privileges and benefits aside from being a partner in the firm. But I knew only too well that he thought the agency had begun to stagnate of late, and he had grown increasingly restless this past year.

I voiced this now.

He listened quietly to everything I had to say. He respected my opinion. I was ambitious for him; I always have been. Now I enumerated some of the reasons why I thought he ought to consider leaving, not the least of which was his frustration with Joe Braddock, the senior partner.

When I finished, he nodded. "You're right, you make a lot of sense. I agree that Joe is hardly the most visionary of men, and especially when it comes to the future of the agency. He's in a time warp these days, living in the past and on past glories."

After taking a sip of his drink, he went on, "Joe didn't used to be like that, and certainly not when I started there twelve years ago. I guess he's just getting too old." He gave me a long, rather thoughtful look. "Tell you what, I'm going to talk to him, mention the various offers I've had this past year. It can't do any harm."

"No, it can't," I agreed.

He hurried on, "Actually it might shake him up a bit. Perhaps he'll come around to my way of thinking about certain aspects of the agency. I know Jack Underwood and Harvey Colton would like me to have a go at Joe. Actually, Mal, they deem it high time he retired, and I'm afraid I have to agree with them. On the other hand, he *is* the last of the original founding quartet, the only one still alive, and something of an industry giant. It's going to be a tough situation to deal with."

I reached over and squeezed his hand. "I'm glad you've decided to talk to Joe. I've wanted you to do that for the longest time, and it'll work out, you'll see. Now, do you want another drink, or shall we go inside and I'll make supper?"

He nodded. "I'm starving! What's on the menu?"

"I was going to prepare spaghetti and a green salad for myself, but if you prefer something else, I can defrost—"

"No, no," he interrupted, "that sounds great. Come on, let's go inside and I'll help you."

Much later, when we had finished dinner and were drinking the last of the wine, Andrew said, "You remember that time my mother talked to you about the only man she'd been seriously attracted to since my father's death?"

"Of course I do. She said he was separated but not divorced—"

"And therefore verboten as far as she was concerned," Andrew interjected.

"That's right. But why are you bringing this up now?"

"I think that man might be your father."

I gaped at him. I was so taken aback I was momentarily speechless. Quickly I found my voice. "That's the most preposterous thing I've ever heard, Andrew. What on earth makes you think such a thing all of a sudden?" I knew he had to have a good reason for this comment, since my husband was not given to flights of fancy, and least of all where his mother was concerned.

Clearing his throat, he explained, "Last Tuesday morning, after you'd gone out and just before I left for Chicago, I asked my mother if she could change a hundred-dollar bill for me. She told me to get her wallet out of her handbag in her bedroom. So I did, but there was an envelope caught in the flap and it fell to the floor. When I picked it up I couldn't help noticing your father's name on the back and his return address in Jerusalem. I thought it a bit odd that he was writing to my mother. Anyway, I put the envelope back in her bag and took the wallet to her. Obviously I didn't say anything. How could I?"

I sat back in my chair, frowning. "It does seem strange," I murmured. "But it might be quite innocent."

"That's true. I sort of dismissed it myself as being a trifle far-fetched, but the other night in Chicago I got to thinking about them, and all sorts of little things kept cropping up in my mind."

"Such as what?" I asked, leaning over the table, pinning my eyes on his.

"Edward's behavior, for one thing. He's very solicitous, gallant with her, and a bit flirtatious, I'd say."

"Oh, come on, he *isn't*! He's actually quite distant with Diana. No, *remote* is a better word. And cool, almost cold even."

"He's really only like that when your mother is present, on those family occasions when we're all together for a short while. Then he is rather . . . " Andrew paused, and I could see him mentally groping for the right word. "Strained," he finished.

I pondered what he had said, staring down into my glass of red wine.

Andrew pressed on: "Listen, Mal, consider the times when he's been in London with us and the twins and Diana. Really think about them. There's a change in him. A subtle change, I have to admit, and it's not noticeable unless one is looking for it, but there *is* a change, nonetheless."

I cast my mind back to those occasions in the past to which Andrew was referring when seemingly quite coincidentally my father had had archaeological business in London at the same time we were there. Now I wondered how coincidental those visits of his had been. Perhaps they had been carefully planned so that we could all be together like one big happy family. Also, looking back, I realized how eager he always was to come to Yorkshire with us. I tried my best to recall my father's demeanor, and as I did I began to see that there was some truth in what Andrew was saying. My father did treat Diana the way an admirer would, and she too, showed another side of herself when he was around.

As I visualized them together, I had a flash of comprehension, and I knew, suddenly, exactly *how* she was different. She didn't flirt with him, nor did she display any signs of affection. It was nothing like that. Diana acted younger when she was in my father's presence. It was as simple as that. And it was barely discernible, so I had not been conscious of it, had not recognized it until now.

"That's it," I said.

"What is?" Andrew asked, looking across at me in bafflement.

"There is definitely a change in your mother when Daddy's around. It's ever so slight, but it's there. She acts younger, she even looks younger. In fact, she's almost girlish. Don't you think so?"

"Yes, you're right, Mal! My mother does seem more . . . *carefree* when Edward is with us, and he appears much younger, too. Actually, that's the difference in him, what I was striving to pinpoint before."

I nodded. Then I asked slowly, "Do you think they're having an affair?"

Andrew began to laugh. "Perhaps they are." His face changed instantly, became sober once more, and he gave a little, noncommittal shrug. "I honestly don't know."

"My mother wouldn't like it if they were."

"For God's sake, Mal, your parents have been separated for donkey's years. They can't stand each other."

"Nevertheless, she wouldn't like it. She's always been terribly jealous of him, and I think she still is."

"Mmmmm. Perhaps that's the reason Mother *isn't* having an affair with your father. It would be too close for comfort for her. She'd feel awkward, embarrassed."

"Yes, she would," I agreed. "And Diana did tell me that she didn't see the special man because he was legally tied to his wife, and so the situation was untenable to her, she said. Well, I guess there's nothing between my father and your mother after all. He was probably just dropping her a friendly note, the way parents-in-law do."

"*Do* they do that, darling?"

I laughed at the skeptical expression on his face. "How do I know?" I lifted my hands in a small, helpless gesture. "Look, getting back to your original statement, Andrew, I'm certain there couldn't be anything between them. You see, I'd *know*. I really would. I'm very close to Diana, and to my father, and I think I'd feel it in my bones." But as I said these words, truly meaning them, I couldn't help thinking that Andrew might well be correct in his initial assumption, and I quite wrong.

Apparently my husband decided the conversation was finished, for he rose suddenly and began to clear the kitchen table. I also got up and helped him to carry the dishes over to the sink. But all the while I kept thinking about Diana and my father, and at one moment I had to turn my head away so Andrew would not see the sudden, pleased smile on my mouth. It gladdened my heart to think that these two people, whom I cared so much about, might be involved with each other. They both deserved a little happiness, considering the bereftness of their years alone.

6

The arc of the sky was the darkest of blues, and it was clear, without a single cloud. The stars were very bright, crystalline, sparkling, and there was a thin sliver of a crescent moon.

It was the most perfect night, and there was even a cool breeze blowing up now as Andrew and I walked over the ridge and down toward the long meadow and the big pond. After helping me tidy the kitchen, he had said he wanted to see the horses, and so a few minutes ago we had set out from the house, walking in silence, holding hands, enjoying the beautiful evening.

Our two horses and the children's ponies were stabled in one of the big red barns near Anna's little cottage. She was an extraordinary gardener whose talent and skill had turned the wilderness surrounding Indian Meadows into a true beauty spot, and she was worth every penny we paid her. We gave her the cottage rent-free in return for caretaking chores and for looking after the horses, feeding and grooming them and mucking out the stalls. Her nephew Billy came to help her every day after school, and we paid him for his work in the stables. Although Anna's true vocation was gardening, she was an enthusiastic and expert equestrian and enjoyed exercising our horses as well as her own.

The cottage was misnamed, since in reality it was a barn, one of the smaller ones which we had remodeled last year, turning it into a comfortable studio with a sleeping loft, bathroom, and kitchen.

Anna loved it, and she had been thrilled to move in with Blackie, her Labrador, and her coffee-colored Persian cat, Miss Petigrew. She had come along at exactly the right time for us, and seemingly so, had we for her. She had just separated from her boyfriend, moved out of his house in Sharon, and was staying with friends at their farm near Lake Wononpakook until she found a place of her own. Our remodeled barn and the offer we made had solved her immediate problems as well as ours.

As we drew closer, I saw there were lights on in the cottage, but she did not come out to speak to us, and since we never intruded on her in the evenings unless there was a specific reason to do so, we wandered on in the direction of the biggest of our barns.

Once we were inside, Andrew turned on the powerful overhead lights and walked forward, moving down between the stalls. He petted and nuzzled Blue Boy and Highland Lassie, and spent a few minutes with them, before going to see the ponies, Pippa and Punchinella. But we did not stay with the horses very long and were soon heading back to the house.

Andrew had not said much on the way down, and he was equally as quiet as we went up the hill. He seemed to be lost in thought, preoccupied, and I decided not to pry. If there was something on his mind, something he wanted to tell me, he would do so in his own good time. From the beginning of our marriage he had always shared everything with me, and continued to do so, as had I with him.

Diana once said that we were each other's best friend as well as husband and wife and lovers, and this was true. We loved each other on many different levels, and even though Sarah was my dearest girlfriend and Andrew was close to Jack Underwood, he and I were inseparable and spent almost all of our free time together. He was not the kind of man who went off on his own, drinking and carousing with his male companions or following his own pursuits; in many ways he was something of a homebody, and certainly he was a wonderful father, very close to his children.

At one moment Andrew put his arm around my shoulders and drew me closer. Glancing up at the incredible night sky, he sighed deeply several times. I recognized that these were sighs of contentment, and I was pleased he felt so relaxed and at peace, as I was now that he was back with me and close by my side.

We lay together, my husband and I, on top of our bed. The room was cool from the air conditioning and dimly lit by two small lamps on each of the bedside tables. But because I had left the draperies open to the night sky, moonlight cast a silvery sheen over everything, bathing the room in a soft radiance.

Andrew moved closer to me, pushed himself up on one elbow, and looked down into my face, moving a strand of hair away as he did. "I missed you this week," he murmured.

"I missed you too, and I hate it when we quarrel."

"So do I. But it was merely a small storm in an even smaller teacup. Let's forget it, shall we, and move on. To more important things."

He paused for a moment or two, and as I looked up at him, I saw a reflective expression settle on his face. He seemed to be thinking deeply. Finally, he said, "There's something I want to say . . . to tell you . . . how I feel about something."

"What? What is it?" I asked quickly, sensing that this was important.

Leaning closer to me, he said softly, "I'd like another child. Wouldn't you, Mal?"

"Yes. Yes, I would," I answered without a moment's hesitation, thinking how like him it was to suddenly voice an idea I had been turning over in my mind of late.

I felt him smile against my cheek, and I knew he was happy at my unequivocal positive response.

"Let me love you," he said against my hair, stroking my cheek as he spoke. Then he touched the strap of my nightgown a little impatiently. "Take this off, darling. Please."

As I pulled the short silk shift up and over my head and dropped it onto the floor, he got off the bed, slipped out of his pajamas, and a split second later he was next to me again, taking me in his arms, bending over me intently, seeking my mouth with his.

He kissed me over and over again, his lips moving from my mouth to each of my eyelids, onto my nose and forehead, and down to nestle in my neck. He stroked my shoulder and my breasts, tenderness in his every movement; then he began to kiss my nipple while his hand slid down onto my inner thigh. An instant later his questing fingers had found the innermost core of me, and he caressed me expertly, delicately, and I felt a sudden surge of warmth spreading through me.

Sighing, I stirred in his arms, arching my body, pressing closer to him, my longing for him paramount in my mind. I put my arms around his neck, and as I did so he began to kiss my mouth again, his passion rising. And I knew that he wanted me as much as I wanted him. It had always been like this between us; our desire for each other had never waned in all the years of our marriage.

He was ready for me now, just as I was ready for him, and I met his passion with intense ardor, arching up, cleaving to him as he entered me. Instantly we found our own rhythm, moving against each other with mounting excitement.

Suddenly, abruptly, Andrew stopped.

I snapped my eyes open and looked up into his face hovering so close. His hands were braced on either side of me, and he was holding his body very still above mine. He stared down at me for the longest time, searching my face.

His eyes were vividly blue, so blue they almost blinded me, and as we gazed at each other, drowning in each other's eyes, neither one of us was able to look away. It was as though we were plunging deeply into each other's souls, merging to become one.

The silence between us was a palpable thing. He broke it when he said in a voice that was low and thickened by emotion, "My wife, my darling wife. I love you, I've always loved you and I always will."

"Oh Andrew, I love you too," I breathed. "Forever." And reaching up, I touched his face, my love for him spilling out of me.

A faint smile flickered onto his mouth and was instantly gone. He brought his face down to mine, kissing me lightly, tenderly. His tongue slid into my mouth, mine curled against his, and we shared a moment of the most profound intimacy.

Sudden heat flared in me again, took hold of me. "I want you," I whispered.

"And I want you," he answered, and in the pale light I saw the need and urgency in his eyes, the excitement on his face.

Slowly, gently at first, Andrew began to move once more. His speed increased, as did mine; our movements became almost violent as we spun out of control.

I closed my eyes, swept along by wave after wave of ecstasy, excited by the things Andrew was whispering to me. We clung to each other, and as I felt that first sharp surge of intense pleasure, I gasped, then called his name.

Like an echo coming back to me, I heard him crying mine, and we rushed headlong toward a rapturous climax, reaching fulfillment together.

We had turned out the lights and lay in the darkness, curled up under the quilt, wrapped in each other's arms. I felt languorous, satiated after our explosive sexual release and overwhelmed by the love I felt for Andrew. He was my life, my whole existence. I was so lucky. There was no woman luckier.

I nestled into him, listening to his even breathing, thankful that it was normal again. During our hectic lovemaking he had started to pant, then gasp, and even after he had collapsed against me, his breathing had been extremely labored.

Now I said quietly, "Your breathing was so strange, I was worried."

"Why, darling?"

"For a split second I thought you were having a heart attack."

He laughed. "Don't be silly. I was very turned on, overexcited. I thought I was going to explode. If you want the truth, Mal, I couldn't seem to get enough of you tonight."

"I'm glad of that," I murmured. "The feeling's mutual."

"I'd rather gathered that." He kissed the top of my head. "Happy?"

"Deliriously, ecstatically." I turned my face, buried it against his chest. "You're the very best."

"I'd better be."

"What do you mean?"

"I don't want you looking elsewhere," he said in a teasing tone, laughing again.

"Fat chance of that, Mr. Keswick!"

He tightened his arms around me. "Oh, Mal, my beautiful wife, you're such a wonder, the best thing that's ever happened to me. I don't know what I'd do without you."

"You won't have to . . . I'll be with you all the days of our lives."

"Thank God for that. Listen, do you think we made a baby tonight?"

"I hope so." I craned my neck to look up at him, but his face was obscured in the murky light. Slipping out of his arms, I pushed myself up until my head was next to his on the pillows. I bent over him, took his face between my hands, and kissed him.

When we finally drew apart, I said with a small smile, "But don't worry if we haven't. Think of all the fun we're going to have trying."

7

I knew immediately that my mother was going to pick a fight with me. I suppose that over the years I have acquired a second sense about her moods, and I recognized she was not in a very pleasant one this morning.

Perhaps it was the set of her shoulders, the tilt of her head, the way she held herself in general, so rigidly, with such tautness. In any case, her body language telegraphed that she was spoiling for a fight.

I was determined not to react, not today, the Fourth of July. I wanted this to be a happy, carefree day; after all, it was our big summer celebration. Nothing was going to spoil it.

She was so uptight when I greeted her on the doorstep that I had to steel myself as I kissed her on the cheek. She was not going to be easy to deal with; all of the signs were there.

"I don't know why you have to have your barbecue so early," she complained as she came inside the house. "I had to get up at the crack of dawn to make it out here."

"One o'clock is not so early, Mother," I said quietly, "and you didn't have to arrive at this hour." I glanced at my watch. "It's barely ten—"

"I wanted to help you," she shot back, cutting me off. "Don't I always try to help you, Mallory?"

"Yes, you do," I answered quickly, wishing to placate her. I eyed the bag she was carrying; she had not said anything about spending the night when we had spoken on the phone yesterday, and I hoped she wasn't planning to do so. "What's in the bag?" I asked. "Are you sleeping over?"

"No, no, of course not!" she exclaimed.

She had such a peculiar look on her face, I wondered if the mere idea of this was distasteful to her. However, I did not say a word, deeming it wiser to remain silent.

She added, "But thanks, anyway, for asking me. I have a dinner date tonight. In the city. So I must get back. As for the bag, I have a change of clothes in it. For the barbecue. I do get so creased driving out here." She glanced down at her black gabardine trousers. "Oh, dear!" she cried. "I hope this dog isn't going to cover me with hairs."

Trixy, ever friendly, was jumping up against her legs. Stifling a sudden flash of annoyance with my mother, I automatically reached for the dog and picked her up.

"The Bichon Frise doesn't shed, Mother." I said this as evenly as I possibly could, exercising great control over myself.

"That's good to know."

"You've always known it," I retorted, unable to keep the acerbity out of my voice.

She ignored this. "Why don't I go into the kitchen and start on the potato salad."

"Oh, but Diana's going to make that."

"Good heavens, Mallory, what does an Englishwoman know about making an all-American potato salad for an all-American celebration like Independence Day? Independence from the British, I might add."

"You don't have to give me a history lesson."

"*I'll* make the salad," she sniffed. "It's one of my specialties, in case you've forgotten."

"Fine," I answered, eager to promote a peaceful atmosphere. My mother began to move in the direction of the kitchen, obviously anxious to start preparing the famous potato salad.

I said, "I'll take your bag up to the blue guest room; you can use it for the day."

"Thank you," she replied, walking on, not looking back.

I stared after her slim, elegant figure, wondering how my father had resisted the temptation to strangle her. Then I hoisted the bag and, still holding Trixy, ran upstairs to the blue room. I came back down immediately, still carrying the puppy, and in the hall outside my little office I kissed the top of her fluffy white head and put her down.

"Come on, Trixola," I muttered, "let's go and attack her, shall we?"

Trixy looked up at me and wagged her tail, and as I so often am, I was quite convinced she understood exactly what I'd just said. I laughed out loud. Trixy was such a gay little animal; she always brought a smile to my face and made me laugh.

As I hurried toward the kitchen with the dog trotting behind me, I was more determined than ever not to let my mother ruin my day. I wondered whether she purposely wanted to upset me or was merely in a bad mood and taking it out on me. I wasn't sure. But then, that was an old story when it came to my mother and me. I never *really* knew where I stood with her.

I found her positioned at one of the counters, slicing the chilled boiled potatoes I had made earlier. She had a cup of coffee next to her, and a cigarette dangled from her mouth. It took a lot of self-restraint on my part not to admonish her; I hated her to smoke around us, and most especially when she was working in the kitchen.

"Where are the children and Andrew?" she asked without looking at me.

"They've gone to the local vegetable stand, to buy fresh produce for the barbecue. Corn, tomatoes, the usual. Mother, do you mind not smoking when you're preparing food?"

"I'm not dropping cigarette ash in the salad, if that's what you're getting at," she answered, still sounding peevish.

Once again, I endeavored to placate her. "I know you're not. I just hate the smoke, Mom. Please put it out. If not for your own health or mine, at least for your grandchildren's sake. You know what they're saying about secondhand smoke."

"Lissa and Jamie live in Manhattan. Think of all the polluted air they're breathing in there."

"Only too true, Mother," I snapped. "But let's not add to the problem of air pollution out here, shall we?" I knew my voice had hardened, but I couldn't help myself. I was furious with her, angered that she was taking such a cavalier attitude, and in my house.

My mother swung her beautifully coiffed blonde head around and stared at me over her shoulder.

There was no doubt in my mind that she recognized the unyielding expression which had swept over my face. Certainly she had seen it enough times over the years, and now it had the desired effect. She stubbed out the cigarette in the sink and threw the butt into the garbage pail. After gulping down the last of her coffee, she carried the bowls of potatoes over to the kitchen table and sat down. All of this was done in a blistering silence.

After a moment or two, she said slowly, startling me with her dulcet tones, "Now, Mallory darling, don't be difficult this morning. You know how I hate to quarrel with you. So upsetting." She proffered me the sweetest of smiles.

I was flabbergasted. I opened my mouth, then snapped it shut instantly. She was the most exasperating woman I had ever met, and once again I felt that old, familiar rush of sympathy for my father.

In her own insidious and very clever way, she had somehow managed to twist everything, had made it sound as if I had been the one itching for a fight. But experience had taught me there was nothing to be gained by taking issue with her or trying to present my point of view. Silence or acquiescence were the only viable weapons that could defeat her.

I walked over to the refrigerator and brought out the other ingredients for the potato salad, all of which I had prepared at six o'clock this morning, long before her arrival. There were glass bowls of hard-boiled eggs, chopped celery, chopped cornichons, and chopped onions; these I placed on a large wooden tray, along with the salt and pepper mills and a jar of mayonnaise.

Carrying the laden tray over to the old-fashioned kitchen table, I placed it in the middle and got another chopping board and knife before taking the chair opposite her. I began to methodically chop an egg, avoiding her eyes. I was seething inside.

We worked in silence for a while, and then my mother stopped slicing a large potato, put the knife down, and leaned back in her chair. She sat gazing at me, studying me carefully.

So intense was her stare, so acute her scrutiny, I found myself reacting almost angrily. She had always had that effect on me; I felt like she was putting me under a microscope and dissecting me like a bug.

I frowned. "What is it, Mother?" I demanded coldly. "Do I have dirt on my face or something?"

She shook her head, exclaimed, "No, no, you don't." There was a little pause, then she went on, "I'm sorry, Mal, I *was* staring at you far too hard. I was examining your skin, actually, gauging the elasticity of it." She nodded quite vigorously, as if confirming something important to herself. "Dr. Malvern is right. Young skin does have a special kind of elasticity to it, a different kind of texture than older skin. Mmmm. Well, never mind. I can't get the elasticity back, I'm afraid, but I can get rid of the sag." As she spoke she began to pat herself under her chin with the back of her hand. "Dr. Malvern says a nip and a tuck will do it."

"Mother! For God's sake! You don't need another face job. Honestly you don't. You look wonderful." I truly meant this. She was still a lovely-looking woman who defied her age. The face-lift she had had three years ago had helped, of course. But she was naturally well preserved. No one would have guessed that this slender, long-legged beauty with the pellucid hazel eyes, high cheekbones, and the most perfect complexion, wrinkleless, in fact, was actually a woman approaching her sixty-second birthday. She appeared to be much younger, easily fifteen or sixteen years younger, in my opinion. One of the few things I admired about my mother was her youthfulness and the discipline she exercised in order to achieve it.

"Thank you, Mal, for those kind words, but I do think I could use just a *little* tuck . . . " Her voice trailed off, and continuing to stare at me, she let out several small sighs. There was an unfamiliar wistfulness about her at this moment, and it took me by surprise.

"No, you *don't* need it," I murmured in a gentler voice, a rush of love for her filling me. She suddenly seemed so open and vulnerable that I felt a rare touch of sympathy for her.

Another silence fell between us as we continued to observe each other; but we were really caught up in our own thoughts and drifted with them for a while.

I was thinking of her, thinking that vain and foolish though she might be, she was not a bad person. Quite to the contrary, in fact. Intrinsically, my mother was a good woman, and she had done her level best to be a good mother. There were times when she had been hopeless at this, others when she was more successful. Admittedly, she had instilled in me some excellent values, which were important to me. On the other hand, we rarely agreed about anything, and frequently she misread me, misjudged me, and treated me as if I were a witless dreamer.

It was my mother who finally broke the silence. She said in an unusually low voice for her, "There's something else I want to tell you, Mal."

I nodded, gave her my full attention.

She hesitated fractionally.

"Go on then," I muttered.

"I'm going to get married," she told me, finally.

"*Married*. But you *are* married. To my father. It might be in name only, but you're still legally tied to him."

"I know that. I mean, after I get a divorce."

"Who are you going to marry?" I asked, leaning forward and staring at her questioningly, unexpectedly riddled with curiosity.

"David Nelson."

"Oh."

"You don't sound very thrilled."

"Don't be silly . . . I'm just taken aback, that's all."

"Don't you like David?"

"Mother, I hardly know him."

"He's very nice, Mal."

"I'm sure he is . . . he's seemed pleasant enough, very cordial on those few occasions I've met him."

"I love him, Mal, and he loves me. We're very good together, extremely compatible. I've been lonely. Very lonely, really, and for a *very* long time. And so has David, ever since his wife died seven years ago. We've been seeing each other fairly steadily for the past year, and when David asked me to marry him, last week, I suddenly realized how much he meant to me. There doesn't seem to be any good reason why we *shouldn't* get married."

Something akin to a quizzical look had slipped onto my mother's face, and her eyes now searched mine; it occurred to me that she was seeking my approval.

I said, "There's no reason at all why you shouldn't get married, Mom. I'm glad you are." I smiled at her. "Does David have any children?"

"A son, Mark, who's married and has one child. A boy, David, named for his grandfather. Mark and his wife, Angela, live in Westchester. He's a lawyer, like David."

A son, that's a blessed relief, I thought. No possessive, overly protective daughter floating around Papa David, one likely to upset the apple cart. Now that I knew about it I was all in favor of this union. I wanted it to go ahead without a hitch. I probed, "And when do you plan to get married, Mother?"

"As soon as I can, as soon as I'm free."

"Have you started divorce proceedings?"

"No, but I'm going to see Alan Fuller later this week. There won't be a problem, considering that your father and I have been separated such a long time." She paused, then added. "Fifteen years," as though I didn't know this.

"Have you told Daddy?"

"No, not yet."

"I see."

"Don't look so pained, Mal. I think he might—"

"I'm not looking pained," I protested, wondering how she could ever think such a thing. I didn't have any pained feelings about anything. Actually, I was pleased she wasn't living in a kind of decisionless limbo any longer.

"I was going to say, before you interrupted me, that I believe your father will be relieved I've finally taken this step."

I nodded. "You're right, Mother. I'm *positive* he will be."

The sound of heels clicking against the polished wood floor of the gallery immediately outside the kitchen made my mother sit up straighter. She brought her forefinger to her lips and, staring hard at me, mouthed silently, "It's a secret."

I gave her another swift, acquiescent nod.

Diana pushed open the door and glided into the kitchen just as my mind was focusing on secrets. There were so many in our family; instantly I pushed this thought far, far away from me, as I invariably did. I never wanted to face those secrets from my childhood. Better to forget them; better still to pretend they did not exist. But they did. My childhood was constructed on secrets layered one on top of the other.

Faking insouciance, I smiled at Diana. It was a beatific smile, belying what I had been thinking. I asked myself if she *was* my father's lover. And if so, would this sudden change in his circumstances affect his life with her? Would the seemingly imminent divorce make him think of marriage—to her? Was my mother-in-law about to become—my stepmother? I swallowed the incipient laughter rising in my throat; nevertheless, I still had to glance away as my mouth twitched involuntarily.

Diana was cheerfully saying, "Good morning, Jessica dear. It's lovely to see you."

My mother immediately sprang to her feet and embraced her. "I'm glad you're here, Diana. You look wonderful."

"Thanks, I feel good," Diana responded, smiled her sunny

smile, and added, "I must say, you look pretty nifty yourself, the picture of good health."

I studied them as they talked.

How different they were in appearance, these two women of middle age, our mothers.

Mine was all blonde curls and fair skin, with delicate, perfectly sculpted features. She was a very pretty woman, a cool Nordic type, slim and lissome with a special kind of inbred elegance that was enviable.

Diana was much darker in coloring, with a lovely golden complexion and straight silky brown hair, pulled back in a ponytail this morning. Her face was broader, her features more boldly defined, and her large, luminous eyes were of a blue so pale and transparent they were almost gray. She was not quite as tall as my mother. "I'm a Celt," she had once said to me. "There's more of my Scottish ancestry in my genes than the English part." Diana's appeal was in her warm, tawny looks; she was a handsome woman by any standard, who, like my mother, carried her sixty-one years well, seeming years younger.

Their characters and personalities were totally different. Diana was a much more serious woman than my mother was, more studious and intellectually inclined. And the worlds they occupied, the lives they lived, were not remotely similar. Diana was something of a workaholic, running her antique business and loving every minute of it. My mother was a social butterfly who did not care to work, and who fortunately did not have to. She lived on a comfortable income derived from investments, family trusts, and a small allowance from my father. Why she accepted this from him I'll never know.

My mother was actually somewhat quiet and shy. At times I even thought of her as being repressed. Yet she was a social animal, and when she wanted to she could exude great charm.

My mother-in-law was much more spontaneous and outgoing, filled with a *joie de vivre* that was infectious. I always felt happy when Diana was around; she had that effect on everyone.

Two very disparate women, my mother and my mother-in-law. And yet they had always been amiable with each other, appeared on the surface to get on reasonably well. Perhaps *we* were the bond between them, Andrew and me and the twins. Certainly they were thrilled and relieved that we had such a happy marriage, that our union had been so successful, so blessed. Maybe the four of us validated their troubled lives and diminished their failures.

The two of them sat down, continuing to chat, to catch up, and I rose and walked to the far end of the kitchen. Here I busied myself at the sink, pulling apart several heads of lettuce, washing the leaves scrupulously.

My mind was preoccupied with marriage, my mother's impending one, to be precise. But then my thoughts took an unexpected curve, zeroed in on my father. His life had not been a happy one, far from it—except for his work, of course. That had given him a great deal of satisfaction and still did. He was proud of his standing as an archaeologist. His marriage had been such a disappointment, a terrible failure, and he had expected so much from it, he had once confided in me. It had gone hopelessly awry when I was a child.

What a pity my father had never been lucky enough to have what Andrew and I have. Sadness for him filtered through me; I was saddened even more that he had never found love with someone else when he was a younger man. He was sixty-five now; that was not old, and perhaps it wasn't too late for him. I sighed under my breath. I blamed my mother for his pain, I always had; he had never been at fault. In my eyes he had always been the hero in a bitter, thankless marriage.

As this random thought surfaced, floated to the front of my head, I examined it as carefully as I was washing the lettuce leaves under the running water. Wasn't I being just a little bit unfair? No one in this world is perfect, least of all my father. He *was* a human being, after all, not a god, even if he had seemed like one to me when I was growing up. He had been all golden and shining and beautiful, the most handsome, the most dashing, the most brilliant man in the world. And the most perfect. Of course. Yes, he had been all those things to me as a child. But he must have had his flaws and his frailties, like we all do, hang-ups and weaknesses as well as strengths. Should I not perhaps give my mother the benefit of the doubt?

This was so startling a thought I took a moment to adjust to it.

Finally, I glanced over my shoulder at her. She was calmly sitting there at my kitchen table, talking to Diana, methodically making her famous potato salad, one she had prepared so religiously every Fourth of July throughout my entire childhood and teenage years.

Unbidden and unexpected, it came rushing back to me, a *fragment* of a memory, a memory prodigiously beaten into submission, carefully boxed and buried and thankfully forgotten. Suddenly resurrected, it was flailing at me now, free-falling into my consciousness. And as it did I found myself looking down the corridor of time. I saw a day long, long ago, twenty-eight years ago, to be exact. I was five years old and an unwilling witness to marital savagery so shocking, so painful to bear I had done the only thing possible. I had obliterated it.

Echoing back to me along that shadowy, perilous tunnel of the past came a mingling of familiar voices which dredged up that day, dragged it back into the present. Exhumed, exposed, it lived again.

My mother is here, young and beautiful, an ethereal, dreamlike creature in her white muslin summer frock, her golden hair burnished in the sunlight. She is standing in the middle of the huge kitchen of my grandmother's summer house in Southampton. But her voice contrasts markedly with her loveliness. It is harsh, angry, and accusatory.

I am afraid.

She is telling my father he cannot leave. Not today, not the Fourth, not with all the family coming, all the festivities planned. He cannot leave her and her parents and me. "Think of your child, Edward. She adores you," she cries. "Mallory needs you to be here for her today." She is repeating this, over and over and over again like a shrill litany.

And my father is explaining that he *must* go, that he has to catch his plane to Egypt, explaining that the new dig is about to start, telling her that as head of the archaeological team he must be there at the outset.

My mother starts to scream at him. Her face is ugly with rage. She is accusing him of going to *her*, to his mistress, not to the expedition at all.

My father is defending himself, protesting his innocence, telling my mother she is a fool, and a jealous fool, at that. Then he tells her more softly that she has no reason to be jealous. He vows that he loves only her; he explains, very patiently, that he must go because he must do his work, must work to support us.

My mother is shaking her head vehemently from side to side, denying, denying.

The bowl of potato salad is suddenly in her hands, then it is leaving her hands as it is violently flung. It is sailing through the air, hitting the wall behind my father, bouncing off the wall, splattering his dark blue blazer with bits of potato and mayonnaise before it crashes to the floor with a thud, like a bomb exploding.

My father is turning away angrily, leaving the kitchen; his handsome face is miserable, contorted with pain. There is a helplessness about him.

My mother is weeping hysterically.

I am cringing in the butler's pantry, clinging to Elvira, my grandma's cook, who is my best friend, my only friend, except for my father, in this house of anger and secrets and lies.

My mother is storming out of the kitchen, running after my father, in her anguish not noticing Elvira and me as she races past the open door of the pantry.

Again she is shouting loudly. "I hate you! I hate you! I'll never give you a divorce. *Never*. Not as long as I live. Mercedes will never have the pleasure of being your wife, Edward Jordan. I swear to you she won't. And if you leave me, you'll never see Mallory again.

Not ever again. I'll make sure of that. I have my father's money behind *me*. It will build a barrier, Edward. A barrier to keep you away from Mallory."

I hear her running upstairs after my father, railing on at him remorselessly, her voice shrill and bitter and condemning.

Elvira is stroking my hair, soothing me. "Pay no mind, honeychile mine," she is whispering, her plump black arms encircling me, keeping me safe. "Pay no mind, chile. The big folks is always mouthing the stupidest things . . . things they doan never mean . . . things no chile needs hear. Pay no mind, honeychile mine. Your momma doan mean not a word she ses."

My father is here.

He does not leave. An armed truce is struck between them; it lasts only through the Fourth of July. The following morning he kisses me good-bye. He drives back to Manhattan and flies off to Egypt.

He does not come back for five months.

I closed my eyes, squeezing back the tears, pressing down the pain this unexpected memory, so long concealed, has evoked in me.

Slowly, I lifted my lids and stared at the kitchen wall. With infinite care, I placed the lettuce leaves in the colander to drain, covering them with a large piece of paper towel. My hands felt heavy, like dead weights, and nausea fluttered in my stomach. Holding on to the edge of the sink, I calmed myself and endeavored to regain my equilibrium before I walked across the kitchen.

Eventually, I was able to move.

I paused at the kitchen table and looked down at my mother.

It struck me, with a rush of clarity and something akin to shock, that she had probably suffered greatly as a young wife. I should stop my silent condemnation of her. All of my father's long absences must have been difficult to endure, unimaginably lonely and painful for her. *Had* there been a mistress? *Had* a woman called Mercedes really existed? Had there been many other women over the years? Most probably, I thought, with a sinking feeling. My father was a good-looking, normal, healthy man, and when he was younger he must have sought out female company. For as long as I could recall, he and my mother had had separate bedrooms, and this situation had existed long before he had left for good, when I was eighteen. He had stayed in that terrible marriage for me. I had long believed this, had long accepted it. Somehow, today, I knew it to be true.

Perhaps my mother had experienced humiliation and despair and more heartache than I ever realized. But I would never get the real truth from her. She never talked about the past, never confided in me. It was as if she wanted to bury those years, forget them, perhaps even pretend they never happened. Maybe that was why she was so remote with me at times. Maybe I reminded her of things *she* wanted to expunge from *her* memory.

My mother was looking up at me.

She caught my eye and smiled uncertainly, and for the first time in my adult life I asked myself if I *had* been unfair, if I had done her a terrible injustice all these years.

"What is it, Mal?" she asked, her blonde brows puckering, a spark of concern flickering in her hazel eyes.

I cleared my throat and took a moment to answer. At last I said in a carefully modulated voice, "Nothing, Mom. I'm fine. Listen, I've just washed all the lettuce. It's draining. Could you put it in the fridge in a few minutes, please?" It seemed important to me at this moment to speak of mundane things.

"Of course," she answered.

"What can *I* do to help, Mal? Should I fix the salad dressing?" Diana asked.

"Yes, please, and then perhaps the two of you could take out the hamburger meat and start making the patties."

"Done," Diana said, immediately jumping up and going into the pantry.

Looking at my mother again, I said, "I'm going to go and set the tables."

She nodded, smiling at me, and this time her smile was more sure. She turned back to her potato salad, mixing in the mayonnaise.

Pushing open the kitchen door, I went outside into the garden with Trixy at my heels, leaving the two women alone.

I paused near the door and took several deep breaths. I felt shaken inside, not only by the memory but by the sudden knowledge that all the years I was growing up I had been terrified my father would leave us forever, my mother and I, terrified that one day he would never come back.

It was very hot and airless in the garden, and within seconds my T-shirt was damp and clinging to me. Even Trixy, trotting along next to me, looked slightly wilted; wisely, she flopped down under one of the trestle tables when we reached them.

Late last night Andrew and I had placed the tables under the trees, and now I was glad that we had.

The maples and oaks which formed a semicircle near my studio were old, huge, and extravagant, with thick, gnarled trunks and widely spreading branches abundant with leaves. The branches arched up to form a wonderful, giant parasol of leafy green that was cool and inviting and offered plenty of protection from the sun. We were going to need such a shady spot; by one o'clock it would be a real scorcher of a day, just as Nora had predicted to me on Friday.

Early this morning I had carried red-and-white checked cloths and a big basket of flatware out here, and now I began to set the tables. I had almost finished the largest table, where the adults would sit, when I heard someone calling, "Coo-ee!"

I recognized Sarah's voice at once and looked up. I waved; she waved back.

She was wearing a white terrycloth robe and dark glasses. Her jet-black hair was piled up on top of her head, and there was a mug in her hand. As she drew closer, I could see that her face was woebegone.

"God, I feel *awful*," she moaned, lowering herself gingerly onto the bench in front of the smaller table.

"I'm not surprised," I said, "and good morning to you, Miss Parfait." This was one of my affectionate nicknames for her.

"Good morning, Little Mother," she answered, using one of her pet names for me.

I grinned and tipped the remainder of the knives and forks out onto the table.

"Oh, please, Mal," she groaned, "have a heart. Hold the noise down. My head's splitting, I feel positively ill."

"It's your own fault, you know, you really did tie one on last night."

"Thanks a lot, friend, for all your sympathy."

Realizing that she wasn't overdramatizing for once, I went and put my hand on her shoulder. "Sorry, I shouldn't tease you. Do you want me to get something for you? Headache pills? Alka Seltzer?"

"No, I've already taken enough aspirin to sink a battleship. I'll be okay. Just move around me very, very carefully, please, tiptoe on the grass, don't clatter the tableware, and talk in a whisper."

I shook my head. "Oh, Sarah darling, you do punish yourself, don't you? Thomas Preston the third isn't worth it."

Sarah paid no attention to my last comment, saying, "I guess it must be the Jewish half of me, the Charles Finkelstein half . . . that's what I inherited from good old Dad, a penchant for punishing myself, a tendency to treat everything like an ethnic drama, lots of Jewish guilt, and dark looks."

"Dark *good* looks," I said. "And have you heard from Charlie Boy lately?"

She smiled and made a moue. "No, I'm afraid I haven't. He's got a new wife, yet another WASPy blonde like my mother, so I'm the last thing on his mind. I'll call him next week to see how he is, and I'll make a date with him and Miranda. I don't want to lose touch with him again."

"No, you mustn't. Not after he's finally forgiven you for taking your stepfather's name. And a WASPy name, at that."

"Forgiven my mother, you mean!" she cried, her voice rising slightly. "She was the one who changed my name to Thomas, not I, when I was seven and not old enough to understand or protest."

"I know she did," I murmured, walking to the far side of the smaller table, which I now began to set for the children.

Sarah took a long swallow of her coffee, then put the mug down. After taking off her sunglasses, she placed her elbows on the table and rested her head in her hands. Her dark brown velvety eyes followed me as I moved about.

"How many are we going to be for lunch, Mal?" she asked.

"About eighteen. I think. Let's see, there's my mother and Diana, you and the twins and Jenny, plus me and Andrew, which makes eight. I've invited Nora, Eric, and Anna, bringing us up to eleven. Then there're three couples, the Lowdens, the Martins, and the Callens, making seventeen, and two more kids. Vanessa, the Callens' little girl, and Dick and Olivia Martin are bringing their young son, Luke. So I guess that makes nineteen altogether."

"All I can say is, thank God *we* don't have to do the cooking."

I laughed at the expression on her face. "I know what you mean. Luckily, Andrew has everything under control, and he's roped in all the men to do the barbecuing. Nora and my mother and Diana will help me to fetch and carry."

"I'm hoping I'll feel better by lunchtime, that I'll be able to pitch in."

"It's not necessary, Sash. Just relax. And in any case, I'm setting up a buffet table here. It'll hold most of the other food, such as the salads, the breads, the baked beans, baked potatoes, and corn. It's only the hot dogs, hamburgers, and chops that'll have to be brought over from the barbecues on the kitchen patio."

Sarah nodded but didn't say anything for a few minutes. She sat staring into space with a reflective expression on her face.

Eventually, she said slowly, "Your mother looks like the cat that's swallowed the canary this morning."

"What do you mean?"

"Her eyes are bright and shiny, and she did nothing but smile at me when I was having my toast. And I couldn't help thinking that it was a very self-satisfied smile. Even a bit smug."

"I guess I can tell you," I began, and then I hesitated.

"Sure you can, you've been telling me everything since the day you could talk."

"It's supposed to be a secret."

"So what, you've always told me your secrets, Mal. Yours and everybody else's, actually."

"Well, so have you too!" I shot back.

"I bet it's to do with a man." Sarah grinned at me and winked.

"I'm impressed. How did you guess?"

She burst out laughing. "She has that look. *The* look, the one that says, 'I have a man and he's all mine.' A guy might not recognize it, but every woman does."

"My mother's getting married."

"Golly gee whiz! You've got to be kidding!"

"No, I'm not."

"Good for Auntie Jess. Who's the man?"

"David Nelson. I think you've met him once or twice when he's been at my mother's."

Sarah let out a low whistle. "He's quite a catch, I'd say. Very good-looking and successful, and younger than her."

"Are you sure he's younger?"

"Yes, I am. My mother said something to me a few months ago about Aunt Jess and David, and she mentioned he was about fifty-eight."

"Oh, only four years, that's not much. Anyway, my mother looks a lot younger than he, don't you think?"

"Yes, she does."

"I can't imagine why she wants to get another face job, though. She doesn't need it, in my opinion."

If Sarah was startled by my comment, she did not show it. She said, "No, she doesn't, but she may feel insecure, worried about her age. That's the way my mother is now that she's turned sixty, always attempting to look younger. A lot of women think that's a milestone, I guess."

I shrugged. "Maybe. On the other hand, sixty's not old. In fact, it's considered young these days. This morning, when my mother mentioned she wanted to have a little nip and tuck, I tried to convince her she didn't need it. But she'll do what she wants. She always has."

"I wonder if she's told my mother? About getting married."

"I don't know. But don't say anything, Sash, just in case she hasn't. As I said, it's a secret. Mom hasn't even informed my father yet, nor has she talked to her lawyer about a divorce. She just made her mind up in the last couple of days ... at least, that's the impression she gave me."

"I won't tell a soul, I promise, Mal. And I'm really glad for Auntie Jess, glad she's happy."

"I am too." I paused, staring at Sarah without saying anything for a moment, then I flopped down opposite her.

"Is something wrong?" she asked, frowning slightly, pinning her beautiful dark eyes on mine.

I shook my head. "No. I had a sort of ... well, a sort of revelation earlier. My mother was fussing with the potato salad, and I suddenly found myself remembering an incident with a potato salad that happened on another Fourth of July morning. When I was five. I'd buried it deep and forgotten all about it. Anyway, the memory came back, at least a fragment of it, and I started thinking about my parents and their relationship when I was little, and I suddenly felt rather sorry for my mother. It struck me she must have suffered greatly when she was a younger woman."

Sarah nodded in agreement. "Looking back, she probably did. She was always alone. You *two* were always alone. At least that's the way *I* remember it."

I was silent for a moment, before murmuring, "I had the most awful feeling inside this morning, Sashy . . . "

"What kind of feeling?"

"I felt sick at heart. I suddenly understood that I'd been unfair, that I'd probably done my mother a terrible injustice—and for years."

"What do you mean?"

"I blamed her for their marital problems, but now I'm not so sure it was always her fault."

"I'm certain it wasn't. Anyway, it takes two to tango, Mal." Sarah sighed under her breath. "Your father was hardly ever in this country, the way I recall it. The normal thing was for him to be sitting on a pile of rubble in the Middle East, examining bits of old stone and trying to ascertain how ancient they were, which millennium they came from."

"He had to be away a lot for his work, you know that, Sarah," I said, then realized I sounded defensive.

"But he *never* took you and your mother with him. He always went off alone."

"I had to go to school."

"Not when you were little, you didn't, and when you were older you could have gone to a local school wherever your father's dig was, or you could have had a tutor."

"Going to a local school wouldn't have been very practical," I pointed out. "I wouldn't have been able to speak the local language, for one thing. After all, I was a little kid, I wasn't fluent in Arabic or Urdu or Portuguese or Greek. Or *whatever*."

"You don't have to be sarcastic, Mal, and look, there are ways to make unusual situations work. Many ways."

"Perhaps my parents couldn't afford a tutor," I muttered.

Sarah was silent.

I studied her for a moment, then asked, "Are you blaming my father?"

"Hey, I'm not placing the blame anywhere, on anyone!" she

exclaimed. "How do I know what went on between your parents. Not even you really know that. Jesus, I didn't understand what was happening between mine, either. Kids never do. But it's always the kids who suffer. Ultimately."

When I said nothing, Sarah continued, "Maybe your mother felt it was better, wiser for you to be brought up in New York, rather than in some broken-down, flea-bitten hotel somewhere in the middle of the Arabian desert."

"Or maybe my father simply preferred to leave us behind, to go off alone. For his own personal reasons." I stared hard at her again.

"Come on, Mal, I never said that, nor did I even remotely imply it!"

"I'm not being accusatory or trying to put words in your mouth. Still, it might well have been so. But I suppose I'll never know about their marriage, what went wrong with it."

"You could ask your mother."

"Oh, Sarah, I *couldn't.*"

"Sure you could. There'll be a moment in time when you'll be able to ask her. You'll see. And I bet she won't bite your head off, either. In fact, she'll probably be glad you asked, relieved to talk about your father and her. People do like to unburden themselves, especially mothers to their daughters."

I doubted my mother would feel this way, but I said, "I hope so, Sash. You know only too well that she and I have our differences. But my mother does love me, and I love her, even though she can be exasperating. And today I felt something else for her, something different—a rush of genuine sympathy, and a certain kind of . . . aching sorrow. I realized that she probably hadn't had it easy with Daddy. It was at that moment it occurred to me that I was being unfair, unjust. I think I've always been somewhat blinded to reality because of my adoration of my father."

"You might have been unjust, yes, but you can't change that now, honey. What's done is done. I'm glad you had this . . . this revelation, as you call it." Sarah cleared her throat, and looking me straight in the eye, she said, "Your father was never there for you, Mal. Your mother *always* was."

I gaped at her, about to protest, but clamped my mouth firmly shut. I realized that Sarah had spoken only the truth. Whenever there had been a crisis during the years I was growing up, my father had inevitably been abroad. It was my mother who had coped with my problems during my adolescence and teenage years and even when I was older.

I nodded. "You're right," I said at last, acknowledging the veracity of her words. Then with a twinge of dismay I realized this was the first time I had ever been disloyal to my father in my thoughts, let alone in my words. But he had most likely been as much at fault as my mother, when it came to the disintegration of their marriage.

She got up and walked around the table to my side, hugged me against her body. "I love you," she whispered.

"And I love you, Best Friend," I said, squeezing her hand, which rested on my shoulder.

Straightening, she said with a light laugh, "I'd better go inside and get dressed. I don't want to be caught in my robe when your guests arrive."

I also stood. "And I must finish setting these tables." As I spoke I picked up a handful of red-and-white checked napkins and began to fold them in half.

Sarah was a few yards away from me when she swung around and said, "It's going to be a good day, Mal. *This* Fourth of July is going to be the best you've ever had. I promise."

I believed her.

9

I could see them through the French doors of the sunroom, play-ing together on the terrace. My beautiful children.

And how glorious they looked this morning. They were like little Botticelli angels, with their sun-streaked blonde hair, the most vivid of blue eyes which echoed their father's, and rounded baby cheeks as smooth and pink as ripe peaches.

I drew closer to the glass, listening to them chattering away together. They were close to each other, quite inseparable, in fact. They were so alike, yet in many ways they were very different.

Lissa was saying, "Yes, Jamie, that's *good*. Give them a flag *each*. We've got a big flag on our house, so they should, too."

"I don't know when they'll *see* their flags," Jamie muttered, casting his sister a quick glance before turning back to the work at hand.

My six-year-old son was sticking a small Stars and Stripes into the top of the wall, trying to secure it between the cracks. "This one's for Tabitha and Henry. But they won't come out to look at it when there are lots of people here, and Mom's having a *big* lot of people for lunch. Vanessa and Luke are coming, too."

"Ugh!" Lissa made an ugly face. "How do you know?"

"Grandma Jess told me."

"Ugh," Lissa said again. Stepping over to her twin, she put her

76

arm around his shoulders in a companionable way and gazed at the flag stuck on top of the wall. "Don't worry, Jamie, the little chipmunks'll see their flag tonight."

"Are you sure?"

"Oh, *yes*. They come out to play at night. They all do, the black snake and the bunny, as well," Lissa reassured her twin, sounding as self-confident as she usually did. My daughter was one of the most positive people I've ever met. "Now," she continued, "let's put the flag in the side of the wall over there, for Algernon. And another one for Angelica."

Jamie nodded and ran to do what she suggested. But almost at once the flag fell down onto the terrace. "It won't stay," he cried, turning to Lissa, as always seeking her guidance. She had been born first and was the more aggressive of the two; Jamie was often diffident, more sensitive about certain things, and he had inherited my artistic nature.

"Does Dad have any of that funny glue he sometimes uses?" Lissa asked. "Mom says it'll stick anything."

"Yes, it will," I said, pushing open the door and stepping out onto the terrace. "But I don't want you messing around with Krazy Glue this morning. It's tricky to use and dries very quickly, and it can stick to your skin."

"But Mommy—" Lissa began.

I cut her off. "Not today, honey. Anyway, I think I have a much better solution to your problem, Jamie. Why not use some of your Silly Putty? You can press a small mound of it onto the wall where you want to place the flag, and then stick the flag into the Silly Putty. I bet the flag'll hold very securely."

"Oh, that's a good idea, Mom!" Jamie exclaimed, grinning from ear to ear. "I'll go and get it."

"Slow down, you'll fall!" I shouted after him, watching him race away as fast as his little legs would carry him. Trixy was hard on his heels, bouncing along by his side.

I looked down at Lissa and smiled, thinking how adorable she was in her pink T-shirt and matching shorts. "So, you decided to give flags to all of our little friends who live in the wall," I said. "That's nice."

She nodded, gazing up at me solemn-faced and serious. "Yes, Mommy. We can't leave them out on the Fourth of July. Every American house should have a flag, *you* said so."

"That I did, and where did you get your flags?"

"Daddy bought them in that shop near the vegetable stand. And he bought you some flowers." She stopped abruptly, her eyes opened wider, and she clapped a hand over her mouth. "Oh, Mom, I shouldn't have told you that. It's a surprise. Pretend you don't know when Dad gives you flowers."

I nodded. "I've just forgotten what you said."

Jamie came back with Trixy in tow, and he began to work with the Silly Putty, breaking off small pieces and making mounds.

Lissa stood watching him for a moment, then she swung her head to me and said, "It's hot, Mommy. Can I take my T-shirt off?"

"I don't think you should, darling. I don't want you to expose yourself to the sun. You know how easily you get a sunburn."

"But it's soooo hot," she complained.

"How about a dip in the pool?" I suggested.

"Oh, yes! Goody! Goody!" She clapped her hands together and beamed at me, then cried to Jamie, "Let's go and get our swim-suits, Fishy."

"*Fishy?*" I repeated. "Why do you call your brother that?"

"Daddy says he's like a fish in the water, the best swimmer, too."

"That's true, but you're not so bad yourself, Pumpkin."

"Mom, can we take Swellen into the pool for a swim with us?"

"Don't be ridiculous, Lissa, of course you can't. Sue Ellen's only a goldfish. She'd drown in the pool. And she'd be scared to death."

"She wouldn't, Mom, honest. And she's a *brave* little fish." Lissa threw Jamie a pointed look, and added, "A very, very, very brave little fish."

"I didn't hurt your fish," Jamie mumbled without looking at his sister.

"Of course you didn't, honey," I exclaimed. Turning to Lissa, I went on, "You really can't take her into the pool with you, even though she is an *extremely* brave little fish. You see, the chlorine might poison her, and you wouldn't want that to happen, would you?"

My daughter shook her head; her blue eyes had grown larger and rounder.

I explained carefully, "Sue Ellen's better off in the goldfish bowl in your bedroom. Truly she is."

"How do you like the flags, Mom?" Jamie stepped back, his head to one side, looking proudly at his handiwork.

"They're great! You've done a terrific job," I enthused.

"Hi, Mrs. Keswick," Jenny said, coming around the corner of the house.

"There you are, Jen dear," I replied, returning her smile. I was going to miss our pretty, young au pair when she went back to England in November. I must talk to Diana about finding a replacement; it wouldn't be easy. Jennifer Grange was unusual, special, and we had all become very attached to her.

"Can I do anything to help with lunch?" Jenny asked, joining Jamie near the wall. An approving expression settled on her face as she glanced at the flags, and she squeezed his shoulder affectionately.

"You can't do a thing, Jen," I said. "Just keep an eye on your charges, make sure they don't get into any mischief. And you—"

"Mommy says we can go swimming," Lissa interrupted.

"But I want you *in* that pool with them, Jenny," I said.

"Of course, Mrs. Keswick. I'd never let them go into the water alone, you know that. I'll just go inside and get their swimsuits."

Lissa said, "We don't have to sit at the kids table, do we?"

"Well, yes, of course you do." I looked down at her, frowning slightly, wondering what this was all about.

"We don't want to, Mom," Jamie informed me.

"Why ever not?"

"We want to sit with you and Dad," he explained.

"Oh, Jamie, there just isn't room, honey. Anyway, you should be with your little guests. You have to look after them."

"Vanessa and Luke. Ugh! Ugh!" He grimaced, squeezed his eyes tightly shut, and grimaced again.

"Don't you like them?" I was baffled by this sudden antipathy toward our neighbors' children, with whom they had frequently played, and quite happily so, in the past.

Opening his eyes, Jamie muttered, "Vanessa smells funny, Mom, like Great-grandma's fur coat."

"*Mothballs*," I said. "Like mothballs?" I stared at him, raising a brow. "How peculiar. Are you sure, Jamie?"

He nodded vigorously. "Yep." He grinned at me. "Maybe they keep *her* in mothballs, Mom, like Great-grandma Adelia keeps her fur coat in mothballs. In that funny wood closet of hers. Ha ha ha ha." He laughed hilariously in the way that only a little boy can.

I had to laugh myself.

Lissa giggled and began to sing, "Smelly old mothballs, smelly old mothballs, Vanessa stinks of smelly old mothballs."

"Ssssh! Don't be naughty," I reprimanded. But I found myself still laughing indulgently. Glancing at Jamie, I now asked, "And why don't you like Luke all of a sudden?"

"He wants to be the boss, and we're the boss."

I threw my son a questioning look.

Jamie said, "Me and Lissa, *we're* the boss."

"I see. However, I think you will have to sit with them for lunch today. There's not much alternative, kids. Come on, do it as a favor to me, please."

"Can the grandmas sit with us?" Lissa asked. "Please, Mommy."

"I don't know . . . Well, maybe. Oh, why not. Okay, yes."

"Oh, goody, we like *them*," Jamie said.

"I'm glad to hear it," I murmured, wondering how I would have coped if they had hated their grandmothers.

"We *love* them," Jamie corrected himself.

"They give us lots of presents," Lissa confided.

"And money," Jamie added. *"Lots of it."*

"They're not supposed to do that!" I exclaimed, shaking my head and averting my face to conceal a smile. There was nothing quite so startling as the honesty of children; it could be brutal, and invariably it took my breath away.

Jamie tugged at my hand.

"Yes, darling, what is it?"

"Who did you belong to before Dad got you?"

"Your grandmother, I guess. Grandma Jess. Why?"

"So we belong to you and Dad, don't we?" Lissa asserted.

"You bet!" I exclaimed.

Hunkering down on my haunches, I swept them both into my arms and hugged them to me. They smelled so sweet and young and fresh. I loved that small child's smell ... of shampoo, soap, and talcum powder, and milk, cookies, and sweet breath. And I loved *them* so much, my little Botticelli angels.

It was Jamie who pulled slightly away, looked into my face intently, and touched my cheek with his grubby, warm little hand. "Mom, will the new baby belong to all of us, or just you and Dad?"

"Baby! What baby?"

"The one you and Dad are trying to make." His fine blond brows drew together in a frown. "And what do you *make* it out of, Mom?"

I was so taken aback I was speechless for a moment. Then before I could think of an answer, Lissa announced with some assurance, "They make it out of love." She smiled up at me, obviously extremely pleased with herself, and nodded her head, looking like a little old woman imbued with wisdom.

"What do you mean, Lissa?" her brother asked before I had a chance to say anything.

I jumped in swiftly. "Well, we are trying to make a baby, that's true. When did your father tell you this?"

"When he was giving us breakfast this morning," Jamie said.

"He was cross with us, we were making too much noise. He said we'd soon have to fend for ourselves, that we'd better start growing up real quick. He said we'd have to look after the new baby when it came, be responsible children and take care of it. Who *will* it belong to, Mom?"

"All of us. If we succeed, of course."

"You mean you might not be able to make it?" Lissa asked.

"Afraid so," I admitted.

"Good. Don't make it. I like it this way, just us and Trixy!" she exclaimed.

"If you do make it and we don't like it, can we give it away?" Jamie asked.

"Certainly not," I spluttered.

"But when Miss Petigrew had kittens, Anna gave them away," he reminded me.

"This is not quite the same thing, Jamie darling. A baby's a baby, a kitten's a kitten."

"Can we call the baby Rover, Mom?"

"I don't think so, Jamie."

"That's a dog's name, silly," Lissa cried.

"But it's my favorite name," Jamie shot back.

"It's the name for a boy dog. You can't call a baby girl that," Lissa told him, sounding very superior.

"If it's a girl, we could call it Roveress or Roverette."

"You're stupid, Jamie Keswick!" his sister shrieked, throwing him the most scornful look. "You're a stupid boy."

"No, I'm not. You're stupid!"

"Stop it, both of you," I admonished.

"Mom." Jamie fixed his vivid blue eyes on me. "Please tell me, how do you make a baby out of love?"

I thought for a moment, wondering how to effectively explain this to them without resorting to a pack of lies, when Lissa leaned toward Jamie and said, "*Sex.* That's what makes a baby."

Startled, I exclaimed, "Who told you that?"

"Mary Jane Atkinson, the girl who sits next to me at school. Her mother just made a baby with sex."

"I see. And what else did Mary Jane tell you?"

"Nothing, Mom."

"Mmmm."

Thankfully, Jenny came back just then, and the conversation about babies was curtailed. Jenny was already wearing a bathing suit and carrying swim wear for the children.

"Come on, put these on," she said, handing Jamie a pair of trunks and Lissa her minuscule pink-and-yellow bikini, which Diana had bought for her in Paris.

"I want them to wear their water wings, Jen, they mustn't go in the pool without them. Or without you," I cautioned.

"Don't worry, Mrs. Keswick, I'll look after them properly." So saying she turned to Lissa and helped her to put her bikini top on, and then she led the twins to the shallow end of the swimming pool. Picking up a set of water wings she slipped these onto Lissa's arms before doing the same for Jamie.

Within seconds the three of them were in the pool, laughing and splashing around in the water, having the best of times.

I watched them for a few minutes, enjoying their antics, pleased they were having such fun. I was about to go into the kitchen to see what was happening when Andrew appeared at my side. After kissing me on the cheek, he handed me a huge bunch of red and white carnations.

"Sorry they didn't have any blue ones to make exactly the right color scheme for today," he murmured against my cheek and kissed me again.

"They only have those odd colors occasionally. Usually on Saint Patrick's Day, when they dye them green," I said. "And thank you, darling." I peered at him closely. "The twins think we're trying to make a baby, Andrew."

"Well, we are."

"They're riddled with curiosity about it. Why on earth did you tell them?"

He laughed. "I didn't mean to, it wasn't planned. Honestly, Puss. It just popped out. They were being impossible this morning, and Lissa's become something of a Miss Know-It-All. I wanted to bring them up short, so I gave them a lecture about being more adult in their behavior. And that's when I mentioned a new baby. The kids were rendered speechless, so it had the desired effect. Momentarily." He chuckled again. "I can tell you this, the grannies were delighted. Absolutely thrilled."

"What did you just call me?" Diana exclaimed, stepping out of the sunroom onto the terrace.

"Oh, hi, Ma," Andrew greeted her. Then another laugh broke free, and he hugged her to him. "*Granny.* I called you and Jessica grannies, Ma. But I have to admit, you're the greatest-looking grannies I've ever seen in my entire life. The most beautiful. And you both have fabulous legs."

"Your husband's quite the flatterer," his mother said to me and winked.

"He's only telling the truth, Diana," I answered and edged toward the sunroom door. "I've got to go in and change for lunch now, if you don't mind."

"Go right ahead, Mal, I'll just sit here and watch my grandchildren frolicking in the water." She sat on a white terrace chair, her eyes immediately focusing on the pool.

"I'll come with you." Andrew said to me. He took hold of my arm, and together we went through the French doors. Trixy followed us automatically, scampering along behind.

As we crossed the sunroom, Andrew whispered in my ear, "Want to try for the baby now? Or don't you have time?"

"Oh, you! You're impossible! Incorrigible!" But despite my words, I smiled up at him.

Bending over me, Andrew kissed the tip of my nose. "I do love you, Puss," he murmured, his expression suddenly serious. Then his face changed yet again, and a mischievous glint flickered in his blue eyes as he said, "Listen, I'm willing to try any time, anywhere. All you have to do is say the word."

I laughed. "Tonight?"

"You've got a date," he said.

10

Connecticut, October 1988

The birds had come back.

A great flock of them had landed on the lawn not far from the swimming pool, just as they had done yesterday. They perched there now, immobile, silent, creating a swath of black against the grass, which was strewn with fallen autumn leaves of burnished red and gold.

I could see them quite clearly through the windows of my studio. They looked for all the world like birds of prey to me. An involuntary shiver ran through me at this thought, bringing gooseflesh to my neck and face.

Putting down my paintbrush, I stepped around the easel and opened the door.

Observing the birds from the threshold, I could not help wondering why they still sat out there. Several hours ago, when I was in the bedroom, I had seen them land, and the amazing thing was that they continued to linger, not moving a single feather nor making the faintest twitter of a sound.

Out of the corner of my eye I caught a flash of color, and I swung around to look over at the house.

Sarah was coming down the steps of the terrace, carrying a tray. She was bundled up against the autumnal chill, dressed in an oversized gray sweater, gray wool pants, and black suede boots. A long, scarlet wool scarf was flung around her neck, and it was this which had caught my attention a second before.

"What were you staring at so intently?" she asked as she drew closer.

"Those black birds over there," I answered, gesturing toward them. "They keep coming back."

Pausing in her tracks, Sarah glanced over her shoulder and grimaced. "They look so strange," she murmured. "So . . . ominous."

"I know what you mean," I said and opened the door wider to let her come into the studio.

"I thought you might like a cup of coffee," she said. "Mind if I join you? Or am I interrupting your work?"

"No, you're not, and I'd love a cup." Turning away from the peculiar gathering of birds, I closed the door and followed her inside. Moving a box of watercolors and a jar of water, I made room for the tray on a small table in front of the old sofa.

Sarah sat down and poured the coffee. As she glanced up and looked through the window, she exclaimed, "Jesus, what *are* those birds doing on the lawn? There're so many of them, Mal."

"I know, and it *is* weird, isn't it? The way they sit like that, I mean. But we do get a lot of wildlife out here these days. The wetlands down there near the beaver dam are a sanctuary, and Canada geese and mallard ducks come and occupy the pond, and sometimes a blue heron pays us a visit. Andrew's even seen a hawk from time to time. At least, he thinks it's a hawk."

"Are those blackbirds?"

"Crows," I replied. "Or maybe rooks. What do you think?"

"Search me, I'm not a bird-watcher, I'm afraid."

I laughed, took a sip of coffee, and bit into a macaroon.

Sarah did the same, then looked over the rim of her coffee cup and asked, "Have you made your mind up yet? About going to London to meet Andrew next weekend?"

"I think so. I'd like to go, Sarah, since he's going to be stuck there for another two weeks. That's if you don't mind coming up here with Jennifer and the twins. Actually, if you prefer it, you could move into the apartment in the city for the few days I'll be gone."

"You know I love to play Mommy, how much I adore Jamie and Lissa, and I'm delighted to come up here. Frankly, these quiet weekends far from the maddening crowd are a blessing. I seem to be able to really recharge my batteries out here. And, God knows, I need to do that these days. There's such a lot of pressure at work. So make your plans. I'll hold down the fort, and very happily. In any case, I—" She broke off and stared out the window facing onto the lawn.

I followed her glance, then sprang up and ran to the door. I pulled it open and stepped outside. The birds had taken off in a great flurry all of a sudden, rising up off the lawn with a flapping and whirring of wings. I craned my neck backward to watch them soar upward into the gray and bitter fall sky. I saw at once that the span of their wings was very wide; they were big birds. They climbed up higher, wheeling and turning against the leaden sky, then circled over the studio, casting a dark shadow across its roof.

"They're not blackbirds or crows," I said. "They're far too large. Those birds are ravens."

"Shades of Edgar Allan Poe," Sarah intoned in a low voice directly behind me.

She startled me. I hadn't realized she had followed me to the door. I swung around to face her. "You made me jump! Gave me quite a start!" I exclaimed. "I didn't know you were standing there. And what do you mean, shades of Edgar Allan Poe?"

"Ravens are very Poe-ish," she said, "always in his writings. They're considered to be birds of ill omen, harbingers of death, you know."

A coldness trickled through me. I felt myself shivering. "Don't say things like that, Sash; you frighten me."

"Don't be so silly," she laughed. "I'm only kidding."

"You know very well I've never liked anything that's macabre or ghoulish or has to do with the occult—" I didn't finish my sentence. Sarah was staring at me, concern reflected in her eyes.

"What is it?" I asked. "Why are you looking at me like that? So *oddly*."

"You've gone quite pale, Mal. I'm sorry, honestly I am. I'd forgotten that you're a bit squeamish about those sort of things."

"And you're not," I retorted, trying to recoup, forcing a laugh. But I was still cold all over, and irrational as it was, I felt a peculiar sense of apprehension.

"Only too true," Sarah agreed. "The more ghoulish and scary something is, the better I like it, whether in a film or a book." She laughed again. "Poe was my favorite until Stephen King and Anne Rice came along."

"I'm afraid I have different tastes," I remarked. Closing the door behind me, I walked back to the sofa.

Sarah strolled over to the long table under the window at the back of my studio and stood looking down at the watercolors spread out on it. "These are terrific, Mally!" she cried, sounding surprised. Her voice was suddenly full of merriment. "Oh, I love these drawings of the creatures in the wall! Here's Algernon, the black snake, with his head in the cookie jar, or I should say the chocolate-covered cherry jar. And how adorable—Angelica in her Easter bonnet off to the Fifth Avenue parade, and the chipmunks making a cradle for the baby they're going to adopt." She turned around; her face was wreathed in smiles. "Mal, you're brilliant, a genius. These are delightful paintings, full of charm and humor. You've missed your way. You should be illustrating children's books."

"That's sweet of you to say, but I have my hands full with so many other things, quite aside from Andrew and the twins," I said. "But I'm pleased you like them. I had fun creating the books, and Andrew helped me with the editing of the stories."

"The kids are going to love the books when they find them in their Christmas stockings," Sarah said.

"I hope so, considering all the time I've put into them."

"You ought to try to get them published, Mal."

I shook my head. "I'm not sure they're good enough."

"Take my word for it, they're good enough."

"I wrote and painted them for Jamie and Lissa—just for them, and that's the way I prefer it."

After Sarah left the studio, I picked up my brush and went back to the portrait on the easel. It was of Diana, and I was painting it as a Christmas gift for Andrew.

I had done the initial drawings in July, when she was visiting us, and taken a number of photographs of her in this pose at that time. Working in oils for the past two months, I was now almost finished. I spent a good hour concentrating on Diana's hair color, trying to capture the reddish lights in it, and once I felt I had it exactly right and couldn't improve upon it, I put the brush down. I needed to step away from the portrait for a couple of hours, to get a new perspective on it; also, it was almost lunchtime, and I wanted to eat with the twins, Jenny, and Sarah.

Taking up a rag, I dipped it in turpentine and cleaned the brushes I had used this morning. When I finished, I turned off the lights, pulled on my heavy cardigan, and headed for the door. But before I reached it the phone began to ring, and I picked up the receiver. "Hello?"

"It's me, darling," Andrew said from London.

"Hi, honey, how are you?" I asked, smiling into the phone, glad to hear his voice.

"I'm okay, Mal, but missing you and the twins like hell."

"We miss you, too."

"You are coming over here next weekend, aren't you?" he asked, sounding anxious.

"Nothing could keep me away! Sarah's agreed to bring the twins and Jenny up here, and they'll have fun together."

"And so will we, Puss, I can promise you that," my husband said.

PART TWO

KILGRAM CHASE

11

London, November 1988

On Thursday morning at nine-thirty I flew to London on the *Concorde.*

Andrew had insisted that I take the supersonic flight because it was so fast, only three and a half hours long, reasoning that since I was going for just a few days, it would give us more time together. He had overcome my objections with the assurance that his office was paying for my very expensive ticket.

I quickly discovered it was a terrific way to fly. I had hardly had a chance to eat a snack, relax, and read my Colette when we were landing at Heathrow. Another good thing about flying Concorde was the way the luggage came off the plane and onto the carousel so quickly. The porter I found was soon stacking my cases on his trolley and whizzing me through customs. As we came out into the terminal I was still blinking at the efficiency and speed with which everything had moved.

I looked around for Andrew and saw him before he saw me. He was standing just beyond the barrier, looking handsome and dashing with a trenchcoat thrown nonchalantly over his shoulders. He wore a gray pinstripe suit, a pale blue shirt, and a plain gray silk tie, and as always he was immaculate, not only in his clothes, but from the top of his well-groomed head to the tip of his highly polished brown shoes.

A rush of excitement hit me at the sight of him. It always did when we had been apart. He was the only man I had ever loved, the only man I would ever want.

Suddenly he saw me, and his face broke into smiles. I raised my hand in greeting, smiled back, and hurried forward as he moved toward me. A split second later he was holding me in his arms, hugging me to him and kissing me. As I clung to him I thought how extraordinary it was that less than four hours after leaving Kennedy I was standing here on English soil, embracing my husband.

We drew apart finally, and I said, "My bags are on the trolley," looking over my shoulder as I spoke.

Andrew glanced at the porter and nodded.

"'Evening, guv'nor," the porter said. "Got a car waiting, have you?"

"Yes, in the parking area just outside this building," Andrew told him.

"Right ho!" The porter went trundling ahead of us, pushing the trolley. We walked after him.

Andrew turned to me and lifted a brow. "You've come for the duration, have you?"

"Duration?"

"Of my stay. You've certainly brought enough luggage."

I laughed. "Only two cases and a makeup bag."

"Rather large cases, though," Andrew murmured, half smiling.

I threw my husband a flirtatious look and said, "But I'll stay if you want me to."

"Will you really, darling?" His face lit up, and there was a sudden eagerness in his eyes, excitement in his manner.

Instantly I regretted teasing him and explained in a more serious tone, "I'd love to stay longer than we'd planned, Andrew, but you know I can't. I've got to go back on Monday."

"Why?"

"I can't leave the children for longer than a weekend."

"'Course you can, darling. The twins'll be fine. They've got Jenny and your mother, *and* Sarah to watch over them."

"Sarah's working during the week," I pointed out.

"Your mother isn't, and Jenny is very reliable. They're as safe as houses with her."

"But we agreed I'd only come here for the weekend," I reminded him. I stopped. Staring hard at him, I said, "I shouldn't have risen to the bait just now, and I shouldn't have teased you, said I'd stay longer. Honestly, it's just not possible. I'd feel uneasy, Andrew."

Suddenly he looked awfully glum, but he made no further comment. We walked on in silence.

Making a snap decision, I stopped again, turned to him, and said, "Look, I'll stay on until Tuesday, honey. I think that'll be all right. Okay? Is that okay with you?"

Smiling, he nodded and exclaimed, "Mal, that's great, just great!" Then taking hold of my elbow firmly, he hurried me forward.

We went through the glass doors of the terminal, crossed the road, and entered the parking area where the porter was already waiting with my suitcases on the trolley.

I shivered. It was a damp November night and quite cold, typical English winter weather.

A dark green Rolls-Royce moved slowly toward us and braked. A uniformed chauffeur jumped out, nodded to me, and said, "Good evening, madam," and went to help the porter load the bags into the trunk before I even had a chance to acknowledge him.

Turning to the porter, I said, "Thanks for helping me," and walked over to the Rolls. Andrew tipped him and followed me. Bundling me into the car, Andrew then stepped in behind me and closed the door. Immediately he took me in his arms and gave me a long kiss, then pulling away, he said, "It's so good to have you here, Mal."

"I know. It's the same for me," I answered. "Wonderful to be here with you."

The chauffeur got in and turned on the ignition. A few seconds later we were leaving the airport buildings behind and heading out onto the main road in the direction of London.

As the car sped along, I glanced at my husband. My eyes lingered on his face, and I saw, on closer examination, that he looked much more tired than I had realized. There were dark smudges under his eyes, and in repose, his face appeared unexpectedly weary. A general air of fatigue enveloped him.

Frowning, I said, "You've had a much rougher time than you've told me, haven't you?"

Andrew gave a quick nod, squeezed my hand, and inclined his head in the direction of the driver, obviously not wanting to speak in front of him. He murmured, sotto voce, "I'll tell you later."

"All right." Opening my bag, I took out two envelopes with *Dad* printed across their fronts in uneven, wobbly, childlike letters. Handing them to Andrew, I said, "Lissa and Jamie have each written you a card."

Looking pleased, he put on his horn-rimmed glasses, opened the envelopes, and began to read.

I leaned back against the soft cream leather of my seat and stared out the window. It was just six-thirty, and dark, so there was not much to see. The road was slick with rain, and the traffic at this hour was heavy. But the Rolls-Royce rolled steadily along at a good speed, and I knew that in spite of the rain, which was now falling in torrents, we would arrive at Claridge's in an hour, or thereabouts.

Later that evening, after I had called Jenny in New York, unpacked, showered, redone my makeup, and changed my clothes, Andrew took me to dinner at the Connaught Hotel.

"For sentimental reasons, Mal darling," he said as we walked from Claridge's to the other hotel, which was situated on Carlos Place.

It was still cold and damp, but the heavy downpour had long since ceased, and I was glad to get a little air after being cooped up on the plane. Anyway, I always liked to walk in London, especially in Mayfair around the dinner hour.

The traffic was far lighter and the streets were much less crowded; in fact, they were almost empty at this time of day. There was something charming and beautiful about this lovely old part of London. Certain streets in Mayfair were still residential, although some of the elegant Georgian mansions had been turned into offices; nonetheless, the section was very special to me, and it held many fond memories of my courtship.

Once we were settled at our table in the restaurant of the Connaught, Andrew ordered a glass of white wine for me and a very dry martini for himself. As we waited for the drinks to materialize, he started to talk about the London office of Blau, Ames, Braddock and Suskind, and without any prompting from me.

"I think I got over here just in the nick of time," he explained, leaning across the table, pinning me with his eyes. "The place is in a mess, as I sort of indicated to you on the phone the other night. It's been badly managed for the last few years. Joe Braddock's son-in-law doesn't know his ass from his elbow, and Jack Underwood and I will have to do a lot of fancy footwork in order to keep it afloat."

I was incredulous. It had always been a financially successful operation. Until recently, apparently. Startled, I exclaimed, "Do you mean you might have to close the London office?"

He nodded emphatically. "Yep, I sure do. Malcolm Stainley's one of the biggest dummies I've ever met. I don't know what got into Joe. Giving him the European end to run was more than foolhardy. It was criminal. And it *is* the European end, not merely the London office, since most of our French, German, and Continental business is handled and billed out of here."

"Nepotism, of course," I said. "That's why Malcolm is where he is." Then I asked, "But what exactly did he do, Andrew?"

"He made one hell of a mess, that's for sure," Andrew muttered, falling silent as the waiter arrived with our drinks.

After we had clinked glasses, Andrew went on, "The trouble with Malcolm Stainley is that he hasn't got a clue about people. He can't keep staff, for one thing, and in my opinion that's because he pits people against one another. Anyway, morale is at rock bottom here, and everyone hates his guts. Then again, he's a bit of a cheap-skate, so he's always trying to save money—in the wrong ways. For instance, he hires second-rate talent instead of going for the best and the brightest. In consequence, we lose out on a lot of bids we make to potential clients, because the presentations are lousy." Andrew shook his head. "He's shown very flawed judgment on many different levels."

"But what's the solution? After all, Malcolm is married to Joe's daughter, and Ellen likes living in London. So you can bet Joe isn't going to remove her husband, or fire him. At least, that's the way I read it."

Andrew looked thoughtful as he sat and sipped his martini without responding.

Finally, he said, "No, I don't suppose Joe is going to do any-thing about Malcolm, so Jack and I will have to render the bugger helpless and take his power away to boot."

"And how do you plan to do that?" I asked, raising a brow.

"Appoint someone else to run the London office, get it on the straight and narrow."

"But Joe may not agree to that. And Malcolm *surely* won't," I ventured.

Andrew gave me a small, very knowing smile. "Joe *will* agree to certain things, Mal. Jack, Harvey Colton, and I have been talking retirement to him, and in no uncertain terms, these last few months, and he will agree to do what we propose. In order to stay on with the agency himself. He loathes the idea of retiring, as I thought you'd realized."

I nodded but made no comment. Joe Braddock was close to senile, in my opinion, and should have been put out to pasture eons ago.

Andrew continued, "You're right, of course, in that Joe won't like seeing his son-in-law demoted or displaced. And neither will Malcolm the Great himself. He'd put up one hell of a bloody fight, no two ways about it, if we said we wanted him to go. So we're not going to do that. Instead we're going to kick him upstairs, give him a fancy title." Andrew paused dramatically, then finished, "And we'll tie his hands. Manacle them, if necessary." He grinned at me conspiratorially. "That leaves the way open for a new, hands-on guy who'll pull the company out of the mire, get it back on course. And lead it to financial security. *We hope*."

"Do you have someone in mind?" I wondered out loud.

"Jack and Harvey wanted me to take it on. However, I said thanks but no thanks. Frankly, Mal, I didn't want to uproot us all, take the kids out of Trinity, move to London for a couple of years. Because that's what it would mean. It's going to take two, maybe even three years to pull this operation around."

"Oh," I said, staring at him. "But I wouldn't have minded living in London for two or three years, Andrew, really I wouldn't. If you haven't already hired someone else yet, why don't you take the position after all?"

He shook his head. "No way, Mal, it's not my cup of tea, cleaning up somebody else's mess. Besides which, Harvey, Jack, and I have been streamlining the New York operation. I want to keep on doing that, it's very important to me." Narrowing those brilliantly blue eyes at me, he said softly, "Oh, hell, darling, you're disappointed, aren't you?"

"No, I'm not," I protested, although he had read my thoughts very accurately.

"I *know* you, Mallory Keswick," my husband said in the quietest of voices. "And I think you *are* disappointed . . . just a little bit."

"Well, yes," I admitted. Then I gave him a reassuring smile. "But I'm not important in this instance. It's your decision. After all, it is *your* career, and you're the one it affects the most. Whatever you decide about where you work, be it agency or city or country, it'll be okay with me, I promise you."

"Thanks for that. I just don't want to live in England," he answered, "but then you've always known this. I love Manhattan and working on Madison Avenue. The rhythm of the city excites and invigorates me, and I love my job. Not only that, I'd miss Indian Meadows, and so would you."

"That's true, I would. So who have you hired? Or haven't you found anyone yet?"

"Jack Underwood. He's going to move over here and tackle the job. In fact, he's flying in next Wednesday so that we can go over things together before I leave. He'll stay on, as of this coming week, and assume the running of the British company immediately. It's going to be a permanent move for him. At least, he'll be here for a few years. I'm going to miss him."

"So you and Harvey will have to cope on your own in New York?"

"That we will. And we do have our jobs cut out for us. But we both believe we can bring the agency back to its former standing. Although it has been losing ground a bit, we're still big in certain areas of advertising, and we have a roster of good and very loyal old clients."

Reaching out, I took hold of his hand, which rested on the table. "I haven't seen you looking so tired for a long time, darling. I guess it has been pretty rough whilst you've been here in London. Much rougher than you've let on to me."

"Mal, that's true to a certain extent." He sighed under his breath. "And I have to admit that very long hours and a disgruntled staff have had their debilitating effect, no two ways about it." Then he winked, taking me by surprise, and in a lighter, gayer tone, he added, "But now you're here, my darling. We're going to have a lovely weekend together, and we're not going to discuss business. Not at all. Agreed?"

"I agree to anything you say or want."

A dark brow lifted, and he laughed a deep-throated laugh. He said, "Let's order another drink, and then we'll look at the menu."

12

It was gray and overcast on Friday morning, and as I left Claridge's Hotel, heading toward Berkeley Square, I glanced up at the sky. It was leaden and presaged rain, which Andrew had predicted before he had left for the office earlier.

Instead of walking to Diana's, which I liked to do, I hailed a cab and got in. Just in time, too. It began to drizzle as I slammed the door and gave the cabbie the address. English weather, I thought glumly, staring out the taxi window. It's always raining. But one didn't come to England for the weather; there were other, more important reasons to be here. I had always loved England and the English, and London was my most favorite city in the entire world. I loved it even more than my hometown, New York.

I settled back against the cab seat, glad to be here. On second thought, it could hail and snow and storm for all I cared. The weather was quite irrelevant to me.

My mother-in-law's antique shop was located at the far end of the King's Road, and as the cab flew along Knightsbridge, heading in that direction, I made a mental note to go to Harrods and Harvey Nichols later in the day, to do some of my Christmas shopping. Since we would be spending the holidays with Diana, I could have gifts for her, the children, and Andrew shipped directly to her house in Yorkshire. Certainly it would save me the trouble of bringing everything with me from New York in December. The stores would probably gift wrap them, too.

Andrew had kept it a secret from his mother that I was joining him in London for a long weekend; when I had announced my presence to her on the phone last night, she had reacted in her usual way. She was full of excitement, so very pleased to hear my voice, and she had immediately asked me to have lunch with her today.

Once we arrived at the shop, I paid off the cabbie and stood outside in the street, gazing at the beautiful things which graced the window of Diana Howard Keswick Antiques.

I feasted my eyes on a pair of elegant bronze *doré* candlesticks, French, probably from the eighteenth century, which stood on a handsome console table with a marble top and an intricately carved wood base, also eighteenth-century French, I was quite sure of that.

After a few moments, I looked beyond these rare and priceless objects, peering inside as best I could. I could just make out Diana standing at the back of the shop near her desk, talking to a man who was obviously a customer. She was gesturing with her hands in that most expressive way she had, and then she turned to point out a Flemish tapestry, which was hanging on the wall behind her. They stood looking at it together.

Opening the door, I went inside.

I couldn't help thinking how marvelous she looked this morning. She was wearing a bright red wool suit, simple, tailored, elegant, and her double-stranded pearl choker. Both the vivid color and the milky sheen of the pearls were perfect foils for her glossy brown hair and tawny-gold complexion.

It particularly pleased me that she was wearing red today, since I had painted her in a scarlet silk shirt and the same choker, which she usually wore and which was her trademark, in a sense. Observing her, I was instantly reassured that I had captured the essence of her on my canvas—her warmth and beauty and an inner grace that seemed to radiate from her. I hoped Andrew was going to like my portrait of his mother, which Sarah says is one of the best things I've ever done.

The moment Diana saw me she excused herself and hurried forward, a wide smile lighting up her face, her pale gray-blue eyes reflecting the same kind of eagerness and joy which I usually associate with Andrew. He always has that same happy, anticipatory look when he is seeing me for the first time after we've been apart; it is spontaneous and so very loving.

"Darling, you're here!" Diana cried, grasping my arm. "I can't believe it, and it's such a lovely surprise. I'm so happy to see you!"

My smile was as affectionate as hers, and my happiness as keenly felt. "Hello, Diana. You're the best thing London has to offer, aside from your son, of course."

She laughed gaily, in that special warm and welcoming way of hers, and we quickly embraced. Then she led me forward.

"Mal, I'd like to introduce Robin McAllister," she said. "Robin, this is my daughter-in-law, Mallory Keswick."

The man, who was tall, handsome, distinguished, and elegantly dressed, inclined his head politely. He shook my hand. "I'm pleased to meet you, Mrs. Keswick," he said.

"And I'm happy to meet you, Mr. McAllister," I responded.

Diana said, "Mal, dear, would you please excuse me for a moment or two? I wish to show Mr. McAllister a painting downstairs. I won't be very long, then we can get off to lunch."

"Don't worry about me," I said, "I'll just wander around the shop. I can see at a glance that you have some wonderful things. As you usually do."

Before my mother-in-law had a chance to say anything else, I strolled to the other side of her establishment, my eyes roving around, taking everything in.

I loved antiques, and Diana invariably had some of the best and most beautiful available in London, many of them garnered from the great houses of Europe. She traveled extensively on the Continent, looking for all kinds of treasures, but mostly she specialized in eighteenth- and nineteenth-century French furniture, decorative objects, porcelain, and paintings, although she did carry a few English Georgian and Regency pieces as well. However, her impeccable credentials and reputation as a dealer came from her immense knowledge of fine French furniture, which was where her great expertise lay. But like every antiquarian of some importance and distinction, Diana was extremely learned in other areas, well versed in a variety of different design periods from many countries.

I noticed that she was currently showing a collection of Biedermeier furniture in the special-display area of the shop, and even from this distance I could see that it was superb. I was instantly drawn down to the far end of the store, near the staircase leading to the upper floors. Here a small raised platform held the furniture, which was roped off.

I stood looking at the German pieces in awe, admiring the rich, gleaming woods and the incredible craftsmanship. I was especially taken by a circular dining table made of various light-colored woods, most likely fruitwoods, and inlaid with ebony. This was a combination often used in Biedermeier designs at the turn of the century, when the furniture was at the height of its popularity.

What I wouldn't give for a table like that, I thought. But quite aside from the fact that it probably cost the earth—I was positive it did—I had nowhere to put it. Not only that, Indian Meadows was furnished with a mixture of antique English and French country furniture, and although Biedermeier was versatile and plain enough to blend with almost any period or style, it wasn't quite right for us, either for our country home or our Manhattan apartment. Pity, though, I muttered under my breath as I walked on.

Pausing in front of an eighteenth-century French *trumeau,* which was hanging on a side wall, I admired its beautifully carved wood frame and painted decorative scene set in the top of the frame, wondering what mantelpiece it had hung over, and in which great house? A château in the Loire, I had no doubt. Then I took a peek at myself in its cloudy antique mirror.

My reflection dismayed me. I decided I looked a bit too pale and tired, almost wan under the mass of red hair, but nonetheless quite smart in my dark delphinium-blue wool coat and dress. No wonder I'm looking tired, I suddenly thought, recalling last night. Andrew and I had been very carried away with each other. A small smile slid onto my face, and I glanced down at the floor, remembering. My husband and I hadn't been able to get enough of each other, and despite his tiredness in general, his fatigue over dinner, he had been imbued with an amazing vitality, a rush of energy the moment we had climbed into bed. If we hadn't made another baby last night, I couldn't imagine when we ever would.

"Hello, Mallory, how are you?" a voice said, and I gave a little start and swung around swiftly. I found myself staring into the smiling face of Jane Patterson, Diana's personal assistant.

Taking a step forward, I gave her a quick hug. "How are you, Jane?"

"I couldn't be better," she said, "and you're obviously in the best of health and thriving."

I nodded and told her I was.

She inquired about the twins. I asked about her daughter, Serena. We stood chatting amiably for several seconds.

Out of the corner of my eye, I became aware of sudden movement. I saw Mr. McAllister striding toward the door. He nodded to us curtly as he went out into the street. Right behind him came Diana, hurrying forward on her high heels, throwing a red wool cape around her shoulders with a flourish as she headed in our direction.

"Shall we go, Mal?" she said to me briskly,

Turning to her assistant, my mother-in-law added, "Percy says he'll be happy to hold down the fort whilst you go to lunch, Janey. I should be back around three."

"No problem, Diana," Jane murmured.

She and I said our good-byes.

Diana rushed out into the street, put up her umbrella, and stood on the edge of the sidewalk enthusiastically flagging a cab, ignoring the rain.

*   *   *

Diana took me to the Savoy Hotel in the Strand for lunch.

Even though it was a bit far from her shop, she knew it was one of my favorite places, and she wanted to please me, as she usually did. I protested. Knowing how busy she was, I tried to persuade her to go somewhere closer, but she wouldn't hear of it. She could be as stubborn as her son at times.

We sat at a window table overlooking the Thames in the main restaurant, which I have always preferred to the famous Grill Room where Fleet Street editors, politicians, and theatrical celebrities frequently lunch and dine. It was quieter in here, more leisurely, and anyway, I could never resist this particular view of London. It was superb.

I gazed out the window. There was a mistiness in the air, and the sky was still a strange metallic color, but the heavy, slashing rain had stopped finally. Even the light had begun to change, now casting a pearly haze over the river and the ancient buildings, bathing them in a gauzy softness that seemed suddenly to make them shimmer; the winter sun was finally breaking through the somber clouds. Light on moving water, Turner light, I said to myself, thinking, as I so often did, of my favorite painter.

I lolled back in my chair. I was relaxed and happy, filled with the most extraordinary contentment. How lucky I was—to be in London with my husband, to be here with Diana at the Savoy having lunch, to have my beautiful children. I might even be pregnant again. My life was charmed. I was blessed.

I sipped my wine and smiled at Diana. And she smiled back, reached out, squeezed my hand.

"Andrew's so lucky to have found you, and I'm so lucky to have you, Mal. The daughter I always wanted. You're the best, you know, the very best."

"And so are you, Diana. I was just thinking how lucky *I* am."

She nodded. "I believe we're both rather fortunate." She sipped her wine, continued, "I was so sorry not to be able to come to your mother's wedding. It was simply the worst time for me. I had made my plans such a long time before she invited me. I had to go to a sale in Aix-en-Provence, and then on to Venice. I just couldn't get out of my commitments."

"It was all right, Diana, Mom understood, honestly she did. To tell you the truth, I think she was relieved to keep it small. That's unusual for her, I must admit, since she's such a social animal, but she seemed glad to have just a few people. Us, and David's son and daughter-in-law and grandson. Oh, and Sarah and her mother, of course. Mom's been close to Aunt Pansy ever since Sarah and I were little kids, babies. She didn't even invite her mother, Grandmother Adelia, but then I don't believe *she* was up to it anyway. She's getting a bit senile, poor thing. Such a pity. She used to be so vital."

"She's very old now, isn't she?"

"Ninety-one."

"Oh, my goodness, that *is* old."

"I wouldn't mind living to that age," I said, "as long as I had all my marbles."

Diana laughed, and so did I.

I said, "David Nelson's a nice man, by the way. I've gotten to know him a bit better over the past few months, and he's very genuine. He really does care for Mom."

"I'm glad Jessica finally got married. She's been so lonely for so very long. Marrying David is the wisest thing she could've done."

I looked across the table at Diana, studying her for a second. And then before I could stop myself, I blurted out, "And *you* must be very lonely too, Diana. After all, you're *alone*."

"I think most women, no, let me correct myself, most *people* who are on their own get extremely lonely at different times in their daily lives," she said, smiling faintly.

There was a slight pause, and I saw a look of sadness creep into her eyes before she said slowly, "In a way, loneliness is another kind of death . . . " She did not finish her sentence, merely sat gazing at me.

I was lost for words myself, feeling her wistfulness, her sense of loss and regret more profoundly than I ever had before. She touched me deeply.

A silence fell between us. We sipped our wine, looked out the window, and quietly ignored each other for a moment or two, lost in our own thoughts.

Quite unexpectedly, I had a terrible urge to ask her about my father, to tell her what Andrew and I had concocted about the two of them this past summer. Yes, I will ask her, I made up my mind. But when I turned my face to focus on her, I lost my nerve. I didn't dare say a word to her. Not because she intimidated me, which she didn't, but because she was essentially such a private person. I could not intrude on her privacy, nor could I probe into her personal life.

She caught my eye and flashed me the most brilliant of smiles. She said cheerfully, "But my loneliness doesn't last very long, Mal, only an hour or two, and it only hits me every now and then. Let's face it, I'm very fortunate to have the business. It keeps me fully occupied night and day—traveling abroad, going to auctions and sales on the Continent, taking clients and would-be clients to lunch and dinner, seeing and entertaining foreign dealers, not to mention running the shop. I never seem to have a moment to spare these days. I'm always flying off to France or Italy or Spain. Or somewhere or other."

"And haven't you ever met someone *delicious* on your travels?" I asked. "A suave, sophisticated Frenchman? Or a lyrical, romantic Italian? Or perhaps a dashing, passionate Spaniard?" I couldn't resist teasing her.

Giggling like a schoolgirl, her eyes as merry as I've ever seen them, she shook her head. "'Fraid not, Mal," she said, then lifted her glass to her mouth and took a sip of the wine, a very good Montrachet. She knew her French wines.

At this moment the waiter appeared with our first course.

Diana had ordered leek-and-potato soup, "to fight the chill in the air," she had said to me a short while before as we studied the menus.

I had selected oysters, and a dozen of the Savoy's best Colchesters were staring up at me temptingly. They looked delectable. My mouth watered. I said to Diana, "Whenever I'm here in London, I manage to make a pig of myself with all of the wonderful fish, I love it so much. And I'm afraid I'm about to become Miss Piggy again."

"It's the best fish in the world, at least I think so; and don't forget, it's not fattening."

"As if *you* had to worry," I murmured. I had always admired Diana's sleek figure. Not that I was fat, but she was very slender and shapely for her age.

Pushing my small, sharp fork onto the shell and underneath a plump, succulent oyster, I lifted it up and plopped it into my mouth. Instantly, I could taste the salt of the sea and seaweed and the sea itself in that little morsel, all of those tastes rolling around in my mouth at the same time. It was refreshing and delicious. As the oyster slid down my throat, I reached for another without pause, and then another, unable to resist. I was going to have to restrain myself, or I would bolt them all down in the space of a few minutes.

Out of the blue, Diana said, "I wonder if your father will get married, now that he's free to do so?"

My eyes came up from my plate of oysters, and I gaped at her. Putting my fork down, I sat back in the chair, my eyes leveled at her. I felt a tight little frown knotting the bridge of my nose.

Finding my voice eventually, I said slowly, "He'd have to have . . . someone . . . someone in his life . . . *someone* to marry, wouldn't he?" I discovered I could not continue. I leaned against my chair, too nervous to say another word. I wanted Diana to tell me, to break the news about her and Daddy. I felt awkward, tongue-tied, and therefore I couldn't probe.

"Oh, but he does have somebody," she said, and that brilliant smile of hers played on her pretty mouth again.

"He *does*?"

"Why, of course. Whatever makes you think that a man like

your father could be alone? He's far too dependent a creature for that." She stopped short, staring hard at me. She must have noticed the expression on my face.

I sat there still somewhat dumbfounded, staring back at her stupidly. I had been rendered mute.

Diana frowned. "I thought you knew ... I thought your mother had told you years ago ... " Once again, her voice trailed off.

"Told me what?" I asked in a tight voice.

"Oh, dear," Diana muttered, almost to herself. "What have I done now? Gone and put my foot in it, I suspect."

"No, you haven't, Diana, truly you haven't!" I protested, eager to hear more. "What did you mean? What did you think my mother had told me?"

She took a deep breath. "That there have been other women in his life. I mean after your mother and he agreed to separate, all those years ago when you were eighteen, when you went off to Radcliffe. Jess once told me about his—affairs, relationships, whatever you wish to call them. I simply assumed that she had confided in you when you grew older. Especially after your marriage."

"No, she didn't. I must admit, though, that I've thought about his life, lately, anyway. Thought about him ... having other women, I mean."

Diana nodded.

"And there's someone now, isn't there? Someone *special* in my father's life."

Again she nodded, as though she did not trust herself to speak, the way I had felt a few minutes before. I could certainly understand why.

Taking a deep breath, I said in a rush, "It's you, isn't it, Diana? Just as Andrew and I have suspected for months now."

My mother-in-law looked as if she'd been struck in the face, stared at me in absolute amazement, and then she burst out laughing. She continued to laugh so much tears came into her eyes. Only by exercising enormous control did she manage to finally stop. Reaching for her bag, she took out a lacy handkerchief and dabbed her eyes.

"Oh, do excuse me, Mal darling," she said after a moment, still gasping slightly. "I'm sorry to behave this way, but that's the funniest thing I've heard in a long time. Your father and I? Good Lord, no. I'm much too practical and down-to-earth, far too sane for Edward. He needs someone a lot more helpless and sweeter than I. He needs a woman who is romantic, idealistic, and fey. Yes, *fey* is a very good word with which to describe Gwenny."

"Gwenny! Who's *Gwenny*?"

"Gwendolyn Reece-Jones. She's a great friend of mine, a theatrical designer, and when she's not up here in London designing sets and scenery and all that sort of thing for plays and shows in the West End, she lives in a sixteenth-century manor house in the Welsh Marshes. She's imaginative and charming and funny and dear, and yes, very, very *fey*."

"And she's Daddy's girlfriend?"

"Correct. She's been good for him, too." Diana cleared her throat and after a pause added, "And I'm afraid I introduced them, for my sins."

"Is it serious?"

"Gwenny is serious, I know that for a fact. She's positively dotty over him. Very much in love." Diana sat back, her head held on one side; a thoughtful look spread itself across her face. "I *think* Edward's serious about her, but I couldn't say definitely. That's why I wondered aloud if he would marry. Perhaps. Hard to say, really."

"Has he known her long?"

"Oh, about four years, thereabouts."

"I see."

After a moment, Diana asked, "Tell me something. What on earth made you and Andrew think *I* was involved with your father? That's a most preposterous idea, and in many ways, I might add."

I told her then about Andrew finding the letter in the summer.

I explained how the two of us had speculated about them, had analyzed the way they behaved when they were together, concluded how different they were when in each other's company. And in consequence of all this had assumed they were having an affair.

Diana had the good grace to chuckle. "If you think I act differently when I'm around Edward, you're perfectly correct. I do. I suppose I'm more of a woman, my *own* woman, less of a *mother*, less of a *grandmother*. I'm more myself in certain ways. What I mean by this is that I'm like I am when I'm alone, when I'm not with you and Andrew and the twins. I behave in a very natural way with him. You see, there's something in your father's personality that makes every woman feel . . . good, and—"

"Except for Mom," I cut in.

"Touché, darling," she said. "And as I was saying, he has that knack, that ability, to make a woman feel her best—attractive, feminine, and desirable. Edward can make a woman believe she's special, *wanted,* when he's around her, even if he's not particularly interested in her for himself. And he's very flirtatious, says flattering things. It's hard to explain, really. I will say this: Your father's very much a woman's man, not a man's man at all. He adores women, admires them, respects them, and I guess that is part of it." She leaned across the table and finished, "It's all about *attitude,* Mal. His attitude."

"Will he marry . . . Gwenny? What's your opinion, Diana?"

"I told you, I don't know." She pursed her lips, looking thoughtful again, but only for a fraction of a second. "If he's smart, he will. She's made him happy, that I do know."

"I wonder if he'll bring her out in the open, now that Mom's divorced him and married someone else?"

Diana threw me an odd look. "He's not made much of a secret about Gwenny in the past. In fact, no secret at all. At least, not here in London. He probably didn't mention Gwenny to you because he didn't want to hurt your feelings."

"Maybe."

"I'm sure that's the case," Diana said in her firmest tone.

It occurred to me that she was suddenly out to defend my father. He didn't need any defense, as far as I was concerned. I had always loved him, and I still did. After all, his marital battles with my mother were old hat. I had grown up with them. Besides which, I was the one who had always thought they should have divorced years ago. I had never understood their behavior.

Clearing my throat, I asked, "Did he ever bring Gwenny to the States? To New York?"

"Not to New York, as far as I know. However, I believe she was with him when he gave those archaeological lectures at U.C.L.A. last year."

"How old is she?"

"About fifty-three or fifty-four, not much more than that."

"Has she ever been married? Tell me something about her, Diana."

Diana nodded. "Of course. It's not at all unnatural for you to be curious. But there's not much to tell. She *was* married. To Laurence Wilton, the actor. As you probably know, he died about twelve years ago. No children. She's a rather nice woman, and she's very interested in archaeology, anthropology, art, and architecture. She shares many common bonds with your father. I think you'd approve of Gwenny."

"I wish he'd trusted me enough to tell me about her," I muttered, dropping my eyes. I ate the rest of my oysters in silence.

Diana dipped her spoon into the soup and took a few mouthfuls. "I'm afraid I've let this grow cold," she murmured.

"Let's get you some more," I suggested, and swiveling in my chair, I endeavored to catch the waiter's eye.

"No, no," Diana demurred. "This is fine, really. It hasn't lost its taste. It's like . . . vichyssoise now, and it's still very good."

I nodded and took a long swallow of the white wine.

My mother-in-law's eyes rested on me, and she studied me for a while. Eventually, she said in a low, concerned voice, "You know, your father has always been a very discreet man, from all that I've heard, and from everything I know about him personally. He's never flaunted his . . . lady friends. And you must always remember that old habits die hard. With everyone. Edward is a gentleman, and so he's discreet. He doesn't know any other way to be. I am quite certain that he thought he was doing the right thing in not telling you about Gwenny. Or introducing you to her. And there's something else. I'm sure he didn't want to upset you."

"I guess so," I agreed, but I was a bit miffed with my father all of a sudden.

I turned my head and looked out the window, staring at the hazy gray sky but not really seeing it. I was disappointed he had not understood that *I* could handle it, had not understood that *I* would have understood everything, understood about Gwendolyn Reece-Jones and his need at this time in his life to have a bit of happiness. I was thirty-three years old, married and a mother, for God's sake. I was a mature, adult young woman, not a little girl anymore.

13

The suite at Claridge's was not all that large, but it was very comfortable, and the sitting room was one of the most charming I've ever seen, redolent of the Victorian period.

What made it so unusual and special was the fireplace that really worked and the baby grand that stood regally in a corner near the tall, soaring windows. These were dressed with plum-colored velvet draperies, handsomely swagged and tasseled, and they punctuated the soft, dove-gray brocade walls, while an oriental carpet spread rich, jewel-toned colors underfoot.

A big, squashy sofa covered in plum silk and matching armchairs, along with an antique coffee table, were arranged in front of the white marble fireplace; here, an eye-catching chinoiserie mirror hung over the mantel and made a glittering backdrop for a gilt-and-marble French chiming clock with cupids reclining on each side of its face.

Adding to the turn-of-the-century mood created by the elegant background were such things as a Victorian desk, a china cabinet filled with antique porcelain plates, and various small occasional tables made of mahogany. In fact, so authentic was the decorative scheme I felt as if I had been whisked back into another era.

Vases of flowers, a bowl of fruit, a tray of drinks, newspapers and magazines all helped to make the room seem even more homey and inviting. It was especially cozy this November night, with the fire burning merrily in the grate and the pink silk-shaded lamps turned on.

A television set stood in a corner on one side of the fireplace; I turned it on and sat down on the sofa to watch the evening news. But it was the tail end of it, with sports coming up, and within a few minutes I became bored and restless.

Turning it off, I wandered through into the bedroom, asking myself when Andrew would manage to get away from the office. We had spoken earlier, in the late afternoon just after I had returned from a visit to the Tate, and he had told me that he had booked a table at Harry's Bar for dinner. But he had not indicated what time the reservation was for, nor had he said when he would return to the hotel.

To while away a little time, I read several chapters of my Colette, and then, realizing it was almost eight, I undressed, put on a robe, and went into the bathroom. After cleaning off my makeup, I redid my face and brushed my hair. I had just finished coiling it up into a French twist on the back of my head when I heard a key in the door. I rushed into the sitting room, a happy and expectant look on my face.

Andrew was hanging up his trenchcoat in the small vestibule of the suite. Turning around, he saw me. "Hi," he said. He lifted his briefcase off the floor and took a step forward.

I found myself staring at him intently. I saw at once that he was totally exhausted. I was appalled. The dark smudges under his eyes seemed more pronounced than ever tonight, and his face was drawn, much paler than usual.

Hurrying to him, I hugged him tightly, then taking hold of his arm, I led him into the room. But he paused by the fireplace, stepped away from me, and put the briefcase on a nearby chair. After leaning toward the fire and warming his hands, he straightened and propped himself against the mantelpiece.

Looking at him closely, I asked, "Don't you feel well?"

"Tired. Bone bloody tired."

"We don't have to go out to dinner," I volunteered. "We could have room service."

He gave me a peculiar, rather cold look. "I don't care whether we go out to dinner or not. What I do care about, though, is dragging myself up to Yorkshire. What I should say is that I'm certainly *not* going to trail up there to my mother's." He said this in a snappish tone that was most unlike him. "I've just had her on the phone, railing on about my working too hard, and insisting we go up there tomorrow. So that I can have a rest, she said. Is that what the two of you were concocting at lunch today?"

"We hardly spoke about it!" I exclaimed a bit heatedly. "In fact, Diana only mentioned it to me in passing."

"Well, she didn't to me!" he snorted, glaring. "She gave me a bloody lecture. She also said *you* wanted to go, that I was not being fair, making you stay in town for the weekend—"

"Andrew," I interjected sharply, "I don't care whether we go or not!" I could tell he was not only tired but angry, and I had an awful sinking feeling it was with me, as well as with his mother.

"I'm glad to hear you feel that way, because we can't go. It's out of the question altogether. I have to work tomorrow, and Sunday as well, most probably."

"Oh," I said, at a loss.

"And what does *that* mean?"

"Nothing, just *oh*. However, if you have to work this weekend, why did you ask me to fly over here? Just to sit in this suite waiting for you? I might as well have stayed in New York with the twins, or taken them out to Indian Meadows."

Instead of answering me, he ran his hand through his hair somewhat distractedly, then rubbed his eyes. "It's been one hellish day," he grumbled in the same belligerent voice. "Malcolm Stainley's been behaving like an idiot. Which he *is*, of course ... goes without saying. He's also a bastard, the worst. And full of himself, has an ego the size of a house. *Ego*." Andrew compressed his lips. "Ego always gets in the way, and it gets more people into trouble than I care to think about," he muttered in a voice so quiet now it was barely audible.

I said nothing.

Suddenly straightening his shoulders, he glanced across at me. "I stumbled on yet another of Stainley's messes this afternoon, and it may take a bit of time to clear up. There's a possibility I'll have to stay in London for an extra week."

"I thought Jack Underwood was coming over on Wednesday," I said. "To take over from you."

"He may need help. *My* help."

I opened my mouth to protest and promptly closed it. I sat down heavily on the sofa, and after a moment I said, "Why don't I call Harry's Bar and cancel our reservation? Obviously you're in no mood to go out to dinner."

"And *you* are. So we'll *go*."

"Andrew, *please*. You're being so argumentative, and I don't know why." I bit my lip, feeling unexpected tears pricking the back of my eyes. Impatiently, I pushed them away, swallowed hard, and said, as steadily as possible, "I just want to do what *you* want. I only want to please you."

"I need a drink," he mumbled and marched over to the console table that stood between two of the high, graceful windows.

I watched him as he poured himself a neat scotch, noticing the taut set of his shoulders, the way he held himself. He gulped it down in two swallows and poured another one for himself, this time adding ice and a drop of water from the glass jug. Then without a word to me of any kind, he walked across the room and went into the bedroom, carrying his drink.

I stared after him speechless.

It had been a long time since I'd seen him in such a contrary and difficult mood. Because my feelings were hurt, because I felt he had been terribly unjust, I jumped up and ran after him. I was furious.

He was standing near the bed, where he had thrown his jacket, and was loosening his tie. Hearing me come into the room, he pivoted swiftly, stood glaring at me.

I said, "I realize you've had a bad day, and I'm sorry for that. God knows, you of all people don't deserve it. But you're not going to take it out on me! I won't let you! *I* haven't done anything wrong!"

"It's a bad couple of *weeks* I've had, not merely a bad *day*," he shot back, adding with ill grace, "I'm going to take a bath," and so saying began to unbutton his shirt.

"And stick your head under the water and keep it there! For several hours!" I shouted, my temper flying to the surface. I turned on my heels abruptly and flounced out, banging the door after me with a resounding crash. The crystal chandelier in the sitting room rattled and swayed slightly, but I didn't care. I had had such a wonderful day, and he had just ruined it, in the space of only a few seconds. I was trembling inside and angrier than I had been in a very long time.

A split second later the bedroom door was wrenched open, almost violently, and Andrew strode over to me, where I was standing by the piano.

Grabbing hold of me by the shoulders, he held me tightly and looked into my eyes. "*I'm sorry,* so very sorry, Mal. I *did* take it out on you, and that was wrong of me, very unfair. There's no excuse for it, really there isn't. The problem is, my mother got my goat tonight. Railing on about going up to spend the weekend with her, complaining she's seen nothing of me whilst I've been in London. That's true, of course, and she means well, but—" He shook his head. "I guess my nerves are pretty raw tonight."

He searched my face.

When I said not one kindly word nor showed a glimmer of friendliness, he murmured in a low, weary voice, "Forgive me, Puss?"

His tiredness was a most palpable thing; all of my anger dissipated as rapidly as it had erupted. "There's nothing to forgive, silly."

Smiling now, his eyes as soft and loving as they usually were, he kissed the tip of my nose. "Oh, Puss, whatever would I do without you?"

"And me you?" I asked.

Lifting my hand, I touched his cheek gently. "Listen, tough guy, let me cancel the dinner reservation, order a good bottle of wine and your favorite soul food, and we can stay here, have supper in front of the fire. Just the two of us. All cozy and warm and loving. So, what do you say?"

"I say okay, you've got a date."

"Good. Now, come on," I bustled. "Let's get you into a nice hot tub. You can soak for a while in some of my bubbly stuff. It's got pine oil in it, and it'll relax your muscles."

"Join me?" he asked, lifting a brow, giving me a suggestive look.

"*No!*"

He laughed for the first time since he had come in, and so did I.

"No hanky-panky tonight, Andrew Keswick. You're far too tired."

"Afraid so, even for you, Puss."

The dinner was perfect. And so was the evening, as it turned out.

Whilst Andrew soaked his weary bones in a tub filled to the brim with the hottest water and a generous portion of my pine bubble bath, I ordered supper from room service.

Wanting to pamper and spoil him, make him feel better, I chose all of his favorite things: Morecombe Bay potted shrimps, baby chops from a rack of lamb with mint sauce, mashed potatoes, *haricot vert,* and carrots. I selected a wonderful red wine, Château Lafite-Rothschild, and to hell with the price. For dessert I picked bread pudding. I wasn't particularly fond of this, but Andrew loved it; it was a favorite of his from boarding school days, and I knew he would enjoy it tonight.

Refreshed, relaxed, and replete with food and wine, my husband was in a much mellower mood by eleven o'clock. Nevertheless, he still took me by surprise when he said suddenly, "Okay! We're going to Yorkshire tomorrow after all, Puss-Puss."

I was lolling against him on the sofa, vaguely watching the television news, and I sat up with a jerk and stared at him.

"But I thought you had to go to the office tomorrow!" I exclaimed. "I thought you had another mess to sort out."

"That's true, yes. But I don't think I can really sort it out by myself. I need Jack as a sounding board. It's financial, which is where his expertise lies. And look, I can take some paperwork with me, clear some of it up on the way to Ma's."

"Are you sure, darling?"

"I'm positive."

"You're not doing it for me, are you? Because you don't want me sitting around the hotel waiting for you? That's not it, is it?"

"I'm doing it for both of us, Mal. And for my mother. Anyway, I think it'll do me good to get away for forty-eight hours. It'll give me a better perspective about everything. And quite frankly, I need to get out of that office, stand away from the situation and take stock of everything."

"If you're really sure . . . " I knew I sounded hesitant, but I couldn't help myself.

"I *want* to do this," Andrew reassured me. "Scout's honor."

"Shall we go on the train?"

He shook his head. "No, I don't think so. I'd like to leave early, about six-thirty, so that we miss the worst of the traffic on the motorway. If we set off then, we'll get to Ma's in the middle of the morning, in time for lunch. I can even work on my papers on Saturday afternoon. We can relax all day Sunday and drive back with my mother early on Monday morning."

"But how are we going to get there tomorrow? We don't have a car, and your mother left earlier this evening. She told me she wanted to be on the road by eight at the latest."

"Yes, I know that. But there's no problem, we're in a hotel, remember, and one of the best in the world." He pushed himself to his feet and walked over to the desk. "I'm going to call the hall porter right now and ask him to have a car and driver outside for us tomorrow morning at six-thirty. How does that sound?"

"Wonderful," I answered and smiled at him. "And your mother's going to be delighted to have us for the weekend."

"Whether your father marries Gwenny Reece-Jones or not doesn't affect you much, does it, Mal?" Andrew asked as he switched off the bedside light and pulled the bedcovers over him.

I was silent for a moment, and then I said, "No, not really. I just want him to be happy, that's all."

"She's very nice."

"I thought you couldn't remember her."

"I couldn't at first. But she's started to come into focus in the past few hours, and I've got a really good picture of her now. Ma's known her for donkey's years. Gwenny's older sister Gladys was at Oxford with my mother, and that's the connection. When I was little we used to go and stay with the family. I vaguely remember an old house that was quite beautiful, in the Welsh Marshes."

"Your mother mentioned it to me earlier. But go on, you said you had a good picture of her. What's she look like?"

"Tall, slender. Dark, like a lot of the Welsh are, with a rather lovely face, a gentle face, and I can visualize pretty eyes, hazel, I think, big and soulful. But she wore odd clothes."

"What do you mean?"

"Long floaty skirts and boots and peasant blouses, trailing scarves, dangling earrings, and flowing capes." I heard him laugh in the darkness, and then he went on in an amused voice, "Looking back, I think she was a cross between a gypsy, a Russian peasant, and a hippie. I mean in her appearance. And she was most eccentric, as only the British can be. But don't get me wrong, she was awfully sweet. I'm sure she still is."

"Yes, and talented, at least, so your mother said."

"Mal?"

"Yes, honey?"

"Don't sound so grudging about Gwenny. I know you're irritated because your father didn't confide in you, but I'm sure it was only because he didn't want to embarrass you or upset you. Ma's right about that."

"I guess so. And I didn't mean to sound grudging. I'm glad Dad has Gwenny. I hope I get to meet her soon. After all, Dad might be in Mexico next year for six months. So no doubt he'll come to New York more often if he's based there."

"Is he going to accept the invitation from U.C.L.A. to be part of the dig in Yaxuna?"

"Possibly. After all, he's had an interest in the Mayan civilization for a long time, as you well know, and I think he'll be glad to get away from the Middle East. He wrote in his last letter that he'd had it out there."

"I can't say I blame him."

"I hope he goes to Mexico. I hope he marries Gwenny, and that they spend a lot of time with us. It'll be nice for the twins to get to know their grandfather better, and I'm sure Gwenny will be a good sport. I got that impression from your mother, anyway— that she's fun, I mean. Listen, Andrew, Dad might come to Yorkshire for the Christmas vacation. Anyway, Diana said she was going to phone Gwenny and invite them. That would be nice, don't you think?"

Andrew did not respond, and I realized that he had fallen asleep. He was breathing evenly but deeply, and this did not surprise me at all, since he was so exhausted. It was a miracle he hadn't fallen asleep over supper.

I lay next to him in the darkness, thinking about my father and Gwenny, hoping they were happy. One thing I was certain of, in this uncertain world, was that my mother was happy with David Nelson. In the beginning I'd had a few misgivings about him, inasmuch as he was a criminal lawyer of some standing and celebrity; he had always sounded too street-smart, too tough and slick in the past. But what a lovely man he had turned out to be, and not in the least like my original impression. Charming without being smarmy, intellectual without being pompous, and brilliant without being a show-off. He had a good sense of humor, but most important, I had discovered he was a kind and compassionate man, blessed with a great deal of understanding and insight into people. He adored my mother, and she adored him; that was good enough for me.

I fell asleep with a smile on my face, thinking how nice it was that my mother had started a whole new life at the age of sixty-one.

14

Yorkshire, November 1988

Andrew worked on his papers all the way to Yorkshire.

Lulled by the warmth and the motion of the car, I dozed on and off as we headed north on the motorway. I roused myself fully at one point, sat up straighter against the seat, and glanced at my watch. I saw that it was almost nine-thirty. This surprised me, and I said to Andrew, "We've been on the road well over three and a half hours. We must be in Yorkshire already, aren't we?"

"That we are, Puss," he answered, looking up from the folder on his lap, giving me a half smile. "And you've slept most of the way. In any case, we left Harrogate behind a while ago."

I swung my head and stared out the car window. I saw that it was a pristine morning, clear and sunny, the sky a high-flung canopy of palest blue and white above the undulating pastoral dales. And as I continued to look out of the window, thinking what a great day it was, I experienced a sudden rush of anticipation and excitement knowing that we would soon be with Diana at her lovely old house just outside West Tanfield.

Ever since our marriage, Andrew and I had come to England at least once a year for a holiday, and we had never left without making a trip to Yorkshire. So, not unnaturally, I was happy we were coming for the weekend. During the last ten years I had grown to love this beautiful, sprawling county, the largest in England, with its bucolic green dales, vast, empty moors, soaring fells, ancient cathedrals, and dramatic ruins of medieval abbeys. It was a rich corner of the north, blessed with immense tracts of fertile, arable land and great industrial wealth, and it boasted more castles and stately homes than any other county in the whole of Britain. Also, I had developed a deep affection and respect for the canny, down-to-earth folk who lived here, and whose pragmatism, dry wit, and hospitality were legendary.

Wensleydale and the valley of the Ure, which we were presently driving through, was the area I knew best, since this was where the Keswick ancestral home was located. The house had been in the family for over four hundred years; even though Michael and Diana had settled in London after their youthful marriage straight out of university, they had spent almost every weekend there with Michael's parents, and all of the main annual holidays as well.

Andrew had been born in the house, as had most of the other Keswicks who had gone before him. "My mother made sure my actual birth took place in Yorkshire, not only because of the Keswick tradition, but because of cricket," Andrew had told me somewhat cryptically, on my first trip to West Tanfield when we had come to England on our honeymoon.

I had asked him what he meant about cricket, and he had chuckled, then explained, "Cricket is Yorkshire's game, Mal. My father and grandfather wanted me to be birthed in the county, because only men actually born within the boundaries of York-shire can play cricket for it. They had high expectations of me, hoped and prayed I might turn out to be another Len Hutton or a Freddy Trueman. You see, Dad and Grandpa were cricket addicts."

Since I knew nothing about cricket, that most British of British games, Andrew had gone on to explain that Hutton and Trueman were world-famous Yorkshire cricketeers who had played for England and had been national champions, if not, indeed, national heroes.

As it happened, Andrew loved cricket and had played it at boarding school. "But I was never inspired, only an average batsman. I just didn't have the talent," he had confided to me on another occasion, a warm summer day the following year when he had taken me to Lords to watch my first test match.

Continuing to gaze out the window, I spotted the shining tower of Ripon Cathedral outlined dramatically against the distant blue horizon. The cathedral was one of the most extraordinary edifices I have ever seen. Founded in the year 650, it was imposingly beautiful, awe-inspiring. Andrew was christened there, and it was in the cathedral that his parents were married. Now the sight of its great tower told me that we were about thirty minutes away from Andrew's family home.

"I'm hungry," Andrew said, interrupting my thoughts. "I hope old Parky has a good breakfast waiting for us. I could eat a horse."

"I'm not surprised," I laughed. "I'm pretty hungry myself, we left London so early. And I hope the hall porter phoned your mother, as you asked him to do. I'd hate to arrive unexpected."

"Good Lord, Mal, you ought to know better than that by now. I'd stake my life on the hall porters at Claridge's; they're the salt of the earth, and very reliable."

"True. Still, perhaps we ought to have stopped on the way up, called her ourselves,"

"Not necessary, my sweet," he murmured. "And it wouldn't matter if we did arrive unannounced. We're going to my mother's, for God's sake."

I said nothing, simply nodded, then I reached for my handbag. Taking out my compact, I powdered my nose and put on a little lipstick. Settling back, I glanced out the window once more to see that we were passing through the marketplace in Ripon. Here, every night at nine o'clock, the horn blower blew his horn at each corner of the neat little square, sounding the ancient curfew, wearing a period costume that came from an era of long ago. It was a centuries-old tradition, which the English, and most especially the locals, took in their stride, but one that an American like me found quite amazing—and extremely quaint.

Within seconds we had left the center of town behind. The

driver pointed the car in the direction of Middleham, following Andrew's explicit instructions, and soon we were out in the open countryside again, making for West Tanfield. This was situated between Ripon and Middleham, but closer to the latter, a place renowned for its stables and the breeding and training of great racehorses; it was also a treasure trove of history, had been known as "the Windsor of the North" at the time of the Plantagenet kings, Edward IV and Richard III.

We continued to barrel along, following the winding country lanes and roads, narrow and a bit precarious under the shadow of those lonely, windswept moors. This morning they looked somber and implacable. In August and September they took on a wholly different aspect, resembling a sea of purple as wave upon wave of heather rippled under the perpetual wind; they were a breathtaking sight.

"We're almost there," I murmured half to myself as the car rolled over the old stone bridge which spanned the River Ure and led into the main street of West Tanfield. It was a typical dales village—charming, picturesque, and very, very old.

I glanced to my left to see the familiar view, a line of pretty stone cottages with red-tiled roofs standing on the banks of the Ure, their green sloping lawns running down to the edge of the river. And behind them, poised against the pale wintry sky, were the old Norman church and the Marmion Tower next to it, both surrounded by ancient oaks and ash and a scattering of evergreens.

I reached over and squeezed Andrew's hand. I knew how much he loved this place.

He smiled at me and began to straighten his papers, quickly putting them back into his briefcase and closing it.

"Did you get a lot done?" I asked him.

"Yes, I did, and probably more than I would have in that damned office. I'm glad Ma put the screws on me yesterday, that I finally made up my mind we should spend the weekend with her. It'll do us both good."

"Yes, it will, and maybe we can go riding tomorrow."

"That's a good thought, Mal. We'll zip up to Middleham and join the stable boys and grooms on the gallops when they're exercising the racehorses. If you don't mind getting up very early again."

"I'm always up early, aren't I?" I laughed. "But Andrew, how stupid I am. I'd forgotten—we don't have our riding gear with us."

"Don't worry about that. I know I've got some historic old stuff at Ma's from years ago. I'm sure it's gungy, but it'll do, and my mother will lend you a pair of her boots and old jeans or riding breeches. And she's got masses of warm jackets, barbours, green Wellies, stuff like that. So we'll manage."

"Yes, it'll be fine." I studied him carefully and asked, "Does it feel good to be home?"

A small frown creased his smooth, wide brow as he returned my steady gaze. "These days, home for me is wherever *you* are, Mal. You and the twins." He leaned into me, kissed my cheek, and added, "But yes, it does feel good to be back in Yorkshire, to come back to my birthplace. I suppose everybody must feel that way—that atavistic pull. It's only natural, isn't it?"

"Yes," I agreed, and turning away from him, I looked straight ahead, peering over the driver's shoulder and out the front window of the car. We had left the village behind a good ten minutes ago and had taken the road which led up to the moors of Coverdale and the high fells. Following a bend in the road, we turned a corner. Now I could see them straight ahead, the high stone wall and the wrought-iron gates which opened onto the long winding driveway leading up to Diana's house.

15

We drove through the gates and progressed up the driveway rather slowly, since there were sheep and fallow deer wandering around the grounds, and the latter were skittish.

Far in the distance, I got just the merest glimpse of the house, of its tall chimneys poking up into the sky.

Its name was Kilgram Chase. It had always been called that, ever since its beginnings. Built in 1563, five years after Elizabeth I ascended to the throne, it was typically Tudor in style. A solid, stone house, it was square in shape yet graceful and with many windows, high chimneys, pitched gables, and a square tower built onto each of its four corners. In every crenellated tower there were only two mullioned windows, but these were huge and soaring, set one above the other, creating a highly dramatic effect and filling the tower rooms with extraordinary light.

Kilgram Chase stood in a large expanse of parkland, its green sweep of lawns and grazing pastures encircling the house, stretching up from the iron gates we had just left behind. Surrounding the edge of the park on three sides, to form a semicircular shape behind it, were dense woods, and rising up above these woods were the moors and, higher still, the great fells. Thus the house, the park, and the woods were cupped in a valley that protected them from the wind and weather in the winter months and, in times past, from political enemies and marauders, since the only access to the house and its park was through the front gates.

The first time I came here I had naturally been intrigued by Andrew's childhood home. Diana had given me the grand tour, told me everything I wanted to know about the house and the family. She was proud of Kilgram Chase and an expert on its history.

Its unusual name came, in part, from the man who had built it 425 years ago, a Yorkshire warrior knight called Sir John Kilgram. A close friend of Robert Dudley, the Earl of Leicester, he was a member of Queen Elizabeth's loyal faction, and one of the *new men,* as they were called, in palace politics. Kilgram had been given the great park and woods by Queen Elizabeth's royal decree for special services to the Crown. But long before Elizabeth Tudor's reign, when the Plantagenets had ruled, it had been a chase, that is, a stretch of open land where wild animals roamed and could be hunted by the local gentry. Later it was owned by the monks of nearby Fountains Abbey; they lost it when Elizabeth's father, King Henry VIII, confiscated all lands owned by the church. After the dissolution of the monasteries it became the property of the Crown.

The house and its park had come to the Keswicks quite legally, through a marriage which took place in the summer of 1589. Sir John had an only child, a daughter named Jane, and when she married Daniel Keswick, the son of a local squire, he gave them Kilgram Chase as part of her dowry. It had been in the family's possession ever since, passed down from generation to generation. One day it would belong to Andrew, and then to Jamie, and Jamie's son, if he had one.

Diana called it a typical country manor and constantly protested that for all of its prestige and historical significance, it was by no means a grand house anymore, and this was true. Architecturally, it was extremely well designed, skillfully planned, even somewhat compact for this type of Tudor manor, and in comparison to some of the great homes of Yorkshire, it was small. Despite its size, for a long time now Diana had found it difficult to run, in many respects. Not the least of it was the cost in time and money for its overall upkeep. For these reasons she lived in only two wings and kept two closed most of the year.

The house was maintained with the help of Joe and Edith Parkinson, who had lived and worked at Kilgram Chase for over thirty years. With their daughter, Hilary Broadbent, they took care of all the interiors, in both the open and closed wings, and did the laundry and cooking. Joe was also the handyman; he did a certain amount of outdoor work as well, looking after Diana's two horses and the sheep and mucking out the stables.

Hilary's husband, Ben, and his brother Wilf were the two gardeners responsible for the grounds; they mowed the many lawns, tended the flower beds, pruned the trees in the orchard, cleaned the pond once a year, and made sure the walled rose garden remained the great beauty spot it had been for hundreds of years.

Roses were my favorite flowers, and I had always gravitated to this particular garden at Kilgram Chase. But I did not plan to visit it this trip; I knew it could only be bereft, without color or life, just as everything at Indian Meadows was brown and faded. It was a bleak period for a gardener like me, these cold, cheerless months when the earth was hard as iron, the air sharp with frost, and all growing things lay dormant and still.

Glancing out the car window, I noticed that many of the giant oaks, which stood sentinel at intervals along the driveway, were already shedding their leaves, now that it was November and the first chill of winter had settled in. Everything was dying. Winter was a time of death in gardens and in the countryside; quite unexpectedly I felt melancholy, and I filled up with sadness. Shivering, I hunched further into my coat, pulling it tightly around me. But the death of the land in winter only meant its rebirth in the spring, I reminded myself, attempting to shake off this curious sense of sadness which had enveloped me. I shivered again. Some poor ghost just walked over my grave, I thought.

And in less than a moment it *was* gone, the sadness, for suddenly there was the house, rising up in front of us in all its glory.

Kilgram Chase. It stood there under the shadow of the moors, proud and everlasting as it had been for four centuries, seemingly untouched by time. My heart lifted at the sight of the lovely old manor. Its pale stones gleamed golden in the clear morning air, and the many mullioned windows shone brightly in the sunlight. I lifted my eyes, saw smoke puffing out of the chimneys, curling up like strands of gray-blue ribbon thrown carelessly into that silky, shining sky.

How welcoming it looked in all its mellowness and charm— my husband's ancestral home, the place where he had grown up.

The car had hardly come to a standstill in front of the house when the great oak door flew open and Diana appeared. She ran down the steps; her smile was wide, her face glowing with happiness at the sight of us alighting.

"Hi, Ma," Andrew cried, waving to her.

I rushed toward her and hugged her close. "Diana!"

"Aren't you the best girl in the whole wide world," she greeted me, "getting this obstinate son of mine to come up here after all."

Laughing, I pulled away from her and shook my head. "Not me, I didn't persuade him, Diana. *He* had a change of heart on his own accord. Late last night, far too late to call you. And we left so early this morning, at six, we didn't want to disturb you. That's why we asked the hall porter to phone. He did, didn't he?"

"Yes, darling." Turning to her son, she embraced him and went on, "As long as you're both here, that's all that matters. We'll have a nice cozy weekend together, and I know Parky plans to spoil you both."

Andrew grinned at her. "We expected nothing less." Leaning closer, he said, "Before I let the car go, should I ask the driver to come back for us tomorrow night? Or can we cadge a lift to town with you on Monday morning?"

"Of course you can. Anyway, it's hardly worth coming up here, if you don't stay through Sunday night. And I'll be glad to have your company and Mal's on the way back to London. In fact, you can drive part of the way, Andrew dear."

"You bet," he said, "and thanks, Ma. There's just one thing: We'll have to leave here fairly early on Monday morning. About six-thirty. Is that all right?"

"I usually set out about that time," Diana answered.

Andrew nodded and hurried off to speak to the driver.

Diana took hold of my arm and drew me toward the stone steps leading up to the front door. Joe Parkinson was hovering at the top of them. He came striding down.

"Morning, Mrs. Andrew," he said, giving me a big smile. "It's lovely to have you back, by gum it is."

"Thank you, Joe, I'm really glad we could come up for the weekend."

"I'll just get along, help Mr. Andrew with the luggage." And so saying Joe moved down the steps, calling out, "Nay, Mr. Andrew, I'll do that. Let me handle them there suitcases."

I glanced back over my shoulder and saw Andrew and Joe shaking hands, greeting each other affectionately. Andrew had been eight years old when the Parkinsons had come to work at Kilgram Chase. Joe had taught him so much about the country-side and nature, and they had always been firm friends. As Andrew said, Joe was the salt of the earth, a real Yorkshireman through and through, hardworking, canny, wise, and loyal.

"It's a raw morning," Diana said, shivering and pulling her cardigan around her. "Come on, let's go in and have a cup of tea."

Waiting for us in the small entrance hall were Edith Parkinson, Joe's wife, whom Andrew had called Parky since childhood, and her daughter, Hilary. Both women welcomed me warmly, and I returned their greetings.

Parky said, "If only the little ones were with you, Mrs. Andrew, they'd be a sight for sore eyes."

Smiling at her, I said, "Don't forget, they'll be here next month for Christmas, Parky. In fact, we're planning on staying through the New Year. Mr. Andrew promised."

"That's just wonderful," Parky exclaimed, beaming at me. "I can't wait to see the wee bairns." Glancing at Diana, she added,

"We'll have to have a *big* Christmas tree this year, Mrs. Keswick, and maybe Joe'll play Santa Claus, get dressed up in his red Santa suit and whiskers, like he does for the Sunday school class at the church."

"Yes, that's a marvelous idea," Diana agreed. Taking my coat, she hung it up in the hall closet. "Now, let's go into the kitchen, Mal. Parky's been busy for the last hour whipping up all sorts of things. Andrew's favorites, of course."

The kitchen at Kilgram Chase was as old as the house itself, and it had altered little over the years. Painted cool white, it was long in shape. The ceiling was low and intersected with dark wood beams. The floor was still covered with the original flagstones, so ancient they were worn in places by the steps of centuries, steps which had gone from the fireplace to the window and across to the door, and back and forth, time and time again, so that deep grooves now scored the stones.

The fireplace at the far end of the kitchen was high to the ceiling and wide, made of local brick and stone and braced with old wood beams to match the ceiling. It had a great, raised hearth, an overhanging mantel shelf, and old-fashioned baking ovens set in the wall next to the actual fireplace. The ovens had not been used for years and years; long ago Diana had installed a wonderful Aga, that marvelous English cooking stove I would give my eyeteeth for. I agreed with her that this was the best stove in the world, and it also helped to keep the rather large kitchen warm the year round. It was welcome, since the kitchen with its thick old walls and stone floor was always cool even in the summer months.

A butler's pantry, which opened off the kitchen, had been updated and remodeled by Diana, so that it better served her and Parky. She had put in a double-sized refrigerator, two dishwashers, and countertops for food preparation; above the counters were lots of cabinets for storing china as well as all of those practical items that made the wheels of a kitchen turn.

A series of mullioned casement windows opened onto a view

of the back lawns, the pond, and the ever-present moors reaching up to touch the edge of the sky. Opposite the window wall an antique Welsh dresser took pride of place, and this lovely old piece was filled to overflowing with willow-patterned china of blue and white. Nearby, in the center of the room, there was an old-fashioned country table with a deal top and stumpy legs, where Andrew and I now sat. A green Majolica jug filled to the brim with branches of bittersweet stood on the table, and I couldn't help thinking how perfect it looked.

Marching along the mantel shelf was a diverse collection of wood and brass candlesticks in the barley-twist style bearing white beeswax candles, and underneath the mantel were all kinds of horse brass that glittered and winked in the bright firelight. And everywhere there was the sparkle of copper in such things as jelly and fish molds and pots and pans all hanging from a rack on the ceiling, and in ladles, spoons, and measuring scoops on a side table.

I had always loved this kitchen, thought it one of the most welcoming I had ever seen; it was not only cheerful in its ambience but comfortable as well. As Diana said, it was the hub of the house, a room you could easily live in.

Diana was over by the Aga stove making a pot of tea; she carried this over to the table but suggested we let it stand for a few moments.

"Aye, that's right, Mrs. Andrew, don't pour it yet, it has to mash," Parky instructed.

"Yes, Parky," I said dutifully and smiled at Andrew. She had been telling me this for ten years.

Pervading the air in the kitchen was the tantalizing smell of bacon sizzling on top of the Aga and the mouth-watering aroma of freshly baked bread just out of the oven. Parky had left the loaves and tea cakes to cool for a few minutes on one of the countertops, and the mere smell made me salivate.

Swinging around to face us, Parky said, "In case you haven't guessed, I'm going to make bacon butties. Your favorites, Mr.

EVERYTHING TO GAIN 137

Andrew." She smiled at him fondly before turning back to her task of lifting the bacon out of the frying pan and onto a large platter. Parky had mothered him as a little boy, and he had been like a second child to her in some respects.

"What a treat, Parky," Andrew exclaimed, and added to me, "*You've* got to make them for me, Mal, when we're home at Indian Meadows."

Diana joined us at the table and poured the steaming hot tea into big blue-and-white cups, and a moment later Parky was beside her, serving the bacon butties. These were thick slices of the warm new bread, spread with butter and with rashers of the fried bacon between the slices—hot bacon sandwiches, really.

"Here goes my cholesterol!" Andrew groaned cheerfully, "But oh, God, how wonderful!" he added after taking the first bite.

"I know, they're *sinful*," Diana said, laughing, then cautioned, "But don't eat too many, Parky's making fish cakes and parsley sauce for lunch."

"With chips," Parky cut in. "To be followed by another of your favorites. Treacle pudding."

"Oh, God, Parky, I think I've just died and gone to heaven," he exclaimed, laughing, enjoying Parky and the fuss she was making over him. He had always had a soft spot for her.

"But, darling, it *is* heaven here," Diana said, smiling at him lovingly. "Or had you forgotten?"

Andrew shook his head, kissed her warmly on the cheek. "No, Ma, I hadn't forgotten. Not only that, I'm here with three of my four favorite women."

"And who's the fourth?" I asked swiftly, staring.

"Why, my daughter, of course," he answered, winking at me.

16

I found the books on Saturday afternoon. And quite a find they were.

After lunch Diana drove off to West Tanfield to do some errands; she asked me to go with her, but I declined, preferring instead to stay at Kilgram Chase with Andrew, only to discover that he wanted to work.

"I must go over the rest of this stuff," he explained apologetically, holding up his briefcase. "I'm sorry, Mal."

"It's okay," I said, although I was disappointed he was going to be poring over the papers in Diana's office for the rest of the afternoon, rather than going out for a walk with me.

"I won't be long, about an hour and a half, two hours at the most." He shook his head as he paused on the threshold of the office. "Some of it's rather complicated, that lousy financial stuff I mentioned to you in London. I could use Jack's nimble brain. He's much better than I am when it comes to figures."

"Maybe I could help you," I suggested.

He smiled at me ruefully. "I'm afraid you can't, darling. Look, you don't mind if I work, do you? At least for a while. We'll go for a walk later, just before tea."

"That's great, don't worry," I said, giving him a quick peck on the cheek. I walked off in the direction of the library, which had always fascinated me. I loved to poke around in there, looking for literary treasures or family memorabilia. Unfortunately, I'd never come across anything remotely interesting or out of the ordinary.

Like the kitchen, the library had not changed much in four hundred years, except, perhaps, for the acquisition of more and more books by the Keswicks over the centuries. And it seemed to me that they never threw anything away. It was larger than most of the other rooms at Kilgram Chase, since it was situated in one of the square towers, the one on the northeast corner of the house, overlooking the moors.

The coffered ceiling was over thirty feet high, balanced by the huge window set in the middle of the center wall, a beautiful window of unusual dimensions and shape which filled the room with the most extraordinary light at all times of the day. Paneled in light oak, the library had floor-to-ceiling bookshelves throughout, and these held many thousands of volumes, most of them very old. A handsomely built fireplace of local limestone was set in the wall facing the window, and around this had been arranged several comfortable chairs, an oak coffee table, and a Knole sofa. Directly behind the sofa stood a library table, also of carved oak, and on this was stacked the latest magazines, many of them to do with antiques, as well as today's *Times,* an assortment of other national and local newspapers, and a few current novels.

I did a cursory check of everything on the table, but there was nothing of particular interest to me, and so I began to wander around the room, my eyes scanning the lower shelves where everything was in easy reach. But, of course, because these shelves were readily accessible to me, I had looked at almost every book countless times before. There was nothing new.

Suddenly realizing it was cool in the library, and shivering slightly, I went over to the fireplace, pulled out the damper, and put a light to the paper and chips of wood under the logs in the grate. Within minutes I had a good blaze going, and soon the logs had caught and the fire was roaring up the chimney.

Glancing around, I saw the set of polished mahogany library steps at the other side of the room, and I pulled these over to the fireplace wall. On either side of the fire there were shelves rising to the ceiling, and since I wanted to stay warm, I decided to investigate these first.

Climbing up, I examined a series of books covered with dark green leather that I'd never noticed before, undoubtedly because they were placed so high. Much to my disappointment most of them were old atlases and maps of Yorkshire and other counties.

Leaning my head back, I looked up, scanned a higher shelf immediately above me, and spotted a large-sized volume bound in purple leather. The royal color of the binding intrigued me, and I climbed a bit farther, until I stood on the top step. I stretched my arm, endeavoring to reach the book; I had no idea what it was, but naturally, because it was beyond my reach, I wanted to look at it.

I tried once more but lost my balance and almost fell. I clutched frantically at the nearest shelf and managed to steady myself. I took a deep breath; my heart was suddenly pounding hard. That had been a close call. After a few seconds, when I recovered, I made a slow descent, moving carefully, having no wish to fall off the library steps. And once I was on the floor, I let out a sigh of relief. Hurrying out, I went in search of Joe.

I found him in the kitchen talking to Parky, and after explaining what I wanted, I returned to the library.

Within a few minutes he came in carrying one of the very tall stepladders he kept in his workshop.

"That *is* a big one, Joe," I said, eyeing it.

He nodded. "Aye, it is that, Mrs. Andrew. I need it for cleaning the chandeliers. And doing some of the windows. I've got a brush with an expanding handle, o'course, but t'brush isn't always long enough, you knows. Windows in the tower rooms, like the library here, are right high, for example, and difficult to get to, by gum they are. Now, then, where exactly do you want this ladder, Mrs. Andrew?"

"Here, Joe, please. I would like to look at that book on the shelf up there." I pointed to the shelf in question.

Joe followed my gaze. "What's it called?"

"I don't know, but it's the purple leather one. Next to the one with the torn, moldy-looking binding."

Almost immediately I realized he wasn't quite focused on the shelf I meant, and so I said, "Don't worry, Joe, I'll go up and get it. Just hold the ladder steady for me." As I spoke, I moved closer to him.

"Nay, Mrs. Andrew, I can't let you climb up there! Goodness me, no! What if you had a fall? Mr. Andrew would be right vexed with me, that he would, and so would Mrs. Keswick. The whole house would be in an uproar, you can bet your last shilling on that." He shook his head vehemently. "Oh, no, no, no, you can't go up there. I'll bring the book down for you. Now, just let me get on the ladder, and then you can direct me to the volume you mean."

"All right," I said, knowing it was no use arguing with Joe. I had tried to do so in the past without success. He was very stubborn, and once he had made up his mind, it was hard to persuade him or to coerce him into doing anything against his wishes. Obviously he thought I was incapable of climbing that ladder, and I wasn't going to make a fuss about it. After all, I'd almost had a mishap on the library steps.

After showing him where to place the ladder immediately behind the shelf, I pointed to the book once more.

"I see it!" he exclaimed, and went up the steps with amazing speed and sureness of foot. Of course he was able to reach it without any problem, since he was taller than I and had much longer arms.

"What is it, Joe?" I asked as he opened it.

"It looks like a ledger. An accounts book, for carpentry items. It says, *nails one halfpenny,* and there are a few other things mentioned, but there's nowt much else in it," he said, leafing through the ledger. "It's got a date in it. 1892. By gum, almost a hundred years ago!"

"Interesting. What's next to it?"

"Looks like another ledger. This one's got a cloth cover." He turned the pages, then glanced down at me. "Definitely a ledger, only one entry. It says *fresh fish two pennies*. No nothing else in it, and no date."

"And that torn book, which is still on the shelf? The moldy-looking one. What's that, Joe?"

He took it down. After a second or two spent scanning it, he said, "Well, this one looks like a diary, aye, summat like that."

"*Diary?* Do you mean it's handwritten?"

"Aye, it is, Mrs. Andrew."

"Could you bring it, Joe, along with the other two, please? The two ledgers. I'd like to take a look at them."

"Right-oh, Mrs. Andrew."

There was a long refectory table in front of the big mullioned window, with a porcelain bowl of flowers in the center and, at either end, a high-backed chair covered in green cut velvet.

I went over to this table, pulled one of the chairs closer to it, and sat down.

Joe brought me the books and put them in front of me.

"Thanks, Joe," I said.

"I'll leave the ladder, shall I, Mrs. Andrew?"

"Yes, do. You can put the books back for me later. After I've studied them. I'll come and find you when I'm ready."

He nodded and went to the door, where he stopped abruptly and swung around to face me.

"Don't start climbing up that there ladder! If you want summat else, another book brought down, come and get me, Mrs. Andrew."

"I will, Joe. I promise."

I looked inside the two ledgers first and quickly laid these on one side. There was nothing much of interest in either of them. But the diary intrigued me, and now I opened this book with its tan leather binding, torn and a bit frayed on the spine. The endpapers were of a feather design, a kind of paisley pattern in shades of brown and ochre, rust and beige, with just the merest hint of blue.

Turning the first few pages, which were blank, I came to a handwritten frontispiece.

Slowly I began to read, filled with growing anticipation and excitement.

I, Clarissa Keswick, wife of Robin Keswick and Mistress of Kilgram Chase, discovered this day the diary and private household book penned by my dear Husband's ancestor, one Lettice, born 1640 died 1683. Fortuitously I stumbled upon her private book in the library here at Kilgram Chase, when my dear Husband asked me to fetch for him a copy of that great tragedy Hamlet *by William Shakespeare. The words of Lettice Keswick were interesting to me and so I bethought myself to copy them in order to preserve them. This is done for the future generations of this family who will follow me and mine.*

I started my work on this tenth day of August in the year 1893 in the glorious and prosperous reign of our great Queen and Empress of India Victoria Regina. God Bless Her Gracious Majesty and Long May She Reign.

Clarissa was a Keswick family name, one we had chosen for our own daughter, and there had been several Clarissas before ours was born six years ago. The Victorian Clarissa whose elegant copperplate handwriting I was now reading had been one of the earlier ones.

Elated by my discovery and eager to read more, I turned the first page, and once again I was staring at a frontispiece, the words set out in the center.

Lettice Keswick
Her Book
Kilgram Chase
Yorkshire

Flipping this page, I read the first words of Lettice's diary, so carefully copied by the Victorian Clarissa nearly a hundred years ago.

> *I, Lettice Keswick, begin this diary on the twenty-fifth day of May in the Year of Our Lord 1660 A.D. On this very day all England rejoices and is glad and light of heart. Our Sovereign, Charles Stuart, returned from Exile and at Dover his feet have trod again on English soil this day.*
>
> *The Monarchy will be restored forthwith. He will be crowned King Charles II and the foul and bloody execution of his father is avenged in part.*
>
> *Death to the traitors who led his father to the block.*
>
> *On this day in Yorkshire and o'er all the land did cathedral and church bells ring forth in praise of our gracious Sovereign, restored to us as if by a great Miracle. And bonfires burned tonight and messengers rode the length and breadth of England to spread the good and glorious news.*
>
> *My dear Husband, Lord and Master Francis, did lead us all in prayer this day, servants and family together, in the blue tower and we gave our grateful thanks to the dear Lord Our God for His Goodness and Mercy. Our true Monarch is safe. We are all reborn.*
>
> *I write my words late this night, well nigh past midnight, by the light of my tallow candle. It was this night that my beloved Husband Francis came to me and took me to him in bodily love and we loved each other well. Perhaps this joyful night I have conceived, God willing, and from our great happiness and love will be born another child. So does my Lord and Husband pray, as do I, and God willing it will be a son and a male heir at last, to carry on the pride of the Keswicks. I pray that it is. I pray.*
>
> *It is growing late. My candle splutters. My Husband sleeps. Outside the May moon rides high across a dark sky.*

*It is very late. I hear my Husband stir. I must put down
my pen and snuff my candle, step over to the bed to sleep,
to share his dreams. This I will do. I will pick up my pen
tomorrow and I will continue.*

I went on reading avidly, my eyes moving swiftly across page after page. I was eager to know more, fascinated by Lettice Keswick's jottings about her life in Yorkshire in the seventeenth century.

There were several more short sections, dated the end of June; then she moved on to cover a few days in July and August. Once more she was writing about her everyday life and her doings. She wrote of her two little daughters, Rachel and Viola, her life as a country squire's wife and the lady of the manor. The last entry for August was a joyful notation that she was at last pregnant and hopeful it was with a son.

I paused for a moment and gazed out the window reflectively. Nothing has changed since time immemorial. We all harbor the same dreams and hopes and desires as those who have gone before us. Here I was, reading about Lettice's desire for another child in 1660, and this was mine and Andrew's dream at the moment, now in 1988. I smiled to myself thinking how very little really changed in life, and, dropping my eyes, I continued to read.

The diary as such stopped quite abruptly. I experienced a genuine sense of disappointment, even irritation, so taken was I by Lettice Keswick's words.

But she had digressed, writing pages of household hints, which I merely glanced at, then listing all sorts of recipes—recipes for making potpourri and pomanders from dried flowers, herbs, and certain fruits and spices. There were instructions on how to make beeswax candles and soap; copious notes about herbs—sweet-smelling herbs for freshening rooms and closets, others for making ointments to treat various ailments, still others to add flavor to the cooking pot.

Her next section was devoted to preserves. Now came Lettice's recipes for rhubarb-and-gooseberry jam, quince jelly, bilberry jelly, lemon curd, mincemeat and sweet apple chutney. Once again I simply scanned these and moved on.

Finally the diary of her daily life began anew, the dates of entry running through October to December. I was completely engrossed as I read about winter life at Kilgram Chase, the various family activities, her needlework and embroidery, her husband's hunting and shooting skills, his expertise with horses. She wrote about the winter solstice, the weather, and her difficult pregnancy.

But before she continued with her daily doings into the new year of 1661, she had indulged in another domestic diversion, writing endless pages about the making of pies, puddings, and pastries, elderberry and nettle wine, even ale.

The diary was a veritable treasure trove, in a variety of ways. Unfortunately, I did not have time to read it scrupulously and in its entirety. At least not now. So I scanned, speed-read the rest of it, still admiring Clarissa's wonderful copperplate handwriting. Not once did it falter; her script was impeccable, a work of art.

As I swiftly turned the pages, I saw that Lettice Keswick's diary covered the early months of 1661 and finished in the spring. She spoke of the birth of her son, Miles, in the April of that year, after a long and difficult labor, and she wrote about her husband's birthday in May.

The very last page was dated May 29. There were no more entries, because there were no more pages left in the book. She had filled it.

Again, I found myself feeling disappointed. Until it struck me that the diary had only ended because the book she was writing in was full. Surely Lettice had continued her diary, for she was a natural writer with an easy, flowing style, almost conversational, and a great eye for detail. There *must* be another volume somewhere here in this library, and Clarissa must have found it and copied it. Just as I wanted to know more, so must she have been riddled with curiosity.

Jumping up, I headed for the ladder, in my anxiety totally

ignoring Joe's warnings about climbing it. I did just that, in fact, until I came to the second-to-last step from the top. I did not dare climb higher, for fear of having an accident.

But I was quite high enough, it seemed. I stood immediately below the shelf from which Joe had taken the ledgers and the diary, and it was easy for me to read the titles of the books which remained. There were two novels by Thomas Hardy, three by the Brontës, and six by Charles Dickens, as well as a volume of sonnets by Shakespeare. But nothing else, just a gap on the shelf where the ledgers and Clarissa's copy of the diary had been.

Liking the look of the book of sonnets, which had a gorgeous red binding with gold lettering, I took this off the shelf. It was then that I saw it. A small, thick book with a black leather cover, which lay just behind the Brontë novels against the back of the shelf. For a moment I thought it was a Bible, but when I looked at it I saw that it had a totally plain front. Certainly no gold lettering proclaimed its title.

Balancing myself carefully at the top of the stepladder, I opened the black book. With a little thrill and a rush of excitement, I recognized it at once. It was the *original* Lettice diary, written in her own hand, the one Clarissa had so carefully copied in 1893. I poked around behind the Brontë, Hardy, and Dickens volumes, but there was nothing else there.

Holding the diary tightly in one hand, I edged my way down the stepladder and hurried over to the table in front of the window. Sitting down, I opened Lettice Keswick's original diary.

I stared at it in awe, turning the pages slowly, carefully, afraid that I might damage it if I handled it roughly.

The diary was over three hundred years old, but to my amazement it was undamaged. Some pages felt slightly brittle, but not very many, and there were tiny wormholes here and there. But for the most part, it was wonderfully intact.

What a miracle it was that it had lasted all this time. But then, no one had known of its existence, and so no one had handled it. Except for Clarissa, of course, who had found it, copied it, and presumably put it back for safety's sake. Then again, the temperature in the library remained the same, year in, year out, exactly as it had for centuries, I was certain. It was always cool and dry; there was no dampness, and certainly the heat from the fire would not cause any damage to any of the old books. It barely warmed the room. No wonder, then, that the seventeenth-century diary had been so well preserved.

The original, written by Lettice herself, was penned in a spidery, rather elaborate script, typical of the century in which she had lived, but her writing was clear and legible. And I discovered, to my delight, that the original diary contained something unique: exquisite little pen-and-ink drawings and watercolors of flowers, fruit, and herbs, and vignettes of Lettice's gardens here at Kilgram Chase, which illustrated the diary throughout.

It was obvious to me that I had stumbled upon a small treasure. Of course, it was of no real value and probably of little interest to anyone except the Keswicks, and I couldn't wait to show it to Diana and Andrew.

Glancing at my watch, I realized that the last hour and a half had sped by. It was almost four o'clock.

Rising, I left the library and went down the corridor to Diana's office. I peeked in. Andrew's grim expression as he spoke on the phone registered most forcibly. He was no doubt talking to Jack Underwood in New York. He sounded angry in that quiet, controlled way of his, and he wasn't even aware that I had cracked open the door. I closed it softly, deeming it wiser to leave him in peace to attend to his business.

I really did need a breath of fresh air now, having been in the house since our arrival that morning, and after the long drive north in the car. In the nearby mudroom I sat down on the bench, took off my shoes, pulled on a pair of Diana's green Wellington boots, and lifted a barbour off the peg. I loved these fleece-lined waterproof jackets that are so snug and can be worn in all kinds of weather. In each pocket I found a woolen glove. After putting these on, I took a red wool scarf off the coat stand, threw it around my neck, and went out through the side door.

It was chilly. The morning sun had long ago disappeared, leaving a sky that was a faded, pale blue, almost without color.

The smell of autumn assailed me: dampness, rotting leaves, and wood smoke, acrid on the air. Somewhere, not far away, one of the gardeners had a bonfire going. It was that time of year, when dead plants and roots, dried leaves, and garden debris in general went into the flames; I had just had my own winter bonfire last weekend at Indian Meadows.

As I turned the corner of the house, I practically stumbled over Wilf, the gardener, who was shoveling dead leaves and roots into a pile, obviously fodder for the fire.

He glanced up when he heard my sharp exclamation.

"Aw, it's you, Mrs. Andrew." He touched his cloth cap and grinned at me. "How you be doing then?" He rested his filthy hands on top of the shovel and stood gaping at me, staring right through me.

"Fine, thank you. And how are you feeling these days, Wilf?"

"Can't complain. Me rheumatism's a bit of a bother, but there's nowt much else wrong with me. I don't expect to be kicking up t'daisies in yon cemetery for a long time." He laughed. It sounded like a cackle.

"I'm glad to hear it." I nodded and hurried away, heading for the pond. There was something odd about Wilf Broadbent. He always seemed to have a baleful glint in his eye when he talked to me. I thought he might be a bit touched. Andrew said he was just gormless, using the Yorkshire word for dumb, stupid. Diana laughed at us when we discussed Wilf. She believed him to be the salt of the earth.

Four brown ducks swam away as I approached the water.

I stood watching them paddling as fast as they could to the far bank, absently wondering if it would freeze by Christmas. The twins so longed to skate on this pond, just as their father had done when he was a little boy. But I didn't think it would be cold enough to freeze; it was a decent-sized body of water.

I set off to walk around the pond, my mind focusing on Lettice and Clarissa, those two other Keswick women who had been the brides of Keswick men, and who had lived out their entire lives here. If only walls could talk to me, what marvelous secrets they would reveal, what tales they could tell.

On the other hand, the *diary* had talked, hadn't it? Only for a short while, but still, it had spoken to me of a time past, given me a bit of the family history.

Even Clarissa's frontispiece, short as it was, and her act of copying it so meticulously had told me quite a lot about her. She must have been a good woman, conscientious, God-fearing, a typical Victorian, but obviously an intelligent and caring person. Certainly she had cared about the diary, had understood what it meant to the family. Also, she had had the foresight to realize that the original might not survive the passage of time; and she had considered it important enough to preserve it for posterity. Of course she lacked artistic talent because she had not copied the drawings or watercolors, but that wasn't so important.

And what did the diary tell me about the diarist herself?

First and foremost that Lettice was a born writer, articulate and with a thorough knowledge of the language and an understanding of its beauty. It was at her fingertips, and she had made excellent use of it. The illustrations indicated that she had been artistically inclined, the household hints and recipes proclaimed her to have been a good housekeeper and cook, not to mention an excellent herbalist and wine-maker. Her many references to her husband and children revealed that she had been a loving wife and mother, and lastly, I decided that she had had a political turn of mind. There were innumerable references to Parliament in her diary, and acerbic comments, and certainly she had been a dyed-in-the-wool royalist, elated, no, *overjoyed* when Charles II returned to England to accept the throne.

It struck me again that there must be another volume of her diary *somewhere* in that vast library. A truly natural writer such as Lettice Keswick would not stop just like that, with such terrible abruptness. But how to find it amongst those thousands of books lining the hundreds of shelves?

There was no time for me to look for it now, not today or tomorrow. Perhaps when we came back for Christmas I could have a stab at it. The effort would be worth it. After all, in my opinion the diary was a little jewel. I knew Diana would be intrigued by it and so would Andrew, if I could ever tear him away from that briefcase and those wretched papers. I couldn't imagine what that awful Malcolm Stainley had done, unless he had been cooking the books, God forbid. If he had, Andrew would go for the jugular, and Jack wouldn't be far behind, wielding a very sharp knife, figuratively speaking.

As I walked up the wide path carved out between the expanse of green lawns, I saw a car approaching the house. It was moving at a snail's pace up the driveway between the giant oaks, and it was not Diana returning, I knew that. This was not her car.

Within a few seconds the car and I had drawn closer. I saw that it was a pale blue Jaguar.

Was Diana expecting a visitor? It was odd that she hadn't mentioned it, if she were. She usually told us if someone was coming to tea, warned us, really, in case we felt we had to escape. Usually Andrew did, since her guests for this truly English ritual were people like the woman who ran the church institute, the vicar and his wife, the head of the garden club, or some such local character.

The car slowed, then came to a standstill at the bottom of the stone steps. I strode across the terrace to the top of the steps and stood looking down expectantly.

The door of the Jaguar finally opened. A woman alighted.

She was tall and slender, with a mass of dark, wavy hair that tumbled around a rather narrow but attractive face. Her eyes were dark, intense, and her generous mouth was a slash of bright red lipstick.

At first glance, her clothes looked like a gypsy's odd assortment, but as my eyes swept over her swiftly, I realized there was a
degree of coordination about them. At least as far as the colors
were concerned. She wore a long, full, green wool skirt, topped by
a short bomber jacket made of red, green, purple, and yellow
patches. Joseph's coat of many colors. Or so it seemed to me. Long
scarves of yellow, purple, and red were wrapped around her neck
and trailed down her back. Her boots were red, her handbag yellow.

I did not have to be introduced to this colorful woman.

I knew exactly who she was.

Gwendolyn Reece-Jones in person.

My father's mistress.

17

We stared hard at each other, she and I. And for a split second neither of us spoke.

I was aware from the expression in her eyes that she knew who I was, had recognized me as Edward Jordan's daughter, but I doubted that she would acknowledge this. Certainly she would not confide her relationship with my father or even say that they were friends. I knew this instinctively.

She spoke first.

Moving closer to the bottom step, she said, "I'm looking for Mrs. Keswick. Rude. To come without calling first. Tried. Your phone's been engaged for a long time. Is Mrs. Keswick in?"

I shook my head. "No, I'm afraid she isn't, she went off to do a few errands. But she should be back any moment. Would you like to come in and wait for her?"

Gwenny bit her lip, and an anxious expression crossed her angular face. "Don't want to impose."

"I'm sure Diana won't be long. I know she'd be very upset if she missed you."

"Frightfully kind. Yes, well, er, thank you. Perhaps I will hang around for a few minutes." She began to mount the steps. Drawing level to me, she held out her hand. "Gwendolyn Reece-Jones."

"Mallory Keswick," I answered, shaking her hand. Immediately I swung around, stepped up to the front door, opened it, and ushered her into the small entrance foyer. "Can I take your jacket?" I asked politely.

"Just the scarves, thank you," she replied, unraveling the three of them from around her neck.

After hanging these in the coat closet, I took her into the parlor next door to the dining room. This was a small, comfortable room, rather cozy, with a Victorian feeling to it, a sort of den, which we used all the time. It was there we watched television and usually had afternoon tea and drinks in the evening.

Parky had turned on the lamps and started the fire. This burned merrily in the grate, and the room looked inviting.

"Please make yourself comfortable," I said. "If you'll excuse me, I'll go and take off my boots and tell Andrew you're here. He'll come and join us. If he's off the phone."

"No rush. Take your time." She reached for the current issue of *Country Life* which lay on the tufted ottoman and sat down in an armchair next to the fire.

Once I had shed Diana's barbour and Wellingtons and put on my shoes in the mudroom, I went in search of my husband. Andrew was still on the phone in Diana's office, but this time when I opened the door he saw me, smiled, and raised an eyebrow questioningly.

"We have a visitor," I said rolling my eyes to the ceiling.

"Just a minute, Jack," he murmured into the receiver and looked across at me, frowning slightly.

"Who is it?" he asked.

"You'd never guess in a million years, so I'm going to tell you. *Gwendolyn Reece-Jones.* She's here looking for your mother. She tried to phone first, but she couldn't get through." I laughed. "For obvious reasons."

"Gwenny!" he exclaimed. "I'll be damned! Since Ma isn't back yet, offer her tea, and I'll join you in a few minutes. I'm just finishing up with Jack."

I nodded. "Give him my best."

"I will."

As I turned away I heard him say, "That was Mal, she sends her love. Well, that's about it, old buddy. Just wanted to run all this by you."

Parky was in the kitchen putting cups and saucers on a large tray; she glanced up as I walked across the floor and hovered next to the table where she was working.

"Hi, Parky," I murmured. "You'll have to add another cup and saucer. A friend of Mrs. Keswick's has just arrived. Miss Gwendolyn Reece-Jones. I'm sure you know her. Anyway, she'll be having tea with us."

"*Oh.*" Parky pursed her lips. "Miss Reece-Jones can't have been expected, or Mrs. Keswick would have told me before she went out. She's very precise about things like that, Mrs. Keswick is."

"She wasn't expected, Parky."

"A bit rude, if you ask me," Parky sniffed, "dropping in like that." She marched into the pantry and came back with an extra cup and saucer. "Most people telephone first."

"She did try to get through," I explained, hiding a smile, amused at Parky's irritation. But then, she was a stickler for good manners; I always remembered that about her. For a reason I didn't quite understand, I felt I had to defend Gwenny, so I now added, "Mr. Andrew's been on the phone to New York for well over an hour, Parky, that's why Miss Reece-Jones was unable to get us."

"Hurrumph," was all Parky said as she went on fussing with the teapot and the other things she needed for afternoon tea. But after a few seconds she threw me a warm smile, and leaning closer, she said, "I've made a luvely caraway-seed cake for tea, Mr. Andrew's favorite. And nursery sandwiches. He did enjoy them when he was little. Four sorts today. Tomato, cucumber, watercress, and egg salad. Homemade scones, too, with homemade strawberry jam and Cornish cream."

"Goodness, we're not going to want any dinner!" I exclaimed, before I could stop myself. "So much food, Parky."

"But it's what I always serve, Mrs. Andrew, and I've been doing so for thirty years," she announced, taking a step back and staring at me. She looked slightly put out.

Realizing that I might have hurt her feelings unintentionally, I said quickly, "The tea sounds wonderful. I just know Mr. Andrew is going to enjoy it, and so will I. Why, my mouth's watering already."

Mollified, she beamed. "In any case, dinner's a simple meal tonight, Mrs. Andrew. Just Morecombe Bay potted shrimps, cottage pie, and a green salad."

"No dessert?" I teased.

Taking me quite seriously, she cried, "Oh, yes! I always make a dessert for Mr. Andrew. You know how he loves them. But I haven't decided which one to make yet—English trifle or custard flan."

"It'll be delicious, whatever it is," I muttered and hurried to the door. "I'll go and keep Miss Reece-Jones company. By the way, Parky, did Mrs. Keswick say what time she'd be back?"

"She's never later than a quarter to five for tea. *Never.*"

"As soon as she arrives perhaps you can serve it," I suggested.

"I will that. And I expect Mr. Andrew'll be needing a bit of sustenance by then, working all afternoon the way he has, poor thing. On a Saturday too."

"Yes," I agreed and slipped out.

Gwenny Reece-Jones was leafing through the magazine when I returned to the parlor. "Andrew will join us in a minute," I told her, closing the door behind me. "And Diana's expected back imminently, so I hope you'll join us for tea, Miss Reece-Jones."

"How nice. Love to."

"Good."

As if she felt she needed to explain her sudden and unexpected arrival, she cleared her throat and said, "Working in Leeds. Doing *A Midsummer Night's Dream*. At the Theatre Royal. Sets. I design sets."

"Diana told me you were a theatrical designer."

"Oh." She looked momentarily taken aback. "Came over to Kilburn today. Know it, do you?"

"I think so. Isn't that the place where there's a giant-sized horse carved into the side of the hill?"

"Correct. On the face of Roulston Scar. Wanted to order a hall table from the Robert Thompson workshop. The great Yorkshire furniture maker and carver. Dead now. His grandsons run the workshop. Continue his work. Thought it a good idea to stop on my way back to Leeds. Say hello to Diana."

"I'm glad you did. As a matter of fact, Diana mentioned you to me only the other day."

"She did?"

I took a deep breath and plunged in. "She told me that you know my father, Edward Jordan, that you're a friend of his. A very good friend."

Startled, Gwenny gaped at me. A bright pink flush spread up from her neck to flood her face. "Good friends, yes," she admitted. She glanced away swiftly and stared into the fire.

I had a terrible feeling that I had embarrassed her, which I hadn't meant to do at all. I simply wanted to have everything out in the open. I said quickly, "I'm glad you and Daddy are friends. I worry about him, worry that he's lonely. It's comforting to know he has some companionship when he's in London, Miss Reece-Jones."

"Call me Gwenny," she said and bestowed a huge smile on me.

I thought I detected a look of relief on her face as I smiled back at her.

At this moment the door flew open and Andrew came in. "Hello, Miss Reece-Jones, remember me?" he said, grinning from ear to ear. "You used to bounce me on your knee when I was a little boy." He strode over to her and shook her hand.

"Never forgot you," she laughed, staring up at him, affection softening her face. "Mischievous." She glanced across at me. "Mischievous boy."

Before I could make any kind of comment, the door opened again, and Diana walked in, obviously not at all surprised to see Gwendolyn Reece-Jones sitting in her parlor. Undoubtedly she had seen the car in the drive.

"Hello, Gwenny dear," Diana said, crossing the room to the fireplace.

Gwenny jumped up and the two women embraced, then Gwenny said, "Rather rude. Dropping in like this. Wanted to say hello."

"Please don't apologize, it's lovely to see you," Diana said in a warm voice. "You must stay for tea. I'll just pop into the kitchen and tell Parky to bring it in. Excuse me for a moment."

"I'll come with you," I exclaimed, moving toward the door. "To help."

Diana looked at me curiously but made no comment, and we left the parlor together.

Of course later in the evening, after Gwendolyn Reece-Jones left and went on her way to Leeds, we held a little postmortem on her. It was only natural, I suppose, given the circumstances.

"She has such an odd way of speaking," I said to Diana, shaking my head. "It's sort of staccato."

"I know, she talks in little sharp bursts, and she has a predilection for using one-word sentences. But she's a good sort, awfully kind and considerate, and she doesn't have a bad word for anybody, or a bad bone in her body, for that matter," Diana answered.

"I liked her very much," I murmured.

"And she liked you," Diana replied. "Furthermore, she was rather relieved that you know about her relationship with your father."

"I hope I didn't embarrass her, I just wanted to level with her, let *her* know *I* knew." I gave Diana one of my piercing looks. "Did she say anything when you went out to the car with her, Diana?"

"Only that you'd taken her by surprise when you'd mentioned

Edward, and what a lovely young woman you were, so pretty. She was very admiring of your beautiful red hair."

"I thought *she* was rather attractive, too, and I can just see her and Daddy together. I approve; she *is* very nice."

"But as eccentric as hell!" Andrew exclaimed. "A genuine character. And whenever I hear the name Gwendolyn, I think of scarves. She's always worn masses of them, rain or shine, all kinds of weather, and as far as I remember they've been made of every type of fabric. Gwenny's a regular Isadora Duncan, if you ask me." He laughed and stood up. "Would you like another glass of wine, Ma?"

"Not at the moment, darling," Diana said, "I've still got half of this one left."

"I think I will," he said and walked across the parlor to the skirted table in the corner, where Parky had put a tray holding a bottle of white wine in an ice bucket and a syphon of soda water. "How about you, Mal?"

"I'm fine, Andrew, and listen, you two, before we have supper I want to show you my finds."

"Finds? What do you mean?" Andrew asked, turning around and smiling at me fondly.

"I was poking around in the library this afternoon, and I found a diary by one of your ancestors, Lettice Keswick, which she wrote in the seventeenth century. Actually, what I found was a *copy* of the original, and it was in the most beautiful copperplate handwriting. It was done by Clarissa Keswick, who copied it in 1893 in order to preserve it."

"Good Lord! So that's what you were doing all afternoon, digging around amongst those moldy old books. Better you than me, my love." Andrew squeezed my shoulder as he came back to the fireplace, bent over me, and kissed the top of my head. "And trust *you* to come across something unusual."

Diana cut in, "But you said *finds,* Mal, in the plural. What else did you unearth?" She had a puzzled expression in her eyes as she looked at me across the room.

"I actually found the *real* diary, as well as Clarissa's copy of it," I said, and I went on to explain what I had done earlier in the day. Then, standing up, walking toward the door, I finished, "Let me go and get them; they're in the library. Once you see both books, you'll understand what I'm talking about."

Firelight danced on the walls and across the ceiling, filling our bedroom with a rosy glow. There was no other light in the room, and I felt relaxed, drowsy, encased in a cocoon of warmth and love as I lay within the circle of Andrew's arms.

Earlier, a high wind had blown up, and now I could hear it howling over the moors. In the distance was the sound of thunder, and lightning flashed spasmodically, illuminating the bedroom with a bright white brilliance for a moment or two.

I shivered slightly, despite the warmth of the bed, and put my arm around my husband, drew closer to him. "I'm glad we're not out in that. Quite a storm's blown up since we came upstairs."

He chuckled. "Yes, it has, and we're in the best place, you and I. Snug as two bugs in a rug. But you know what? When I was little I always wanted to be out in it, in the rain and the wind and the hail, don't ask me why. I just loved storms. Maybe the inherent drama of such dreadful weather appealed to something in me. And once, when I was about seven, my father told me that it was our ancestors in their armor crashing about up there in the heavens, that their ghosts were riding out to conquer their enemies, as they had done centuries ago. I'm certain that must've sparked my imagination when I was a kid."

"And *did* you go out in the storm when you were a boy?"

"Sometimes I managed to sneak out of the house, but not if Ma could help it. She was always a bit overprotective."

"What mother isn't? Anyway, I don't blame her; storms can be dangerous. People have been struck by lightning—"

"Like I was, when I first met you!" he interrupted, putting his hand under my chin and turning my face to his. He kissed me softly, tenderly on the mouth, then broke away. "The French call it a *coup de foudre*, that instantaneous falling in love just like that." He snapped his thumb and a finger together. "In other words, struck by lightning."

I smiled against his chest. "I know what it means."

There was a small silence. We were content to lie together like this, so at peace with each other.

After a few minutes I said, "It's been such a lovely weekend, Andrew, I'm glad we came to Yorkshire, aren't you?"

"I am, and anyway, it's not over yet. We still have Sunday here. We can go riding tomorrow morning if you like, up on the gallops as I promised. And then we can take it easy for the rest of the day, be lazy. We'll have a good Sunday lunch, read the newspapers, watch television."

"You're not going to do any work?" I asked, my voice rising a fraction in my surprise.

"Certainly not. Anyway, I've done as much as I can. Now I've got to wait for Jack to come in from New York next week."

"I have a feeling you've discovered something about Malcolm Stainley, something awful."

When he was silent, I went on, "Something . . . unpleasant, unsavory, perhaps?"

His answer was simply a long, drawn-out sigh.

"What is it? What's he done?" I pressed, riddled with curiosity. I turned my face to look at his in the firelight, but it betrayed nothing.

"I don't want to go into it now, darling, honestly I don't." He sighed again. "But always remember: Beware of guys selling snake oil."

"He's crooked, Andrew! That's what you mean, isn't it?"

Pushing himself up on one elbow, he bent over me, smoothed the hair away from my face, and kissed me full on the mouth. Then he stopped and stared deeply into my eyes. "I don't want to discuss it. I've got other, more important things on my mind right now."

"Such as what?" I teased.

"You know *what*, Mrs. Keswick," he murmured, a half smile playing around his mouth.

I looked up into his face, that beloved face which was so dear to me. His expression was intense, and his extraordinary blue eyes had turned darker, almost navy in the firelight; they overpowered me.

"*You*," he said at last. "I've got you on my mind. I love you so much, Mal. You're my whole reason for being."

"I love you, too." I stroked his face. "Make love to me."

Bending over me, he brought his mouth down to mine and kissed me for a long time, gently at first. But his desire overtook him, and his kisses became wilder, more passionate.

"Oh, Mal, oh, my darling," he said between his hot kisses. Then pulling the bedcovers away, he slipped off the straps of my nightgown and released my breasts, stroking them. "Oh, look at you, darling, you're so beautiful, my beautiful wife." Lowering his head, he kissed my nipples, and his hand slid down my thigh, along the silky length of my nightgown until he caught the hem of it in his fingers. He raised it to my waist, began to kiss my stomach, then my inner thighs. And all the while his hand stroked my body in long caresses, and I trembled under his touch.

Eventually, his mouth came to rest at the center of me, and I felt myself stiffen with pleasure. I was swept along, lost in my love for him. He came and knelt between my legs and brought me cresting to a climax, then he stopped suddenly and slid inside me, filling me. We clung together, and as always we became one.

The fire had burned low, and the shadows had lengthened across the bedroom walls. Outside, the wind howled and rain slashed violently against the panes of glass. It was a wild November night here at the edge of the moors, and growing wilder, by the sound of it.

Andrew stirred against me and murmured, "Shall I put another log on the fire?"

"Not unless you're cold."

"I'm fine. And we should let the fire die out anyway."

Sitting up, I climbed out of bed, padded over to the window, and pulled the cord to close the draperies, shutting out the storm. As I walked back, I said, "That was nice of your mother, wasn't it?"

"Inviting Gwenny for Christmas, you mean?"

"Yes." I got into bed, pulled the covers over me, and snuggled up to Andrew. "I hope she'll come, and that she'll bring Daddy with her. That way it'll be a real family occasion."

"I don't think your father could stay away. And the twins are going to love it here. It's going to be a wonderful Christmas, Mal. The best."

PART THREE

NEW YORK CITY

18

New York, December 1988

"Have a wonderful baby shower, and we'll see you tomorrow," Andrew said, moving across the hall to the front door of the apartment.

"It won't be the same without you, but I do understand your reasons for fleeing," I said, laughing.

He laughed with me. "Sixteen women in this apartment is a bit too much even for me to cope with." He picked up Trixy's lead and his canvas bag and opened the front door. "Come on, kids, let's get this show on the road. It'll be teatime before we get to Indian Meadows, if we don't leave soon."

"Coming, Dad," Jamie said, buttoning his quilted, down-filled jacket but getting the buttons in the wrong holes.

I bent down to help him do it correctly, then kissed him on the cheek. He looked at me through solemn eyes and asked, "Is it *our* baby shower, Mom?"

I shook my head. "No, Alicia Munroe's. She's the one having the baby, honey."

"Oh," he said, and his little face fell. "Any news of our baby, Mom? Have you made it yet?" he asked, fixing me with his bright blue eyes, a hopeful look flashing across his face.

"Not yet," I answered, standing up. I glanced at Andrew and we exchanged amused looks, and he winked at me.

Lissa said, "Don't forget to feed Swellen, Mom, will you?"

"No, I won't, darling, I promise." I hunkered down on my haunches and kissed her. She put her little arms around my neck and showered me with fluttery kisses on my cheek. "Butterfly kisses for you, Mommy, like Daddy gives me," she said, then holding her head on one side in that old-fashioned way she had, she continued, "Did you tell Santa to bring me the big baby doll?"

"Yes. Well, at least Daddy told him."

"Will Santa know where to come?" she asked, suddenly sounding anxious. Her expression grew worried when she added, "Will he find Nanna's house in Yorkshire?"

"Of course. Daddy gave Santa her address."

She beamed at me, and I buttoned her coat and pulled on her blue woolen cap that exactly matched her eyes. "There! You look beautiful! You're my beautiful little girl, the most beautiful girl in the whole wide world. Now, put your gloves on. Both of you," I said, glancing at Jamie. "And I don't want either of you running outside to play without your coats when you're in the country. It's far too cold. And don't give Trixy any tidbits from the table."

"No, Mom," they said in unison.

"Hear that, Trixy?" I said, glancing down at the puppy. Our little Bichon Frise looked up at me through her soulful black eyes and wagged her tail. I picked her up and cuddled her, kissed the top of her head, then put her back down on the floor.

I walked with them to the front door and stood in the outside foyer waiting for the elevator to come. Andrew hugged me and kissed me on the cheek, then asked, "Did you put the list in the canvas bag? The list of the things you want me to bring back tomorrow?"

"Yes, I did. And there's not much, really, just a few items for the twins and our shearling coats, yours and mine, to take with us to Yorkshire."

"Okay, no problem, Puss." He kissed me again and ushered the kids and the puppy into the elevator. "See you."

"Drive carefully," I said just as the elevator doors started to close.

"I will," he called back. "And I'll ring you when we get there, Mal."

It was quiet in the apartment now that they had left. I went to my desk in the bedroom, sat down, and carefully wrote the card to go with Alicia's gift.

Alicia Munroe was a good friend of Sarah's and mine and had been at Radcliffe with us. A fellow New Yorker, she had married Jonathan Munroe two years ago and moved to Boston with him. She had come to Manhattan for the weekend to see her parents and to attend the baby shower Sarah and I were giving in her honor at the apartment.

When he heard, three weeks ago, what we were planning, Andrew had exclaimed. "It's the country for me, Mal! In any case, I want to give Indian Meadows the once-over before we take off for Yorkshire for Christmas. I'll take the twins and Trixy with me, get them all out of your hair, and you can have a real girls' weekend with Sarah."

When I had worried out loud how he would manage without Jenny, our former au pair, who had finally returned to live in London, he had grinned at me and said one word: "*Nora.*" And, of course, hearing her name had set my mind at ease at once. Nora loved the twins and enjoyed cooking for them, fussing over them. She would be in her element without me hovering around, as would Eric, who was devoted to Jamie and Lissa.

I glanced at the small calendar on my desk. Today was Saturday the tenth. In exactly eleven days we were flying to London and then taking the train to Yorkshire the following morning.

Diana had invited Sarah to join us for Christmas, and she had been thrilled to accept, and we were all going to stay at Kilgram Chase until early January. Gwenny Reece-Jones and my father were going to be with us too; in fact my father had called me yesterday from London. He had wanted to tell me how much he was looking forward to spending the holidays with me, Andrew, and his grandchildren. He had also told me how glad he was I liked Gwendolyn.

There were still quite a lot of preparations to make for the trip, and tomorrow Sarah and I were going shopping for last-minute gifts. Now I began to make a list on a yellow pad and was stumped when I came to Gwenny's name. Last night, tongue in cheek, Andrew had suggested we buy her a scarf. And although he had been joking, it wasn't a bad idea after all, since she did seem to like them. Perhaps I would find something special and unusual at Bloomingdale's.

Once I had finished the list, I put the card in the shopping bag with the gift for Alicia, an antique silver christening cup. Then, carrying the bag, I went into the living room.

Josie, our housekeeper, a lovely, motherly woman from Chile, was already plumping up cushions on the two big traditional sofas and armchairs.

She glanced up as I came in and said, "I've dusted the dining room, and I'll get to the kitchen next, Mrs. Keswick."

"Thanks, Josie, but perhaps you'd better make the beds and tidy the bedrooms first. Miss Thomas should be here any minute, and then we'll start preparing some of the food. I guess you ought to leave the kitchen until last."

"You're right, and I can help with the sandwiches as soon as I've finished cleaning."

"Thanks," I said, and went into the adjoining dining room, where I put the shopping bag in a corner. I added, "I'm going to start setting the table for the tea."

By the time Sarah arrived half an hour later, I had already put out cups, saucers, and plates, as well as crystal flutes, since we had called the shower a champagne tea, and we were going to serve Veuve Clicquot.

"You haven't left me very much to do," Sarah said, as she surveyed my handiwork in the dining room.

"Don't kid yourself," I shot back. "There's a lot to do yet. Roll your sleeves up, and let's go to the kitchen."

But the first thing we did was to have a cup of coffee together. This we drank at the table in front of the window, chatting about the shower and Sarah's hectic week and gossiping in general.

Finally, fifteen minutes later we started to work on the food, cutting the slices of smoked salmon into small pieces, boiling eggs for the egg salad, slicing cucumbers and tomatoes, and mashing sardines. All of these things we would use for the tea sandwiches later in the afternoon, just before the guests were due. They had been invited for three o'clock and it was still far too soon to make the sandwiches.

At one moment Sarah said, "I'm glad we made it early, Mal. Everyone'll be gone by six, no later than six-thirty, and maybe we can go to a movie, have supper out somewhere."

"Great idea. And how about a snack now? I don't know about you, but I'm starving." I looked at the clock on the wall. "It's nearly one thirty-five."

"I'm on a diet. In readiness for Christmas."

I laughed. "But Sarah, you look fantastic. You are *svelte*."

"I could still lose a few pounds. But okay, why not? I'll have a taste of the smoked salmon."

"Coming up," I said, reaching for a slice of bread. The phone rang, and I picked it up.

"Hello, Puss, it's me, and we're here," Andrew said. "And guess what, it's snowing! Mal, it's gorgeous, just like a fairyland. All white. And the snow is glistening in the sun. I promised the kids a snowball fight later."

"That's great, but make sure they wear their Wellies and are wrapped up well, honey, won't you?"

"I will, don't worry so, Puss."

"Is Nora there, Andrew?"

"She certainly is, and so is Eric. He's got the fires going throughout the house, and Nora made a wonderful vegetable soup and baked a loaf. We're going to have lunch in a few minutes. And this soup! It smells delicious! So don't worry your little head about us, everything is fine at Indian Meadows."

"Just goes to show how well you can manage without me," I muttered.

"Oh, no I can't," he asserted, his voice dropping. "There's *no way* I can manage without *you,* Mal."

"Nor me you," I responded. "I love you."

"And I love you. Big kiss, darling. And a big kiss to Sarah. I'll see you both for supper tomorrow night. Tell her I'm looking forward to her spaghetti primavera."

"I will, and have a nice time with the kids."

19

It was snowing again, as it had yesterday. But tonight the snowflakes were light, and as I glanced out the window, I noticed that they were melting the moment they hit the pavement. So it couldn't be the weather which was making Andrew late getting home.

Putting my glass of white wine down on the coffee table, I left the den, crossed the entrance hall, and went into the kitchen.

Sarah swung around when she heard me come in. "I've turned off the water for the spaghetti. No point boiling it yet. I'll make everything at the last minute, once Andrew and the twins arrive."

I nodded, and automatically my eyes went to the kitchen clock. It was ten past eight. "I can't imagine where he is, why he's not home yet, Sash," I said.

"Anything could be holding him up," Sarah answered, putting the lid on the pot of hot water. "Traffic. Snow."

"It can't be the snow. I just looked out the den window, and it's not even settling on the ground."

"Not on East Seventy-second Street, maybe, but if it's snowing in Connecticut, it could be slowing Andrew down, and everyone else who's coming back to the city on Sunday night. There's probably a backup of cars."

"That's true, yes," I said, seizing on this possibility, wanting to ease my worry. But the fact was, Andrew was rarely, if ever, late, and that was what troubled me now. Sarah knew it as well as I did, but neither of us was voicing this thought at the moment.

I said, "I'm going to try Anna again, maybe she's home by now."

"Okay, call her," Sarah agreed.

Lifting the receiver off the wall phone in front of me, I dialed the gardener's number at Indian Meadows. It rang and rang as it had earlier this evening. I was about to hang up when the phone was finally answered.

"Hello," Anna said.

"It's me. Mal," I said. "You must have been out, Anna, I've been trying your number for ages."

"I was in Sharon. I went to visit my sister, and I—"

"Did you see Andrew before he left today?" I interrupted, wanting to get to the point.

"Yes, I did. Why?"

"What time was that?"

"About two, somewhere around there."

"*Two.* But that's over six hours ago!" I cried, and looking across at Sarah, I couldn't help transmitting my anxiety to her. She came and stood next to me, her face suddenly as full of concern as mine was.

"You mean he's not arrived home yet?" Anna asked.

"No, he hasn't, and I'm starting to worry. It never takes more than three hours at the most, and Andrew does it in less time than that."

"There's snow up here, Mal, and he may have hit more of it on the way down to the city. Oh, and there's another thing, he did say something about needing to do some Christmas shopping. That could've delayed him."

"That's true, yes, and maybe he did stop off at a couple of shops on the way in. Everything's open at this time of year, and stays open late. I guess that's what happened, and thanks, Anna, you've made me feel less anxious."

"Try not to worry, Mal, I'm sure he'll be there any second. And you'll call me before you leave for England, won't you?"

"Yes, during the week. Bye, Anna."

"Bye, Mal."

We hung up, and turning to Sarah, I said, "Andrew told Anna he needed to do some Christmas shopping. I'm sure that's the explanation. Don't you think?"

Sarah nodded, giving me a reassuring smile. "He loves all those little antique shops in the area. Also, the twins might have wanted to go to the bathroom, or wanted something to eat, and so he could've stopped several times. We often stop, if you think about it, for those very reasons."

"But why hasn't he called me? It's not like him not to be in touch, you know that," I muttered, biting my lip.

The doorbell rang several times.

Sarah and I looked at each other knowingly, and we both broke into happy smiles.

"There he is! And wouldn't you know he doesn't have his key!" I exclaimed, laughing with relief as I hurried into the entrance hall.

As I unlocked the front door and pulled it open, I cried, "And where have all of you be—" The rest of my sentence remained unsaid. It was not my husband and children who stood there, but two men in damp overcoats.

"Yes?" I stood staring at them blankly, and even before they told me who they were, I knew they were cops. As a New Yorker, I recognized them immediately, recognized that unmistakable look. They were plainclothes police officers from N.Y.P.D. My chest tightened.

"Are you Mrs. Andrew Keswick?" the older of the two cops asked.

"Yes, I am. Is there—"

"I'm Detective Johnson, and this is Detective DeMarco," he said. "We're from the Twenty-fifth Precinct. We need to talk to you, Mrs. Keswick."

They both showed me their shields.

I swallowed several times. "Is there something wrong?" I managed to say, my eyes flying nervously from him to his partner. I dreaded the answer; my heart began to clatter.

"Can we come in?" Detective Johnson said. "I think it would be better if we spoke inside."

I nodded, opened the door wider, and stepped back to let them enter the apartment.

DeMarco closed the door.

Sarah, who had been hovering in the background, said, "I'm Sarah Thomas, an old friend of Mrs. Keswick's, a friend of the family, actually."

Detective Johnson nodded, and Detective DeMarco murmured, "Ms. Thomas," and inclined his head, scrupulously polite.

I led them into the living room and said, "Is there some sort of problem? My husband's late getting home. I, we, that is, Sarah and I, have been a bit worried. He's not been in an accident, has he?"

"Let's sit down, Mrs. Keswick," DeMarco said.

I shook my head. "Just tell me what's wrong, please."

DeMarco cleared his throat and began, "Something tragic has happened. I think we should sit down."

"*Tell me.*" My voice quavered as I spoke, and a dreadful trembling took hold of me. Sudden fear surged through my body, and reaching out, I gripped the top of the wing chair to steady myself.

"We found your husband's Mercedes on Park Avenue at One Hundred Nineteenth Street. Your husband was hurt—"

"Oh, my God! Is he badly injured? Where is he? Oh, God, my children! Are they all right? Where are they? Where's my husband?"

My heart was racing. Filled with a mixture of panic and dread, I moved forward and grasped DeMarco's arm. Urgently, I said, "Why didn't you bring my children home? Which hospital is my husband in? The twins must be frightened. Take me to them, please."

Gasping, fighting my tears, I swung to Sarah and cried, "Come on, Sash, let's go! We must go to the twins and Andrew. *Come on!* They need me."

"Mrs. Keswick, Ms. Thomas, just a minute," DeMarco said.

I stopped, looked at him. There was something odd in his voice. My stomach lurched. He was going to say something awful, something I didn't want to hear. I knew it instinctively.

He said, "I'm sorry to have to tell you this, Mrs. Keswick, but your husband has been shot. He's—"

My eyes opened wide. "*Shot!* Who shot him? *Why?*" The blood was draining out of me; my legs had gone weak.

My eyes flew to Sarah. Her face had turned the color of bleached bone. In an unusually high voice, she exclaimed, "I thought the car was in some sort of accident."

I stood staring at her; somehow I had thought the same thing.

"No, Ms. Thomas," DeMarco said.

"He's not badly hurt, is he?" Sarah asked, endeavoring to speak in a more controlled voice.

"Where are my children?" I demanded before either of the detectives could answer her. "I want to go to my children and my husband."

"They're all at Bellevue," Detective DeMarco said. "And so is your dog. I'm very sorry to have to tell you this, but your—"

"My children ... are ... all right ... aren't they?" I interrupted, speaking very slowly, fearfully.

Detective Johnson shook his head. He looked dour.

DeMarco said, "No, Mrs. Keswick. Your husband, your children, and your dog were all fatally shot this afternoon. We're very sorry."

"No! No! Not Andrew! Not the twins! Not Jamie and Lissa! It's not possible! It can't be true," I cried, gaping at DeMarco, uncomprehending. I began to shake.

I heard Sarah saying over and over again, "Oh, my God, my God!"

I stepped away from DeMarco, stepped away from the chair, and went lurching across the room to the entrance hall, shaking my head from side to side, denying, denying. Blindly I reached out, grabbing at air, at emptiness.

I had to get out of here.

Get to Bellevue.

Bellevue.

That's where they were.

My husband.

Get to Andrew.

To Lissa and Jamie.

Get to my children.

My children needed me.

My husband needed me.

My little Trixy needed me.

He'd said they were dead.

All dead.

The four of them.

NO!

The room became very bright, and it began to sway and move.

I heard it then. The noise.

It was a terrible, piercing scream that went ripping right through me. A bone-chilling scream rising higher and higher. It sounded like the scream of an animal being tortured, of an animal in torment.

It grew louder and louder until it filled my mind absolutely. And it deafened me.

As the floor came up to hit me in the face, I knew that it was I who was screaming.

20

When I regained consciousness, I was lying on one of the sofas in the living room.

As I opened my eyes, it was Sarah's face I saw. She sat in a chair next to me.

"Mal," she whispered, reaching out, taking hold of my hand. "Oh, Mal, darling." Her voice broke, and tears welled in her dark, compassionate eyes. I saw the pain on her face.

I grasped her hand tightly, pinning her with an intense gaze. "Tell me it's not true, Sash," I pleaded tearfully. "Tell me it's not. They're all right, aren't they? It's been a horrible mistake, hasn't it?"

"Oh, Mal," was all she could say, in a muffled voice. She was unable to continue speaking, and tears trickled down her strained white face.

I saw him then.

Detective DeMarco.

He was standing near the living room window, looking across at me. Fleetingly, a look of pity washed over his face and was instantly gone; but I knew without a doubt that it was true.

It *had* happened.

It was not a bad dream from which I had just awakened.

It was *real*, this nightmare.

My eyes shifted. Through my tears I could see his partner, Johnson. The older detective was standing by the small antique desk in front of the window overlooking Seventy-second Street. He was speaking on the phone. I heard him say, "Yes, that's correct."

I shouted in a shrill, angry voice, "I want to go to my husband and my children. I want my family. I want my dog. I want to be with them." I tried to struggle off the sofa, but Sarah put her arms around me, held me still, endeavored to soothe me.

"I want my babies," I shouted through my wracking sobs. "I want my family. I'm going to them now." I continued to struggle against Sarah, but she held me tightly.

"Yes, we *are* going, Mal, in a few minutes." Sarah's voice was low, drained. She went on. "The detectives are going to take us to the mor—to Bellevue. I just gave Detective Johnson your mother's number. He's been talking to her and David. They're coming now; they'll be here in a couple of minutes."

I clung to Sarah, sobbing against her shoulder. I wanted Andrew, I wanted the twins. What had happened this afternoon? I didn't understand. Who had shot my family? And why? Why had this happened to us? Why would anybody shoot a decent man like Andrew? Shoot innocent little children and a dog? *Why?*

Suddenly I heard the front door and my mother's voice exclaiming, "Where's my daughter? Where's Mrs. Keswick? I'm Mrs. Nelson, her mother."

I pulled away from Sarah. My mother was rushing toward me across the living room. Her face was stricken, ashen, her eyes full of horror and disbelief.

"Oh, Mom!" I cried out. "Oh, Momma! Andrew and the twins have been shot. And Trixy. Why, Mom? I don't understand."

My mother sank down heavily on the sofa, wrapped her arms around me, and held me close to her. "It doesn't make sense," she whispered, and she kept repeating this like a litany. She began to weep, and we held on to each other desperately, struggling with our pain and heartbreak.

Between sobs, my mother said, "I don't know how to help you, Mal, but I'm here for you, darling. Oh, God, how can anybody help you? This is too much for anyone to bear." She rocked me in her arms, weeping, and whispered in a cracking voice, "I can't believe it. Lissa and Jamie gone, Andrew gone. It doesn't make any sense. What has this world come to? It's godless. *Godless.*"

After a few minutes, David left the detectives and came over to the sofa, knelt down on the floor in front of us, and put his arms around my mother and me.

His voice was gentle, caring. "I'm so very, very sorry, Mal. I'm here for you and your mother. I'll do anything to help you both. All you have to do is ask me. Anything at all, Mal."

Eventually I managed to sit up. Gently, I extricated myself from my mother's arms. She lay back against the sofa; her face was haggard.

David rose, came and sat in a chair near me. "Take your time, Mal, we're in no hurry."

I looked at him, tried to speak, but I couldn't say anything. I began to weep once more. Wrapping my arms around my body, hugging myself, I moved backward and forward on the sofa, making low, keening noises. I was distraught, I was in an agony of mind, soul, and body. Every part of me felt as if it had been bludgeoned.

Finally I stopped moving and leaned back, closing my eyes. But the tears kept coming, seeping out from underneath my lids.

Opening my eyes at last, I gazed at David helplessly. He gave me his handkerchief.

After I wiped my eyes, I said in a shaky voice, "I want to see my family."

"Of course, and you shall," David said. "The detectives are ready to take you to Bellevue, Mal. We'll all come. Your mother and Sarah and I. We'll be with you."

I could only nod my understanding.

David said, "Can I get you anything? Anything to drink? Brandy, maybe?"

I shook my head. "Just water, please."

My mother stood up shakily. "I'll get it, I need a glass myself."

Sarah said, "I'll come with you, Auntie Jess."

David took hold of my hand, held it tightly in his, wanting to comfort me. His light gray eyes were full of sympathy, and his tactfulness and concern were palpable. I was thankful he was here. I had grown to know him quite well since he'd married my mother, and he was kind and considerate. He was also quick, efficient, and smart, and as a criminal lawyer he knew how to properly and effectively deal with the police.

After a second, he said, "I need to talk to the detectives, Mal. I didn't learn much from them on the phone. My fault, I didn't give them a chance to fill me in. Your mother and I just raced around here within minutes of receiving their call."

He started to get up, but I wouldn't let go of his hand.

Puzzled, he looked at me closely. "What is it, Mal?" he asked.

"Can you bring them over here? I want to hear what they have to say."

Nodding, he rose and strode across the floor. He stood talking to Johnson and DeMarco for a few minutes, and then the three of them came back and sat down near me.

Detective Johnson said, "We don't know what happened, Mrs. Keswick." He threw David a quick glance, and went on in a low voice. "It could have been a crime of opportunity, such as robbery, we're just not sure. And we won't be able to give you any real answers until we've done a proper investigation."

David said, "You told me you found the car on Park Avenue at One Hundred Nineteenth Street. At the traffic light there."

"Yes," Johnson said.

"Was the family in the car?"

Johnson said, "Yes. Mr. Keswick was in the front seat, the driver's seat, and he'd fallen across the passenger seat. His door was open, and his legs were out of the car, as if he'd been trying to get out. One back door was also open, and the children were on the backseat together, with the dog."

I pushed myself to my feet. On shaking legs I half walked, half staggered out of the living room. I managed to get to my bathroom. Closing and locking the door, I knelt on the floor and vomited into the toilet, retching until there was nothing left inside me. Then I fell over on my side and curled into a ball, sobbing my heart out. I was in shock, disbelieving. This couldn't be happening, it couldn't. This morning I had been talking and laughing with Andrew on the phone, and now . . .

"Mal, Mal, are you all right?" Sarah called, knocking on the bathroom door. "We're concerned about you."

"Give me a minute." I dragged myself to my feet, splashed cold water on my face, and looked at myself in the mirror. The face staring back did not look like mine. It was stark, the cheekbones sticking out like blades, and it was as white as chalk under all the freckles. I felt stunned, dazed, and my glazed eyes reflected this.

Not me, that's not me. But then, I would never be me again.

There were two medical examiners waiting for us at Bellevue Hospital, where the New York City Morgue was located. I followed them into the morgue, accompanied by Detectives Johnson and DeMarco as well as David Nelson.

I had protested to Detective DeMarco, begging him to let me go in alone except for the two doctors. It was Johnson who had explained the law; the police officers who were the first to arrive on the scene of a crime must be present at the identification of the body or bodies. It was mandatory.

David had insisted on coming in with me, and I hadn't had the strength to argue. In any case, the medical examiners seemed to think his presence was essential.

When they pulled out Andrew's body and showed it to me, I gasped and cried out in anguish, then pressed my hands to my mouth. I felt my legs buckle, but David was there, standing right behind me, and he put his arm around my waist, held me upright.

Oh, Andrew, my darling, my heart cried out.

My eyes were streaming as they led me to the next two compartments, pulled out the slabs, and showed me Lissa and then Jamie. My children, my darling babies. I could barely see their faces for my blinding tears. They were so still, so quiet, so cold. All I wanted was to keep them warm, to keep them safe. Oh, my poor babies.

Looking at one of the medical examiners, I gasped through my tears, "They didn't suffer, did they?"

He shook his head. "No, Mrs. Keswick. None of them suffered. Death was instantaneous."

Detective Johnson was edging me away, edging David and me away from my children.

"I want to stay with them," I whispered. "Please let me stay."

"We can't, Mrs. Keswick," Johnson said. "You can be with them tomorrow at the funeral parlor, after we've released them." Then he added, very quietly, "Your dog's here. Normally it would have gone to an animal hospital, but it was required for evidence."

"She," I said. "She's a she, not an it."

"You must have a vet, don't you?" Johnson said. "We'll need the name and address. The dog can go there tomorrow."

All I could do was nod. I was sobbing uncontrollably.

One of the doctors took me to Trixy, showed her to me. I bent over her and touched the top of her furry head, and my tears fell down on my hands.

Trixy. My little Trixola.

I was still weeping when David guided me out into the corridor. He led me down to the waiting room, but I could barely walk; waves of shock and heartbreak were washing over me.

As we went into the waiting room, my mother stood up and so did Sarah. They both hurried over.

"Oh, Mom, oh, Momma," I wept. "It is them. They're dead. Whatever am I going to do without them?"

21

"Park and One Hundred Nineteenth Street is a very bad area, Mrs. Keswick; there's drug dealing on the street, prostitution. So, what do you think your husband was doing up there on Sunday afternoon?" Detective Johnson asked.

I stared at him, clenching my hands in my lap, endeavoring to control their constant trembling. "I know what he was doing up there," I said quietly. "He was on his way home with our children. He was coming from Connecticut."

"Where in Connecticut?" DeMarco inquired, shifting slightly in his chair, leaning back in it. There was a sympathetic look in his eyes.

"Sharon," I said. "We have a house there."

Detective Johnson frowned. "And did he usually drive through the heart of Harlem?"

I nodded. "Yes. Andrew always takes—" I stopped, steadied myself, and went on, "Andrew always took Route 684, which leads into the Saw Mill River Parkway and then the Henry Hudson Parkway. That's an absolutely straight line from Sharon to Manhattan. And by going through Harlem he came out at the top of Park Avenue."

"Where did he get off the Henry Hudson?" Johnson asked.

"At the One Hundred Twenty-fifth Street exit, in order to zip right over to the East Side. He never varied this route, and we would go all the way across One Hundred Twenty-fifth, past Twelfth Avenue and Amsterdam, until we came to Park."

DeMarco said, "Did he go under the elevated section of the Metro North railway tracks at One Hundred Twenty-fourth, passing North General Hospital and the Edward M. Horan School around One Hundred Twentieth?"

"That's right. Then my husband would drive all the way down Park Avenue, turning right on Seventy-second Street. He believed it was the quickest way to get home. And it is."

"It's a well-traveled route. A lot of New Yorkers use it to hit the East Side quickly, but that area around One Hundred Nineteenth Street has become very dangerous lately," DeMarco said. "Huge quantities of crack cocaine are sold up there, underneath those stone arches of Metro North, just near the traffic light where your husband's . . . car was found."

"He wasn't on drugs," I exclaimed angrily. "Furthermore, he had our children with him. He wasn't doing anything wrong. He was simply driving home." My mouth began to tremble, and I covered it with my hand. I felt the tears sting the back of my eyes.

"We know he wasn't doing anything wrong, Mrs. Keswick," Detective Johnson said in a kindly voice, and I glanced at him in surprise. His partner had seemed to be the nicer of the two.

"Why were my husband and children shot?" I asked again, repeating the question I had been asking nonstop for two days.

DeMarco cleared his throat. "Your husband either stopped for the red light there, or he was forcibly stopped by one or more perpetrators. He was either getting out of the car, to see what was going on, or the door of the car was wrenched open. Then the shootings occurred, around four-thirty, five o'clock, according to the medical examiners. And we're not sure why he and the children *were* shot, Mrs. Keswick."

I stared at him. I could not speak.

Johnson said, "We think it might have been a carjacking gone wrong, in other words, an *attempted* carjacking."

"Carjacking?" I repeated. "What's that?"

"It's a crime that's occurring more and more frequently these days," Johnson explained. "It usually happens when a car is waiting at a red light or is parked in a rest area. The car is attacked, usually by several perpetrators. The occupants are made to get out, and the car is driven away. What might have happened, in your husband's case, is that the perpetrators were startled by something or someone, or taken by surprise, and so they fled without the car. It's possible they left the scene of the crime in panic or fear, or both, because one of them or more got trigger-happy. There might have been witnesses, and we're hoping someone will come forward."

DeMarco said, "We know from Mr. Nelson that your husband always wore a gold Rolex and carried a wallet. These items were missing, as we informed Mr. Nelson yesterday. But was there anything else in the car? Luggage?"

"Our shearling coats, Andrew's and mine. A few small items, clothing and a pair of riding boots, things like that, which he packed in a suitcase. Nothing very valuable, as far as I know," I said.

"Those things were not found in the car. It was empty," DeMarco reminded me, and continued, "The car will be released tomorrow, so you should have it back in another day. It was dusted for fingerprints on Sunday, and these have been sent to the FBI to be checked."

I did not respond. I did not want the car. I never wanted to see it again.

Johnson rose. "I'll be back in a minute," he said to DeMarco and went to the door. As he opened it and walked out, the din of the Twenty-fifth Precinct penetrated the quiet office.

Detective DeMarco said, "I've got to ask you a few other questions, Mrs. Keswick."

"Yes."

"Ruling out a possible carjacking, an attempted carjacking, that is, can you think of any reason why someone might want to shoot your husband? Why someone might wish to do him harm?"

I shook my head.

"Did he have any enemies?"

"No, of course he didn't," I said.

"Did he have any bad business dealings with anyone?"

"No."

DeMarco cleared his throat. "Any girlfriends, Mrs. Keswick?"

"What?"

"Could your husband have had a relationship with another woman? I realize that you might not have known about it, but was it a possibility?"

"No, it wasn't, Detective DeMarco. No, he didn't have any girl-friends. We were very happily married," I said in a cold little voice, and once again it was all I could do not to burst into tears. I resented the fact that I'd had to come to the precinct to be questioned rather than making a statement to them at home. But last night David had told me that I must go, that it was simply police procedure.

A moment or two later Detective DeMarco escorted me out into the corridor, where Sarah was sitting on a bench waiting for me. After I'd said good-bye to DeMarco, who told me he'd be in touch if there were any developments, Sarah took my arm and hurried me out of the precinct.

Once inside the car waiting for us outside, she told the driver to take us back to Park Avenue and Seventy-fourth Street, where my mother lived. I had been staying with her and David since Sunday night; my mother had not wanted me to be alone. In any case, her apartment, which David had moved into after their marriage, had been my home until I married Andrew. I had grown up there.

I leaned back against the car seat, feeling weak and drained. Since the shooting I had been trying to hold myself together as best I could, but most of the time I felt as though I was flying apart. I could not let that happen—not until after the funeral, any-way.

Sarah held my hand and glanced at me worriedly from time to time, but we were silent as the car sped down Park.

Finally, I looked at her and said, "The police think it might have been an attempted carjacking."

"What?" She stared at me in puzzlement. "What's that?"

"Apparently a carjacking is a relatively new crime that's been recurring constantly lately. The thieves attack a car that's either parked or at a red light, usually at gunpoint, and after they've made the occupants get out, they steal the car."

"Good God!" Sarah looked at me aghast.

"Johnson and DeMarco think Andrew's car was attacked in this manner, but that the thieves got scared off." I went on to repeat everything the two detectives had told me.

"Nobody's safe anymore," she said quietly, when I had finished, and I felt a shiver run through her.

22

My father was the first person I saw when I entered my mother's apartment with Sarah.

He must have heard my key in the door, for he came out of the small library. Anxiousness and concern ringed his mouth, and his thin, patrician face was taut with strain.

Sarah said, "Hello, Uncle Edward," and disappeared in the direction of the kitchen before he could answer, discreetly leaving us alone.

"Mal!" my father exclaimed, hurrying across the entrance hall. But there was no joy in his voice at the sight of me, only anguish.

"Oh, Dad," I cried and ran to him. I threw myself into his arms and held on to him tightly. "Oh, Daddy, I can't bear it. I can't. I can't live without Andrew and Lissa and Jamie. I should have been with them. Then I would have been killed too, and we would be together." I broke down, sobbed against his chest.

He stroked my hair, trying to console me. But I was inconsolable. He held me for a few moments. At last he said, "When Diana reached me I couldn't believe it. It's *not* believable . . . that such a thing could happen to Andrew and the twins—" He stopped, unable to continue, his voice broken; tears shook him, and we stood there in the middle of the entrance hall, weeping and clinging to each other.

After a short while we both managed to gain control of ourselves, and we drew apart.

My father took out his handkerchief and wiped away my tears, tenderly, as he had when I was a child. Then he wiped his own eyes and blew his nose.

After helping me off with my black wool coat, which he hung in the closet, he put his arm around my shoulders and walked with me into the library.

Looking up at him, I said, "Where's Diana? I thought you traveled together from London."

"We did. She's in your mother's bedroom, freshening up. The minute she walked in and saw your mother, she began to cry. So did your mother, of course. It's difficult to comprehend that we don't have Andrew and our grandchildren anymore—" My father's strong, resonant voice faltered, and I saw the tears glistening at the back of his eyes.

Silently, we sat down next to each other on the sofa. My father said, "I wanted to comfort you, to help you, but I'm afraid I'm not doing a very good job of it, am I, darling?"

"How can you?" I replied in a strangled voice. "You're grieving too. We're all grieving, Dad, and we're not going to stop, not ever."

He nodded, took my hand and held it tightly in his. "When David picked us up at Kennedy this morning, he explained that you'd gone to the precinct to make a statement, that this was just normal procedure. But did they tell you anything? Pass on any new information?"

"No, they didn't, except that they thought the shooting was a carjacking."

My father looked as puzzled as Sarah had. I explained and repeated everything the detectives had told me.

He shook his head in wonder, his tanned, freckled face registering a mixture of pain and anger. "It's so horrific one can hardly bear to think of it, never mind comprehend it." A deep sigh escaped him, and he shook his head again.

"And all for a watch, a wallet, and possibly a car, until something, or someone, made them run." My voice wavered, and fresh tears surfaced. "And they may never be caught."

My father's voice was gentle and loving as he said, "I'm here for you, darling. I'll do whatever I can to help you bear this . . . this . . . this unbearable sorrow and pain."

"I don't want to live without them, Dad. I don't have anything to live *for*. Life without Andrew and the twins is no life for me. I want to die."

"Ssssh, darling," he said, gentling me. "Don't say that, and don't let your mother and Diana hear you. It will destroy them afresh if they hear you speaking in this way. Promise me you'll put such thoughts out of your head."

I remained silent. How could I make a promise I knew I couldn't keep?

When I did not answer him, my father said, "I know that you—"

"Mal!" Diana said from the doorway, and it sounded like a cry of pain.

I leapt up and went to her as she came toward me.

All of her emotions were on her face; I could see her raw grief, her immense suffering. I tried to be strong for her as I put my arms around her and embraced her.

"You're all I have left now, Mal," she said in a low, shaking voice, and the tears came and she wept in my arms, just as I had wept in my father's a few minutes ago.

He rose and came to us and led us both back to the sofa, where she and I sat down.

Daddy took a chair opposite us and said, after a few moments, "Shall I go and get you a cup of tea, Diana? And one for you, Mal?"

Diana said, "I don't know . . . I don't care, Edward."

I murmured, "Yes, why not. Go and get it, Dad, please."

"All right." He got up and strode across the carpet but paused in the doorway. "Your mother's in the kitchen, helping the maid make sandwiches. Not that I think anyone is going to eat them."

"I can't, and I'm sure Diana feels the same way."

Diana said nothing. She dabbed her eyes with her handkerchief and blew her nose several times. "I simply can't absorb it, Mal," she began, shaking her head. "I can't believe they're . . . gone. Andrew and Lissa and Jamie. My son, my grandchildren, cut down like that—so senselessly, so cruelly."

"They didn't suffer," I managed to say in a tight voice. I was so choked up it took a moment for me to continue. "I asked the medical examiners if they had, and one of them assured me they hadn't, that death had been instantaneous."

Diana bit her lip, and her eyes filled, and at that precise moment I realized how much Andrew had resembled his mother. I covered my mouth with my hand, pressing back the tears.

"I don't know what I'm going to do without him," I whispered. "I loved him so much. He was my life, the twins were my life."

Reaching out, Diana clasped my hand. "I know, I know. I want to see them. I want to see my son and my grandchildren. Can we go and see them, Mal?"

"Yes. They're at the funeral home. It's nearby."

"And the service is tomorrow, your mother said. In the morning. At Saint Bartholomew's."

"Yes."

Diana said nothing more. She simply sat there staring at me, stupefied. I knew she was in shock, as was I. As we all were, for that matter.

Swallowing a few times and trying to get a grip on myself, I said, "I need you to do something for me, Diana."

"Oh, Mal, anything, anything."

"Will you come to our apartment? I have to choose . . . choose . . . their . . . clothes . . . the clothes they'll wear . . . in their coffins," I managed to say brokenly, the horror of it all sweeping over me yet again, as it had constantly in the past forty-eight hours.

"Of course I'll come," Diana said in a choked voice that sounded suddenly exhausted and old.

Without warning and without another word, she jumped up and rushed out, and I knew she was barely managing to hold herself together.

I knew exactly how she felt.

I leaned back on the sofa, and my gaze turned inward as I sat and reflected about my life and how it had been destroyed beyond redemption.

PART FOUR

INDIAN MEADOWS

23

Indian Meadows, January 1989

I was alone.

My husband was dead.

My children were dead.

My little pet, Trixy, was dead.

I should be dead too.

And I would have been if I had come with them to Indian Meadows that weekend in December. But I had stayed in the city to give the shower for Alicia Munroe, and because of that I was alive.

I didn't want to be alive. I had nothing to live for now, no reason for being.

A life without Andrew had no value.

A life without my children had no meaning.

I did not know what to do without them; I did not know how to cope with the business of everyday living, or how to function properly.

It seemed to me that I walked around like a zombie, doing everything automatically, by rote. I got up in the morning, showered, dressed, and drank a cup of coffee or tea. I made my bed and attended to chores in the house, helping Nora as I always had.

Sometimes I visited Anna and the horses in the stables; I spoke on the phone to my mother and Sarah. Several times a week I called Diana, or she called me, and my father was more in touch with me than he had ever been, phoning me constantly.

But for the most part I did nothing. I had no strength, no initiative; I was filled with apathy.

Occasionally I did come to my small office at the back of the house, where I sat now, trying to answer some of the condolence letters I had received. There were hundreds of them, but I could face only a few at a time, they were so harrowing to deal with.

Frequently I sat upstairs in my sitting room, thinking about Andrew, Lissa, and Jamie, grieving for them and for Trixy. My little Bichon Frise had been my constant companion before the children were born, forever at my heels, following me everywhere. She had been a genuine little presence.

I could not understand why this terrible thing had happened to us. What had we done to deserve it? Why had God allowed them to be murdered? Had I done something to offend Him? Had we all done something wrong? Something which displeased Him?

Or was there no God?

Was there only evil in this world?

Evil was man's invention, not God's. It had existed since the beginning of time and would continue to exist until this planet blew itself up, which it would, because man was evil and destructive, intent on killing and destroying.

My life, *our lives,* had been touched by evil when that animal had pulled the trigger, wiping out two innocent children, a little puppy, and a decent man who had never done any harm to anyone in his forty-one years.

Andrew had been cut down in the prime of his life, my children at the beginning of their lives, and it made no sense to me. Some of my friends had told me that it was God's will, and that we should never question Him. Or ask why He did certain things, that we must *accept* them, however painful.

How could I accept the deaths of my husband and my children? And so I kept on asking *why*. I wanted to understand why it had happened. I needed to know why God permitted the human race to commit the crimes it did. *Did God want us to suffer?* Was that it? I did not know. I had no answers for myself. Or for anyone else.

Perhaps there were no answers; perhaps there was no God, which was something I'd been pondering for five weeks. My mother said we lived in a godless world, and she might just be right.

We knew now from the ballistics report that the gun used to shoot my family had been a nine-millimeter semiautomatic hand-gun, which carried seventeen or eighteen bullets in the clip and did not have to be reloaded. DeMarco had told David this, explaining that it could be bought on the streets quite easily, adding that it was the gun of choice.

Gun of choice.

What had we come to? Had we learned nothing over the centuries?

According to DeMarco, the same type of bullet had killed all of my family, so he and Johnson were fairly certain there had been only one gunman. But that did not rule out an attack by a gang, DeMarco had told David. Unfortunately, there were still no suspects. And no witnesses had come forward.

Nothing was happening, as far as I knew, despite the intense media coverage, which still continued. The shooting of my family, the funeral service, and the police investigation had attracted the media in droves; it had become a circus in the end, with newspaper and television reporters hounding us on a daily basis. Even the British press had descended on us, much to our distress.

I no longer read the newspapers or watched the television news. I did not want to get caught by surprise by something about me or mine. Certainly I no longer cared what was happening in the world. The world was irrelevant.

I had fled to Indian Meadows.

I had also wanted to escape the apartment and New York,

which I now loathed. The city filled me with disgust and fear.

David had told me not to be too disdainful of the media and their constant coverage of this tragedy.

"They're keeping the pressure on the police," he had pointed out again just the other day. "Be glad about that, Mal. The N.Y.P.D. doesn't want to get roasted alive. They'll only intensify their efforts to find the perp." After a pause, he had thought to add, "Mind you, DeMarco and Johnson are hell-bent on solving this crime, and DeMarco especially has made it a personal crusade."

Everything David said was true. And DeMarco did seem to be very personally committed. Yet I doubted that the monster who had so cold-bloodedly taken the lives of my family would ever be tracked down.

He was long gone with his lethal weapon.

He was free.

Free to live his evil life. And kill again, if the whim took him.

And I was left to grieve.

I grieved for my husband and my children, grieved for the lives they would never lead, grieved for the future which had been stolen from them, grieved for all that might have been and never would be now.

I wanted to die.

And I was going to die.

Soon. Very soon.

I had been unable to kill myself up until now because I had not been left alone for a moment. There was always someone with me.

Did they all suspect my intentions?

I had been surrounded since the day after the funeral, when I had driven up to Sharon with Diana and my father. Sarah had followed with my mother and David, and they had stayed for days.

They had given me love. And they had tried to comfort me, as I had endeavored to console them. But none of us had succeeded. The loss was too great, the pain too excruciating. It lingered deep inside, never beginning to fade.

Eventually they had all left, although some of them only temporarily, such as my mother, David, and Sarah. She had had to go to work at Bergman's, David to his law office. But they were all back within a few days, and Nora and Anna were never far from my side. Even Eric, Nora's husband, seemed to hover constantly when he was not at work.

Diana had decided to return to London toward the end of December. She had wanted to stay with me here, at least to help get me through the holidays, as had my father. I had pointed out that my mother, David, and Sarah would be coming to Indian Meadows for Christmas, and that they should go, should try to get on with their lives as best they could.

"Perhaps you're right, Mal," Diana had said. "You and I will only feed on each other's pain and grief if I remain here." It struck me she was only saying this to help me feel better. Certainly I knew it was heart-wrenching for her to leave me. In fact, at the last minute, just before she and my father had set out for Kennedy, she had begged me to quickly pack a bag and go with her to London, then up to Yorkshire.

My father had also pleaded with me to accompany them. He had asked me to spend Christmas with him, Diana, and Gwenny at Kilgram Chase, or, if I felt that that was impossible, he would take us all away. We could go somewhere in France, he had said.

But there was nothing for me in London or Yorkshire or France or anywhere else for that matter. I was no longer comfortable on this earth. I craved another, distant place.

And so I had shaken my head, kissed them both good-bye, and sent them on their way. I wanted to be here with my memories. And I wanted to make my plans for my death.

There was another reason why I had not done it yet. I was waiting for something to be delivered. It had not arrived. But once it did, I would kill myself and join my husband and babies. We would be together, and the pain would end.

I glanced at today's date in my engagement book. It was Tuesday, January 17. The package was due to arrive tomorrow, the eighteenth.

There was no doubt in my mind that I would do it on the nineteenth.

So be it.

I got up and walked out of the office, down the corridor to the coatroom, where I kept boots and raincoats. Earlier this morning Anna had asked me to go down to the stables, and now seemed as good a time as any. Before I reached the coatroom I ran into the ever-present Nora carrying a tray.

"Mal! I was just bringing you this bowl of soup."

"I don't really want it, Nora, I'm not hungry. Thanks. Anyway, I'm going out."

"No, you're not," she said, blocking my way. "Not until you've got something inside you." She stared me down. "You've not eaten a thing for days. Tea, coffee, a slice of toast. What good is that going to do you? You're going to have this soup."

"All right," I said. I couldn't be bothered to argue with her. Anyway, she had that obdurate look in her eyes, which lately I had come to know only too well. Also, it occurred to me that she might physically prevent me from going outside unless I ate the soup.

She softened a bit. "Where do you want it?"

"In the kitchen," I said.

Without saying anything, she turned on her heels and went in the direction of the long gallery, which in turn led into the kitchen.

I could tell from the way she held herself that she was annoyed with me, hurt even, and this troubled me. I wouldn't offend Nora for the world. She was a good woman, and she too was grief-stricken and sorrowing. She had adored the twins to the point of distraction and had cared deeply for Andrew. She, Eric, and Anna had come to New York for the funeral service, and they had been devastated ever since.

Wanting to make amends for my curtness, I said as I sat down, "I'm sorry, Nora. I didn't mean to speak so crossly to you."

She placed the tray on the kitchen table in front of me and put her hand on my shoulder. She began to speak, but there was a catch in her throat, and she hurried away before I could say another word.

Even though it was the middle of January, it was not very cold, and so far this year there had been little snow. A light dusting of it covered the flat ground near the house, but it was not particularly deep on the lawns, only on the hill which sloped down to the barns, the pastures, and the pond.

Eric had cleared a path through the snowdrifts which covered the hill and had put down sand and salt. I followed this path, heading for Anna's cottage. I was almost there when she came out of the stables, turned, saw me, and waved.

I waved back and increased my pace.

After greeting me affectionately, as she always did, she said, "It's about . . . the ponies, Mal. You told me to do what I wanted about them, and . . . well, I have a customer."

I frowned. "A customer? What do you mean, Anna?" I asked, staring hard at her.

"I have someone who wants to buy them," she answered quickly, and there was a baffled expression in her soft brown eyes.

"Oh, I couldn't sell them!" I exclaimed. "*Never.*"

My voice must have sounded harsh, for she colored and stammered, "I guess I misunderstood."

I put my hand out, touched her arm reassuringly. "No, no, you didn't misunderstand, Anna. *I* didn't make myself clear. And I'm sorry if I spoke harshly just now. When I told you to do what you wanted about the ponies, I meant that you should give them away. I could never sell Pippa and Punchinella."

Her face broke into a smile. "I have this friend who wants them. She'll take good care of them, Mal, and her children will, too. It's a lovely gift, thank you."

I nodded. "Is there anything else you wanted to talk about?"

"No, that was it," Anna replied.

"I think I'll go in and look at the ponies, say good-bye to them," I muttered half to myself as I walked across to the stables.

Anna had the good grace not to follow me.

I went to the stalls and pulled a carrot out of my pocket for Punchinella, then another one for Pippa. After feeding them, patting their heads, and nuzzling them, I whispered, "Go off to a new home. And be sure you give two other children the same pleasure you gave mine."

Slowly I walked back up the hill to the house.

When I reached the top I sat down on the seat under the apple tree. It looked so bare, so bereft at this time of year, but in the spring and summer it was leafy and filled with delicate white blossoms. A beautiful tree, I have always thought.

This was one of my favorite spots at Indian Meadows. Andrew had called it Mommy's Place, for whenever I had a moment or two to spare I would come here—to relax, to think, to read, occasionally to paint, and very often just to sit and daydream. Eventually it had become theirs, too, the children's and Andrew's. If ever I was missing for a while, it was here they usually found me, and they always wanted to stay, to share this place.

Underneath this tree I had told the twins fairy tales and read to them, and sometimes we had had picnics on the grass. It was never anything but cool and shady even on the hottest of summer days, and it was one of the prettiest spots I had ever known.

And it was here that Andrew and I had come just to be alone, especially on warm nights when the sky was inky and bright with stars. Enfolded in each other's arms, we had sat together quietly talking about the future, or not talking, if we didn't want to, always at peace here.

How we had all loved it beneath the old apple tree.

I closed my eyes, shutting out the powder-blue sky and the January sunlight, squeezing back my tears.

24

"Mal, there's a truck here, a delivery truck," Nora said, bending over me and touching my shoulder.

I sat up with a start, blinking.

"I'm sorry I had to wake you up. I know you hardly ever sleep these days. But the delivery guy needs these papers signed, and he wants to know where you want the safe."

Pushing myself to my feet, I said, "Up here. I want it up here, Nora, in my clothes closet."

"Oh," she answered, throwing me a puzzled glance. "Why do we need a safe, Mal?"

"I have things I want to put in it," I replied. "Private papers, jewelry, documents." This was a lie, but I had to give her some sort of answer.

"You'd better come down and speak to him," she muttered, handing me the papers she was holding.

I followed her out into the corridor and down the stairs, relieved that the safe company had delivered my order on time. I had placed it several weeks ago, sent a check immediately, and had been waiting for it patiently.

The truck had driven up to the back door, and the driver was standing in the kitchen when Nora and I walked in.

She disappeared into the pantry. I said, "Hi, I'm Mrs. Keswick.

205

I want you to bring the safe upstairs, but it might be a problem. The staircase is narrow."

"I got my helper in the truck," he said gruffly. "Can you show me where it's going?"

"Come with me."

I took him upstairs to my little sitting room, led him into the deep, walk-in closet where I kept my clothes, and said, "I want it against the back wall. There." I indicated the spot.

"Okay," he said and went back downstairs.

I was hard on his heels. In the kitchen I sat down at the table, gave the papers a cursory glance, found a ballpoint pen near the phone, and signed them.

Nora poked her head around the pantry door and asked, "Is Sarah coming tomorrow or Friday?"

"She's not coming this weekend."

"Oh." Nora looked taken aback. After a second she said, "So your mother's coming."

I shook my head. "No, I'll be by myself."

"But it's the first time you'll have been alone." She stood there uncertainly, staring at me, looking worried.

"I'll be fine," I reassured her. "There are things I have to do."

She did not move for a second, and then she turned and went back into the kitchen, a helpless expression settling on her face.

A moment later the delivery man from Acme and his helper were rolling in a dolly with the safe on top. "I'm gonna take the door off," the delivery man announced, and he proceeded to do just that. Once the door had been lifted off its hinges, he placed it on the floor. Then he laid the safe flat on the dolly, and he and his helper pushed the dolly through into the long gallery, heading toward the stairs. They returned for the door, and within fifteen minutes the safe had been reassembled and stood in my walk-in closet exactly where I wanted it.

Once I was alone, I practiced opening and closing it, following the instruction chart the delivery man had given me. When I had the knack of it, I erased the factory code and entered my own into the digital panel, using the date of my marriage.

It seemed to me that it was taking Nora longer than ever to finish up today.

Several times I looked at the clock on the mantelpiece in the office, baffled as to why she was still here. It was now four o'clock.

I had the answer in a flash. Eric was probably coming to see me, as he so often did during the week these days, and she wanted to be here when he arrived from work.

Now that the safe was here, I could clear up all my affairs, and I was writing checks, fulfilling my obligations. When I had finished paying the bills, I added up everything on my yellow pad, entered the balance, closed the checkbook, and put it in my desk drawer.

Without Andrew's monthly salary check, I had nothing coming in, and my funds were getting extremely low. And I had not yet received the money from his insurance policy. There was some money in our savings account, but it wasn't much, certainly not a fortune. Andrew and I had always lived life to the hilt, and frequently beyond our means.

Anyway, what did it matter now? I wasn't going to need money. I was going to be dead.

My mother would sell the apartment in New York and this house, pay off the two mortgages, and use whatever money remained to settle any other debts that were left. Everything would be neat and tidy; that was exactly how I wanted it to be.

I had had my last will and testament drawn up a few days ago, using a local lawyer in New Milford rather than the law firm in Manhattan which handled my mother's affairs. It would only throw her into a panic if she knew I'd made a will.

She and Sarah were the executrixes, and my mother would get the bulk of my estate, such as it was. But I had left my pearls and most of my jewelry to Sarah, except for my engagement ring, which I had willed to Diana. After all, it was a Keswick heirloom and had been hers before it was mine. I had made other small bequests, such as small pieces of jewelry and some of my own paintings to Nora, Eric, and Anna. The rest of the paintings my mother could dispose of as she wished.

I loved Sarah. She was my closest and dearest friend, the sister I had never had. I knew only too well that she was going to be devastated and that she would miss me. But I couldn't bear to go on living, not without my family.

The office door suddenly opened, and Eric stuck his head around it. "Hi, Mal, how're you doing?"

"I'm all right," I answered, attempting a smile without much success. "And you?"

He made a face, shook his head. "Things are a bit tough down at the lumberyard. The boss had to lay a couple of guys off this week. But so far so good, I'm not too concerned."

"I'm glad *you're* okay, Eric. Nora's upstairs; I heard her footsteps a few minutes ago."

He grinned. "I'll see her shortly. I'm going down to the basement to bring up some more logs, then I'll take a look at that third heater in the stables. Anna told Nora it's been on the blink for the past few days. Got to keep the barns warm for the horses."

"We certainly do, and thanks, Eric, I appreciate it."

"No trouble, Mal. Just let me know if there's anything else you need fixed. The furnace isn't acting up again, is it?"

"It seems to be running fine, thanks."

"I'll pop in and see you before I leave." He smiled and was gone.

Eric Matthews was a kind man. Ever since I had been living permanently at Indian Meadows, he had gone out of his way to do all of the jobs Andrew had done and which were too hard for Nora or me. Like his wife and Anna, he was grief-stricken, and although he tried to be cheerful whenever he came to say hello, I could see the pain of loss in his eyes.

*   *   *

Nora and Eric had finally driven off, she in her ramshackle old Chevy, he in his battered pickup truck, and as much as I cared for them, I breathed a sigh of relief.

At last I was alone.

After locking the doors, I ran upstairs and went to the chest of drawers in my bedroom where I kept T-shirts and sweaters. The bottom drawer was deep, and in it, at the back, I had hidden the four cardboard boxes.

Taking them out one by one, I carried them carefully into the sitting room adjoining the bedroom and put them on the sofa.

First I opened the box with the vet's label on it and took out the small cream-colored can. Next I opened the three others, which bore the name of the crematorium. Placing the four canisters on the coffee table side by side, I sat down on the sofa and looked at them. When David had collected them and brought them out here to me, I had immediately labeled each container, writing the name and the dates of birth and death of Andrew, Lissa, Jamie, and Trixy.

There they were—all that I had left of my family. Four cans of ashes.

Tears rushed into my eyes, but I pushed them back, reached for a tissue, and blew my nose.

Immediately getting a grip on myself, I picked up the two canisters containing Lissa's and Jamie's ashes and carried them into the walk-in closet. I placed them on the shelf in the safe, then I went back to the sitting room, returning a moment later with Andrew's ashes. Finally I brought in Trixy's.

After I had arranged the four of them next to one another, I closed the door, locked it, and put the key in my pocket.

"You're safe now. Absolutely safe. No one, nothing, can hurt you ever again," I said out loud, talking to my family as I did frequently these days. "Soon I'm going to be with you. We'll be together forever."

*   *   *

The following day I passed the morning making phone calls.

I spoke to Diana in London, my mother and Sarah, who were both in New York, and finally to my father, who was in California, attending meetings at U.C.L.A.

I chatted to them all pleasantly, made sure I sounded cheerful, and told each of them that I was feeling much better.

I think they believed me. I could be very convincing when I wanted to be.

In the afternoon I wrote my farewell letters to the four of them. There was a fifth letter to David Nelson, thanking him for all that he had done for me and asking him to look after my mother, to cherish her. I also gave him instructions about our ashes. Sealing the envelopes and writing each name on them, I placed these in the desk drawer next to my checkbook.

Tonight I would kill myself. My body would be discovered tomorrow morning. And not too much later the letters would be found.

I lay on the sofa in my upstairs sitting room, sipping a vodka and listening to Maria Callas sing *Tosca*. It had been one of Andrew's favorite operas.

The winter sun had long since fled the pale wintry sky, and the light was rapidly fading. Soon it would be twilight—*the gloaming,* Andrew had called it. A northern name, he had once said.

A deep sigh escaped me.

Soon my life would be over.

I would shed this mortal coil. I would be free. I would go to that other plane where they waited for me. All my suffering would finally cease. I would be at peace with them.

In the dim light of the room I could see Andrew's face looking down at me from the portrait I had painted of him. I smiled, loving him so much. And then my eyes shifted, and I gazed at the portrait I had done of the twins. Jamie and Lissa. How beautiful they looked, my little Botticelli cherubs. I smiled again. They had been my two small miracles.

Reaching for the glass, I gulped down some more of the vodka, closed my eyes, and let myself drift with the music.

When this side of the disc ended, I would end my life.

"Mal! Mal! Where are you?"

I sat up with a jerk, dropping the glass of vodka I was clutching, startled out of my mind.

Before I could recover myself, Sarah came bursting into the little sitting room, her eyes anxious, her face pale.

"No wonder you couldn't hear me banging on the front door!" she exclaimed. "What with Callas screaming her lungs out like that!" Stepping over to the stereo, she lowered the volume. "I've been outside for ages. Banging and banging on the door."

I was stunned that she was here. "How did you get in?" I asked in a faint voice.

"Through the kitchen door."

"But it was locked!"

"No, it wasn't, Mal."

"But it was!" I cried, my voice rising shrilly. "I locked it myself." As I spoke I cast my mind back to this afternoon. I had walked Nora across the kitchen, we had said good-bye as I saw her out. I had then closed the kitchen door and swung the bolt. Demented I might be, but there was no question in my mind about that door. Who had unlocked it?

Sarah was standing there, looking down at me.

I said, "What are you doing here, anyway?" She had spoiled my plans, and I was furious.

Throwing her coat onto a chair, she came and sat next to me on the sofa, took my hand in hers. "Why am I here, Mal? Because I was worried about you, of course. Very worried."

I stared at her speechlessly.

25

Sarah had obviously come to Indian Meadows for the weekend. As we went into the kitchen, I saw her suitcase, which she had dumped on the floor near the back door.

The first thing I did was to walk over and check that door. I turned the knob, and it opened. "I guess you didn't lock this before you came upstairs looking for me," I said.

"No, I didn't, Mal. It was open, so I left it open. Sorry."

"It's okay. I just don't understand. I did lock it earlier. It's a mystery."

Sarah made no comment. She walked over to the pine cabinet, took out a glass, and poured herself a vodka. Looking at me, she asked, "How about you, Mal? Do you want one?"

"Why not," I replied. If I couldn't kill myself tonight, I might as well get drunk. I could put myself out of my misery for a few hours at least.

Opening the freezer, I took out a tray of ice and gave it to Sarah, then went back and peered into the refrigerator.

"There's some hot pot here," I said. "Nora made it this morning. Or I can fix you an omelette."

Plopping ice cubes in our drinks and adding chunks of lime, Sarah said, "No eggs, thanks. I'll try the hot pot. What're you having?"

"The same," I murmured, although I wasn't even hungry. I

never was these days. After I had emptied the hot pot into a pan and put this on the stove over a low light, I said, "It's going to take about half an hour to heat up."

Together we headed for the sunroom. Although it had a lot of windows and French doors, it was warm, centrally heated like the rest of the house. As we went in, I switched on the lights and noticed that it was snowing outside. The lawns had a coating of white; the trees looked as if they had just burst into bloom with white blossoms.

I sat down on a side chair with my back to the window.

Sarah took a big armchair, propped her feet on the coffee table, and lifted her glass in silence.

I did the same.

Sarah didn't say anything, and neither did I; we sat together like that for quite a while.

Finally rousing herself and focusing her eyes on me, she said, "My cousin Vera's coming back to New York, Mal."

"Oh," I said, looking at her swiftly. "Didn't she like the West Coast?"

"Yes, but her husband's left her. Moved in with another woman. Apparently he wants a divorce, so she's decided to pack up and come home."

"I'm sorry," I murmured, wanting to be polite.

Sarah went on, "Vera's flying to New York in about two weeks. To look for an apartment, and driving up here tonight it suddenly occurred to me that yours might be perfect for her. She has a teenage daughter, Linda, if you remember, and a housekeeper who's been with her for years. Your apartment is just the right size."

I took a sip of my vodka and said nothing.

"So, what do you think?" Sarah asked, eyeing me.

I shrugged indifferently.

"Do you want to sell it, Mal?"

"Yes, I guess so."

"You sound uncertain. But weeks ago you told me you never

wanted to see New York ever again, that you hated the city. Why keep an apartment in a city you hate?"

"You're right, Sash. If Vera wants to buy the apartment, she can. Show it to her whenever you want. Or my mother can. She has a set of keys."

"Thanks, Mal." She smiled at me. "It'll be nice if I do you both a good turn."

"What do you mean?"

"Vera wants a nice place to live. And I'm sure you can use the money, can't you?"

I nodded. "Andrew's insurance policy is not a big one."

"There's a mortgage on the apartment, isn't there?"

"Yes," I said. "And one on this house."

Sarah gave me a long stare. "How're you going to manage?" she asked quietly, her concern apparent. "What are you going to do for money?"

I won't need it, I'll be dead, I thought. But I said, "There's a little bit coming from the advertising agency, but not much. Jack Underwood told me they're in trouble. They've lost a number of big accounts, and there are all kinds of financial problems at the London office. But you knew that. Andrew told you, when he came back in November."

"When did you talk to Jack?"

"He came out to see me a couple of days ago. He'd just returned from London. He's been heartbroken about Andrew—they were very close—and distressed about the agency. He and Harvey are leaving. They're going into business for themselves. Andrew had instigated the whole thing . . . " My voice trailed off, and I stared at her blankly, then sitting up, I finished in a stronger, firmer voice. "And so they're going ahead with their plans, even though Andrew's no longer here."

Sarah was silent. She sat sipping her drink, gazing out the window at the snow-covered lawns, her face miserable.

I got up and lowered the lights, which were a little too bright for me tonight. Then I sat down again.

"I'm worried about you, Mal," Sarah suddenly said.

"You mean about the money, the fact that I haven't got any?"

She shook her head. "No, not that at all. Auntie Jess and David will help you, and so will I. You know anything I have is yours. And your father and Diana will chip in until you're on your feet."

"I guess so," I said. Of course this would never be necessary; I would not be here.

Sarah said softly, "I'm worried about your well-being, about your health. But, most importantly, about your state of mind. I know you're in the most excruciating pain all the time, that your sorrow and suffering are overwhelming. I just want to help you. I don't know how."

"Nobody can help me, Sash. That's why it's better if I'm alone."

"I don't agree, honestly I don't. You need someone with you, to comfort you whichever way they can. You need someone to talk to, to cling to if necessary. You mustn't be alone."

I did not answer her.

"I know I'm right," she pressed on. "And I know *I'm* the right person. It's *I* who should be with you. We've known each other all our lives, since we were babies. We're best friends . . . I should be with you now when you need someone. It's *me* that you need, Mal."

"Yes," I said softly. "You're the best one. And the only one who knows how to cope with me, I suppose."

"Promise me I can come every weekend, that you won't try to push me away, as you have several times lately."

"I promise."

She smiled. "I love you, Mal."

"And I love you too, Sash."

A small silence fell between us once more.

"It's the nothingness," I said finally.

"Nothingness?"

"That's what I face every day. *Nothingness*. There's just nothing there. Only emptiness, a great void. For ten years my focus has been on Andrew and our marriage and his career, then later it encompassed the twins. But now that they're gone, I have no focus. Only nothingness. There's simply nothing left for me."

Sarah nodded. Her eyes had welled up, and she was obviously unable to speak for a moment. But also she would never offer me meaningless pap, the kind of empty words that I had heard from so many of late.

I stood up. "Let's not talk about this anymore."

We ate supper in the kitchen. Actually, only Sarah ate—I just picked at my food. I had lost my appetite, and it had never come back. But I had opened a bottle of good red wine, and I drank plenty of it as the meal progressed.

At one moment Sarah looked at me over the rim of her glass and said, "Not now, because I don't think you're up to it, but later, in six months or so, maybe you could work. It would keep you busy. I know it would help you."

I merely shrugged. I wasn't going to be around in six months, but I could hardly tell her that. I loved her. I didn't want to upset her.

"You could work out here in the country, Mal, doing what you love."

I stared at her.

She continued, "*Painting.* You're very talented, and I think you could easily get some assignments illustrating books. I have a couple of friends in publishing, and they'd help; I know they would. You could also sell some of your watercolors and oils."

"Don't be silly. My paintings are not good enough to sell, Sash."

"You're wrong, they are."

"You're prejudiced."

"That's true, I am. But I also know when someone's good at what they do, especially in the artistic field, and you're good, Mallory Keswick."

"If you say so," I murmured, pouring myself another glass of Andrew's best French wine.

26

It snowed again on Sunday.

Even though I was low in spirits, I could not help noticing the beauty of the grounds at Indian Meadows. They were breathtaking. They resembled a monochromatic painting in black and white below a crystal-clear sky of the brightest blue washed over with golden sunlight.

As I walked down to the pond with Sarah, my heart tightened. I thought of Lissa and Jamie, and how much they would have enjoyed playing in the snow with Andrew, making snowballs, building a snowman, and sledding down the hill below the apple tree.

I missed them all so much; my yearning for them was constant, ever-present in my heart.

But now I pushed my heartache away, burying it deep inside me, hoping to conceal it. I did not want to burden Sarah. She was so loving and understanding, and she worried about me all the time. I felt I must act as normal as possible around her today. She was going to Paris tomorrow with her fashion team from Bergman's, and I wanted her to leave feeling that I was in a better frame of mind.

"I've never seen so many ducks here before!" she exclaimed when we got to the pond. "There must be at least two dozen!"

"Yes, and they're mallards. They've made Indian Meadows

their home this winter," I answered. "Obviously because we're feeding them every day."

As I spoke I put the shopping basket I was carrying down on the snow, took out the plastic container of scratch feed and turkey-grower pellets, and went to the edge of the pond.

The ducks took off immediately. Some rose up into the air and flew to another part of the property, others hopped onto the portion of the pond that was frozen and waddled away.

Our first winter at Indian Meadows, Andrew had installed a recirculating pump at one end of the pond. Electrically operated, it constantly churned the water surrounding it and thus prevented that area from freezing, even when it was below zero.

Sarah came and stood with me as I scattered the grain at the edge of the water, then she took a handful herself and walked to the frozen part, throwing it down for them.

"Silly ducks," she said, looking at me over her shoulder. "They're not coming to eat."

"They will, once we leave."

She joined me again and stood staring at the pump agitating the water.

"This really works," she said, glancing at me quickly. "What a good idea it was, to put it in for the ducks and the other wildlife that come around in winter. How did you know about it?"

"Eric told Andrew. In fact, they installed it together. This kind of pump is mostly used by farmers, who need to keep small parts of their ponds unfrozen, so that their cows can drink in winter," I explained.

"Hi, Mal! Hi, Sarah!"

We both swung around and waved to Anna, who waved back as she walked toward us across the snow.

She was as heavily bundled up against the weather as we were, dressed in a crazy collection of clothes, and I had a flash of Gwendolyn Reece-Jones in my mind's eye.

Like Gwenny, Anna was sporting lots of bright primary colors this morning, noticeable in the three scarves wrapped around her neck. These were turquoise-blue, red, and yellow, and they matched her long jacket, which looked as if it had been made from an Apache blanket. On her head was a royal-blue woolen ski cap with yellow pom-poms, and she wore a pair of jodhpurs, riding boots, and green wool gloves. Could she be color-blind?

"Anna, I love your jacket," Sarah exclaimed as Anna drew to a standstill next to us. "It's not only beautiful but very unusual. Is it authentic American Indian?"

"Not really," Anna said. "Well, maybe in its design."

"Did you get it out West? Arizona?"

Anna shook her head. "No, I bought it from Pony Traders."

"Pony Traders," Sarah repeated. "What's that? A shop?"

"No. Pony Traders is a small crafts company, up near Lake Wononpakook. I know one of the two women who own it, Sandy Farnsworth. They make jackets, capes, skirts, waistcoats, even boots and moccasins. Everything has an Indian look to it. And I fell in love with this jacket."

"I don't blame you, it's great," Sarah responded. "I'm off to Europe tomorrow, but maybe when I get back you'll take me up to meet them. Perhaps I'll put in an order for the store."

"Hey, that'd be fantastic," Anna said. Turning to me, she went on, "I thought you might like to come in for a cup of hot chocolate, or coffee, whatever you'd like, Mal." She eyed the basket and added, "I see you've got carrots for the horses. Why not come to my barn first?"

I was about to decline her invitation but changed my mind. She was trying to be nice, and I didn't want to offend her. She had always been so sweet with my children and had spent a lot of time with them when they rode, helping them to handle their ponies correctly. And so I said, "I won't say no to a cup of coffee, Anna. What about you, Sarah?"

"I crave the hot chocolate, but it'll have to be black coffee," Sarah said, grimacing at Anna. "I'm always watching my weight."

Anna laughed and shook her head, "You're a beautiful woman, Sarah. *You* don't have to worry."

Together the three of us walked toward the small renovated barn where Anna lived. It had been months since I had been here, and as I followed her inside, I was instantly struck by its rustic charm and comfort.

She had a big fire going in the fieldstone hearth, and her black Labrador, Blackie, lay stretched out on the rug in front of it. He got up when he heard us and came trotting over, nuzzling at Anna's legs and wagging his tail furiously at me.

"Hello, Blackie," I said, stroking his head. The Labrador looked past me to the door, his tail still wagging. I experienced a sudden pang as I realized he was expecting to see Trixy, who had always accompanied me wherever I went on the property.

I think Anna had probably realized the same thing. She looked at me, her eyes worried, and said in a brisk, cheerful voice, "Come on, give me your coats, and I'll get us the coffee. It's already made. Would you like anything to eat?"

Sarah muttered, "I would, but I won't."

"Just coffee, Anna, thanks," I said. I sat down on the sofa in front of the fire.

"Can I look around, Anna?" Sarah asked. "It's ages since I've seen your home."

"Sure, feel free. Go up to the sleeping loft if you like."

I leaned my head against the Early American quilt that covered the back of the big red sofa and closed my eyes, thinking of Lissa and Jamie. They had loved Anna, had loved to come here for milk and cookies and special treats. She had loved the twins in return, had always spoiled them, and had cared for them like they were her own.

Later, walking back up the hill to the house, Sarah said, "The barn looks great. Anna's done wonders with it. It's packed to the hilt with stuff, but somehow she's made it all work."

"Yes, she has," I murmured, shrugging further into my quilted coat, feeling the nip in the air all of a sudden.

"You know, Mal, she's very pretty, all that blonde hair, those soft brown eyes, doe eyes. Very appealing, really. But she could be absolutely stunning if only she wore a bit of makeup, especially eye makeup. Blondes always look so faded, so washed-out, if they don't do their eyes right."

"I know exactly what you mean, Sash. But I don't think she really gives a damn how she looks most of the time."

"No incentive, you mean?"

I shook my head. "No, I don't mean that." I hesitated thoughtfully, then said finally, "I think Anna's happy with *herself.* And with the way she looks these days. Healthy, full of vitality, no black eyes or bruises. She had a really bad experience with that guy she lived with, before she came here. And I think she gave up on men a long time ago. He used to beat her up constantly. He was *extremely* abusive, actually, and she was smart to get away from him when she did."

"I remember your telling me about it at the time. Well, I guess it's better to be on your own without a man than—" She broke off and stared at me, looking horrified, then grabbed hold of my arm. "I'm sorry, Mal, I'm so thoughtless."

I turned into her, put my arms around her, and hugged her to me. "You can't keep watching yourself, Sash, watching every word and what you say all the time. Life does intrude, I'm very aware of that."

"I'd give anything to make you feel just a little bit better," she murmured. "Anything, Mal, anything at all." She stood gazing at me, her dark eyes moist, brimming with emotion, all of the love and friendship she felt for me spilling out of her.

"I know you would, Sarah darling, and it *is* easier when you're around," I replied. I wanted to reassure her, and so ease her worry about me.

The stillness in the house was so acute it was tangible.

I stood in the middle of the long gallery, listening to that stillness, letting it wash over me, and I began to feel less agitated than usual.

Ineffable sadness dwelt within my heart, and yet I felt oddly comforted all of a sudden.

It was the house, of course.

It had always been a peaceful place, tranquil, benign, enfolding my family and me in its loving embrace. Ever since I had first set eyes on it, I had thought of it as a living thing, an entity rather than an edifice. I had never believed we had found the house all by ourselves, rather, that it had beckoned to us, drawn us to it, because it wanted us to occupy it, to love it and give it life.

And we had for a while.

My children had laughed here and run along its twisting corridors and played in its many rooms; Andrew and I had loved each other here and loved our family and our friends, and for a short time the house had truly lived again, had been happy. Certainly it had given us joy.

I walked from room to room, looking at everything for the last time before locking the outside doors and switching off the lights. Then I slowly climbed the stairs to my upstairs sitting room.

When I pushed open the door and went in, I saw that the room was dim and filled with shadows. It had grown much darker outside in the last hour or so since Sarah had left. But the logs spurted and hissed in the grate and threw off sparks, and there was a lovely warmth up here on this icy night.

I turned on a lamp and undressed, put on a nightgown and robe.

After pouring myself a vodka, I sat down in front of my portrait of the twins and studied it for a long time. I really had captured them on the canvas; this realization pleased me.

Eventually, my gaze settled on Andrew's portrait hanging over the fireplace. It was not quite as good as the one I had done of the twins, but the likeness was there, and I had caught his extraordinary blue eyes perfectly. They were exactly right.

I finished my drink, poured another one, lingered over this, then drained the glass suddenly, in one big gulp.

Rising, I went into the bathroom. I turned on the taps and ran a bath. When it was full, I took off my robe, threw it across the bath stool, and walked across to the sink.

My art knife was there, where I'd put it earlier, its razor blade encased in a sheath of plastic. The blade was sharp, very sharp. I knew. I had used it for cutting thick paper, posterboard, and sometimes canvases. It would do the job nicely.

I had read somewhere that this was a painless way to die, if one can think of dying as painless. Lying in a tub of water, slitting each wrist, bleeding gently until unconscious, until death came. *Painless.*

Picking up the knife, I examined it before stepping over to the bath. I placed it on the edge of the tub near the taps and lifted my nightgown.

As I began to pull it up over my head, I heard the faintest sound. It was laughter. *Someone was laughing.* In the next room. I was so startled I was frozen to the spot. Finally I let the hem of my nightie fall.

I went out into the sitting room.

Lissa stood there in the center of the floor wearing her nightgown.

"Mommy! Mommy!" she cried and laughed again, her light, tinkling laugh. It was the same laughter I had heard a moment ago.

"Lissa!" I took a step forward.

She laughed and ran out into the corridor.

I rushed after her, calling her name, shouting for her to stop, to come back, as I followed her down the stairs, along the entrance gallery and into the kitchen. She wrenched open the back door and flew out into the snow, laughing, saying my name.

It was dark outside.

I couldn't see her.

I stumbled around in the snow, calling and calling her.

Suddenly she was there, standing right next to me, tugging at my nightgown. "Hide and seek, Mommy, let's play hide and seek."

She ran away, ran into the house.

I chased her. My heart was pounding, my breath coming in gasps as I raced up the stairs. I saw her dash through the door of my upstairs sitting room, but when I got there the room was empty. I looked in the bathroom, hurried into the adjoining bedroom, only to discover I was alone.

Shivering, I glanced down at my nightgown.

It was soaking wet at the bottom, and my feet were frozen. I had run outside with nothing on my feet. My teeth began to chatter, and I got my robe and put it on. I dried my feet on a towel and found a pair of slippers in my clothes closet.

Where was Lissa hiding?

I went from room to room on this floor and covered every room downstairs. I even made it to the basement.

The house was empty except for me.

I'm not certain exactly how long I searched for her, but eventually I gave up. Returning to my little sitting room, I threw some logs on the fire and poured a vodka to warm myself.

Puzzled by what had just happened, I sat down on the sofa to think.

Had it been a dream? But I hadn't been asleep.

I had been in the bathroom, and I had been wide wake.

Was it wishful thinking? Possibly. No. Probably.

Had I just seen Lissa's spirit? Her ghost?

But were there such things?

Andrew used to say this house was full of friendly ghosts. He *had* been joking, hadn't he?

I didn't know anything about parapsychology or ectoplasm or psychokinesis. Or the occult or any of those things. All I knew was that I had seen my daughter, or thought I'd seen her, and that the image had been so strong I had believed her to be real.

Baffled, sighing to myself, I finished the glass of vodka, lay back against the sofa's cushions, and closed my eyes. Suddenly I felt exhausted, wiped out.

"Mommy, Mommy."

I paid no attention. Her voice was in my head.

"Butterfly kisses, Mommy," she said, and I felt her child's soft lips against my cheek, felt her warm breath.

Snapping my eyes open, I sat up with a jerk.

Lissa was standing there, looking at me.

"Oliver's cold, Mommy," she said, handing me her teddy bear, and then she climbed onto the sofa and snuggled down into my arms.

Sunlight streaming in through the lace curtains awakened me, and I turned and stretched, almost falling off the sofa. Pushing myself up into a sitting position, I glanced around, feeling completely disoriented.

I had obviously fallen asleep on the sofa. I had a crick in my neck, my back ached, and my mouth was dry. I felt parched. My eye fell on the half-empty bottle of vodka, and I shuddered.

It was then that I remembered.

Everything came rushing back to me. Lissa had been here last night. She had been in her nightgown, holding Oliver, and she had said he was cold; she had given him to me and had crept into my arms.

I *had* held her. I know I had.

No, it was a dream. A hallucination. My imagination playing tricks. The vodka.

I heard Nora's step on the stairs and her voice calling, "Mal, Mal, are you up there?" And when I glanced at the clock, I saw to my shock that it was nine-thirty.

Nine-thirty.

I hadn't slept like this since Andrew had been killed. In fact, I had hardly slept at all until last night.

"Freezing cold out," Nora announced coming into the sitting room. She stood in the doorway, eyeing me. "Not like you not to be up and about," she went on, "lolling around like this. You haven't even made the coffee this morning."

"No, I haven't. I only just woke up, Nora. I must have fallen asleep on the sofa. I've been on it all night."

She glanced at the vodka bottle, said succinctly, "Not surprising. But a good sleep was what you needed."

"I'll be down soon."

"Don't rush. Coffee takes a few minutes," she said as she hurried out.

I went into the bathroom and bent over the tub to flip the plug and saw, to my amazement, that the bath was empty.

But it couldn't be. I'd filled it last night. Filled it to the brim. I had been going to kill myself last night by slitting my wrists with my art knife.

The knife was not there.

This is ridiculous, I thought, looking around for it. I had put the knife on the edge of the tub near the taps. It was gone.

I spent a good twenty minutes searching for my art knife, but without success. It had vanished.

The whole business of the empty tub, the missing knife, and the kitchen door both puzzled and disturbed me. Demented with grief I might be, but I knew I wasn't crazy.

27

"I'll be in my studio if you want me," I said to Nora a little later that morning.

"Oh, that's good to hear," she said, and there was a pleased note in her voice.

"I'm going to clean out some of my stuff, not paint," I said, looking at her as I pulled on my barbour.

Her face fell, but she made no comment, simply went back to preparing the vegetables for yet another one of her interminable soups. She was determined to feed me, and about the only thing she could get me to eat was soup or porridge. I was never hungry these days.

The icy wind stung my face as I walked quickly down the path which led past the terrace and the swimming pool. The studio door was locked, and as I fumbled with the key I shivered. Nora had been correct again. It was freezing cold today, below zero.

Warm air greeted me as I stepped inside my studio.

Last year I had installed gas heating, and I kept it at fifty degrees in the winter months. I went over to the thermostat and pushed the switch up to sixty-five.

Glancing around the studio, I saw that Nora had made an effort to tidy it since I had last been in here in November. But even so, there was a lot of mess and clutter. Brushes were lying around, and there were palettes with dried paint on them, a stack of new canvases piled haphazardly on a table, and several of my oils propped up against the side of the old sofa.

Taking off my barbour, hanging it on the coat stand, I ignored the mess I had supposedly come to clean. Instead I looked for another art knife with a razor blade. I was certain there was a new one in a drawer of the chest I used for storing supplies. But I was wrong. All I could find were new sable brushes, crayons for drawing pastels, small pots of oil paints, a new paintbox of watercolors, and a lot of colored pencils.

I stood staring at the chest, biting my lip. Apparently the only art knife I had was the one which had gone missing.

How was I going to cut my wrists if I didn't have a blade?

I could gas myself instead. My eyes focused on the gas fire set in the wall.

The intercom on the phone buzzed, and I picked up the receiver, "Yes, Nora?"

"Were you expecting your mother, Mal?"

"No."

"Well, she's here. At least her car's coming up the front drive."

"Okay. I'll be right there."

"Good thing I'm making this soup for lunch," she said, then hung up.

After lowering the heat in the studio, I went out, locked the door, and ran back up the path to the house. It was not like my mother to come without calling me first; also, I was surprised she had ventured up to Connecticut in this bitterly cold and snowy weather.

She was coming in the front door as I strode into the long gallery.

"Mom, this is a surprise," I said, embracing her. "What's brought you up here on a day like this?"

"I wanted to see you, Mallory. I thought you might try to put me off if I phoned first. So I just came."

"You know you're always welcome, Mom."

She gave me an odd look but didn't say anything, and I took her heavy wool duffel coat and carried it out to the coatroom in the back of the house near my office.

"Would you like a cup of coffee?" I asked when I returned.

"Tea would be nice," she answered, following me into the kitchen. I went to put the kettle on.

Nora said, "Hello, Mrs. Nelson. Roads bad, are they?"

My mother shook her head. "No, they've been well plowed. And good morning, Nora, how are you?"

"Not bad. And you?"

"As well as can be expected, under the circumstances," my mother responded. She half smiled at Nora, then looked at the stove and sniffed. "Your soup smells delicious."

"It's lunch," Nora said. "And I can make you a sandwich. Or an omelette, if you like."

"Anything will do, thanks, Nora. I'll have whatever Mal's having."

Nora went over to one of the cupboards and took out a cup and saucer for my mother's tea. Looking over her shoulder, she asked, "What about you, Mal? Do you want a cup too?"

"Yes, it'll warm me up," I said, and turning to my mother, I asked, "How's David?"

"He's well. Very busy right now."

"Has he heard anything? From DeMarco?"

"No. Have you?"

"No."

We stared at each other. I saw the tears rising in my mother's eyes. She blinked, pushed them back, and took a deep breath. "Are you feeling a bit better, darling?"

"Yes, I'm doing fine," I lied.

I walked over to the kitchen stove, turned off the kettle, and made the pot of tea. I began to put everything on a wooden tray, and looking up, I said to my mother. "Let's go into the sunroom. It's really very pleasant in there today."

"Wherever you wish, Mal."

*   *   *

We sat opposite each other on either side of the big glass coffee table, sipping our tea.

When she had finished her cup, my mother put it down on the table, looked across at me, and said, "Tell me the truth, Mal, are you really all right?"

"Of course, Mom!"

"I do worry about you, and about your being alone out here all the t—"

"I'm not alone. Nora's here, and Eric's in and out almost every day, and there's Anna down in the barn."

"They're not with you at night."

"True, but I'm okay, honestly. Try not to worry so much, Mother."

"I can't help it. I love you, Mallory."

"I know, Mom."

"And then there are the weekends." She stopped, studied me for a moment, then asked, "Don't you want David and me to come out anymore?"

"Yes. Whenever you like. Why do you say that? And in such a peculiar tone?"

"I've felt that you've been pushing us away recently."

"Not true. I told you before, you're welcome anytime, and so is David."

"It disturbs me that you're alone so much," she said again.

"I'm not. And Sarah's always here. She was here this weekend."

"I know. She called me last night when she got back to the city. She wanted to tell me about her cousin Vera, about Vera looking at your apartment. So you are going to sell it, then?"

"Why not? I don't want to live there."

"Yes," she said quietly. "I understand."

"Vera's coming to New York in a couple of weeks, so Sarah said. Do you mind showing her the apartment? That is, if Sarah's working or away on business."

"I'll be happy to do it, darling."

"I guess Sarah told you she was going to Paris today?"

My mother nodded. "You and Sarah are very lucky, you know."

I stared at her. *I* was *lucky*?

"To have each other, I mean," she said swiftly, no doubt noticing the startled expression on my face. "To be so close—"

"Yes, we are," I agreed, cutting her off.

"To be best friends," she continued. "To be lifelong friends, to have such unconditional love for each other. You're both so fiercely loyal, and in many ways you're very dependent on each other."

"We bonded long ago, Mom."

"Yes, it's rare, that kind of friendship."

"But surely you have it with Auntie Pansy?"

"To a certain extent, but we were never as close as you and Sarah. I don't think Pansy wanted that kind of intimacy. She's not a bit like her daughter. Sarah's much warmer."

"Well, there's nobody like my Sarah, I must admit. They threw the mold away."

"She is unique, Mal, I agree. But I've been wondering lately—do you think she's enough?"

"I don't know what you mean, Mom." I sat up straighter and focused my eyes on her. "What are you getting at?"

"I'm not talking about friendship, darling. I'm talking about your pain and grief, your heartbreak. Maybe you need more help than Sarah or I can give you. Perhaps it would be a good idea to see a professional. A psychiatrist."

"A *psychiatrist*. Do you think I need one, Mother?"

"Perhaps. For grief counseling. There are many who specialize in that, and I understand they help people come to grips—"

"I don't want to see a shrink," I interrupted. "You go if you want."

"Perhaps we can go together."

"No, Mom."

"There are groups, you know, who counsel mothers and fathers who have lost children to violent crimes."

I sat staring at her, saying nothing.

She went on, "I've heard of this young woman who lost her child in a car accident. She was driving, and walked away alive. She's started a group. People in similar circumstances, who have lost children, get together to talk. My friend Audrey Laing wants me to go. Do you want to come with me, Mal? It might help you."

"I don't think so," I said in a low voice. I began to shake my head vehemently. "No, no, it wouldn't help, Mom, I'm sure of that. I know you mean well, but I just couldn't . . . couldn't talk about Lissa and Jamie and Andrew to strangers, to people who had never known them. Honestly, I just couldn't."

"All right, I understand what you're saying. But don't dismiss it out of hand. At least think about it, will you?"

"I much prefer to talk to you and Sarah. And Diana, Daddy when he calls. People who know firsthand what I've lost."

"Yes, darling." My mother cleared her throat. "I do worry about you so. Maybe I should get you another dog."

"Another dog!" I cried, jumping up, gaping at her. "I don't want another fucking dog! I want *my* dog! I want *Trixy*. I want my *babies*! I want my *husband*! I want my *life* back!" I glared at my mother, then swung around and flew to the French doors. Opening them, I ran outside. Something inside me had snapped, and I was crying and shaking with rage.

I stood there in the snow, pressing my hands to my face, sobbing as if my heart would break. I was oblivious to the icy wind and the snow, which was falling again.

A moment later I felt my mother's arms around me. "Come inside, Mal. Come inside, darling."

I let her lead me back into the sunroom, let her press me down onto the sofa. She sat next to me, pulled my hands away from my face, and looked into my eyes. I looked back at her, the tears still trickling down my cheeks.

"Forgive me, Mal. I didn't mean it the way it came out, the way it sounded. I really didn't," she whispered in a choked-up voice.

Her own grief and heartache stabbed at me, and my anger dissipated as swiftly as it had flared inside me. "I know you didn't,

Mom, and there's nothing to forgive. I know you'd never hurt me."

"Never," she wept, clinging to my arm. "I love you very much."

"And I love you, Mom."

She lifted her head, looked into my eyes again. "It was always your father with you—" she began and stopped short.

"Perhaps I favored him because he was hardly ever there, and so he seemed very special to me. But I've always loved you, Mother, and I know you've always been there for me."

"And I still am, Mal."

A few days after this visit of my mother's I fell into a deep depression.

I became morose, filled with a strange kind of melancholia, and I felt listless, without energy. I could hardly bear to move, and my limbs ached as if I were an old woman suffering from an ague. It was a kind of physical debilitation I was unaccustomed to, and I was helpless, almost an invalid.

All I wanted to do was curl up in my bed and sleep. And yet sleep always eluded me; I only ever dozed. I would soon be wide awake, my mind turning and turning with endless distressing and painful thoughts.

Wanting to end my life though I did, I discovered I did not have the strength to get out of bed, never mind actually kill myself. Apathy combined with a deep-rooted loneliness to render me useless to myself.

There were moments when despair overwhelmed me, brought me to tears again. I was alone, without purpose. I had no future. The absence of my family appalled me, and the loneliness, the yearning for them was destroying me.

At times different emotions intruded, bringing me to my knees: Guilt that I had not been with them, guilt that I was alive and they were dead; rage that they had been victims of street violence, rage that I could not avenge their deaths. These were the moments I felt murderous, wanted to kill whoever had killed my children and my husband.

On those occasions I would call the Twenty-fifth Precinct to talk to Detective DeMarco, wanting to know if any new evidence had turned up.

He never sounded anything but regretful, even sad, when he told me no. He promised they would break the case. He meant well. But I was unconvinced. I never believed him.

Memories were my only source of comfort. I fell down into them gratefully, recalling Lissa, Jamie, Andrew, and little Trixy with the greatest of ease. I relived our life together and took joy from this.

But then one abysmal day the memories would no longer come at my bidding. And I was afraid. Why could I no longer recall the past, our past? Why were my children's faces suddenly so blurred and indistinct? Why did I have such trouble picturing Andrew's face in my mind's eye?

I did not know. But when this loss of total recall persisted for a week, I knew what I had to do. I must go to Kilgram Chase. I wanted to be in Andrew's childhood home, the place where he had grown up. Perhaps there I would feel close to him once more, perhaps there he would come back to me.

PART FIVE

KILGRAM CHASE

28

Yorkshire, March 1989

Spring had come early, much earlier than anyone here at Kilgram Chase had expected.

I had arrived from Connecticut toward the end of January to find everything covered in snow, and the first part of February had been bitter, with sleet, freezing rain, and intermittent snowstorms. But the weather had changed in the middle of the month. The rain and harsh winds had ceased unexpectedly; there had been a general softening, a warming much welcomed by everyone here, most especially the farmers.

Now, on this first Friday in March, the trees were bursting with tender green shoots and the first fluttering little leaves. Grass was beginning to sprout, and the borders at the edges of the lawns were alive with purple, yellow, and white crocuses and delicate, starlike snowdrops. Daffodils danced down near the pond and under the trees in the woods. Tall and graceful as they nodded in the light breeze, their brilliant yellow bonnets reflected the bright afternoon sun.

I stood at the mullioned window in the library, looking out toward the moors, thinking that perhaps I ought to take a walk later.

I had not been able to go out much since I had arrived almost five weeks ago. Within the first few days I had fallen sick, felled by a bad bout of flu, and I had spent over ten days in bed.

Diana, Parky, and Hilary had nursed me through it, done the best they could to make me better. But I had been a bad patient, not very cooperative at all; I had refused almost all of the medicines they had offered me and done little to speed my recovery, hoping to catch pneumonia and die. I had not. But then neither had I been very well; I was slow to get up on my feet and about. When I first arrived I had been exhausted and undernourished, and the aftermath of the flu virus left me feeling even weaker. This physical debilitation combined with my mental apathy to make me more listless and enervated than I had been at Indian Meadows.

Although I was here in Andrew's childhood home, I continued to face dreary empty days and sleepless nights, and that awful nothingness was ever-present.

Not even Diana could cheer me up very much when she came back to Yorkshire on the weekends, after working at her shop in London all week. How right my mother had been when she had told me that you don't leave your troubles behind you when you go to another place.

"Pain and heartache travel well," she had said to me the day she took me to Kennedy to catch my plane to London. And indeed they did.

Yet I did feel closer to Andrew here at Kilgram Chase, as I had believed I would. My memories of him and my children now came back to me unbidden, and their well-loved faces were clear, distinctive in my mind's eye once again. Very regularly my thoughts turned inward, and I was able to live with them within myself, in my imagination.

The days passed quietly, uneventfully. I did very little. I read occasionally, watched television; sometimes I listened to music, but for the most part I sat in front of the fire in the library, lost in my own world, oblivious to everyone most of the time. Of course Diana made her presence felt when she was here and tried to rouse me from my lethargy. I really made an effort, tried to perk up, but

I wasn't very successful. I had no one and nothing to live for. I simply existed. I had even lost the will to kill myself.

Now, moving away from the window, I crossed to the fireplace and piled more logs on top of those already crackling and burning up the chimney. Then lifting the tray with the coffee things on it, I took it back to the kitchen.

Parky looked up as I came in and exclaimed, "Nay, Mrs. Mal, you needn't have bothered with that! I would have sent Hilary or Joe for it later."

"It's no trouble, Parky, and thank you, it was a lovely cup of coffee. Just what I needed."

"You didn't eat much lunch, Mrs. Mal," she said, her eyes filled with worry. "Picking at your food is no way to improve your health and get your strength up."

"I know, I do try, Parky. And what I did eat I really enjoyed. The grilled plaice and chips were delicious."

She went on rolling out the pastry on the big slab of marble, saying, "It's a right bonny afternoon. Too bonny to stay cooped up in that there library, if you don't mind me saying so. You should get out, have a good blow on the moors. It'll do you good, that it will, Mrs. Mal."

"I was just thinking about taking a walk, actually, Parky."

She smiled at me, nodded her approval, and continued. "Mrs. Keswick will be arriving a bit earlier than usual this weekend. About four-thirty, or thereabouts. In time for tea," she said.

"That's nice," I answered. "Parky, can I ask you something?"

"Of course you can, Mrs. Mal."

"I've been wondering why you and Joe and Hilary and the gardeners call me that? For ten years I've been Mrs. Andrew to you all. But since I came back in January, it's been Mrs. Mal. Why?"

She stared at me, flushing slightly and looking discomfited. "It's just that . . . that . . . well, we didn't want to upset you further," she began haltingly. "We thought that to keep mentioning Mr. Andrew's name would be . . . well, painful."

"No, Parky," I interrupted softly. "It wouldn't. I *am* Mrs.

Andrew, and I really would prefer you to keep on calling me that."

"I'm sorry if we've upset you," she said, sounding concerned. "We'd never do anything to hurt you. We were only trying to be mindful of your feelings."

"I know you were, and honestly, I do appreciate that, and I am grateful to you for the kindness you've shown me these last few weeks."

"You were in such a bad way when you got here, and we didn't want to distress you anymore than you already were. We felt we had to be careful. It was like . . . like walking on eggs."

"I'm sorry, Parky."

"Oh, there's no need to apologize, Mrs. Mal, I mean Mrs. Andrew. We understand. We loved Mr. Andrew and the wee bairns—" Her mouth began to tremble and her eyes filled, but she took a deep breath and finished. "Such a tragedy, so hard to live with . . . "

"Yes, it is." I coughed behind my hand, trying to control myself. I knew I might easily break down if I didn't keep a tight grip on my emotions. My grief was never very far below the surface.

Parky said quietly, almost to herself, "Like my own child, he was," and then she put down the rolling pin and hurried into the adjoining pantry. "Got to find that big pie dish for the steak-and-kidney pie," she called to me in a muffled voice without looking around.

"I shall go for a walk," I said, and went out of the kitchen swiftly, knowing it was wiser to leave her by herself to recoup. Otherwise we'd both be in a flood of tears.

I headed in the direction of the mudroom. Once there, I took off my penny loafers, pulled a pair of Wellingtons on over my jeans, and struggled into one of Diana's old barbours. Wrapping a scarf around my head, I went outside.

It was a clear day, crisp but not really cold, and there was the lightest of breezes rustling through the trees, making the new leaves flutter and dance. I dug my hands into the pockets of the barbour and struck out toward the pond down near the woods. Behind the pond there was a narrow path, which the gardeners had cut through the dense mass of trees some years ago, and this led up to the lower moors.

The grounds were deserted, I noticed as I walked.

Usually Ben and Wilf were somewhere or other, digging, planting, and pruning, or burning leaves. This afternoon they were nowhere in sight.

But by the time I got closer to the pond, I saw Wilf pushing a wheelbarrow along the path that led from the orchard up to the house. When we drew level with each other, he stopped and touched his cap. "Afternoon, Mrs. Mal."

"Hello, Wilf."

"You're not going up on yon moors?"

"Yes, I was thinking about it," I answered.

"Aye, no, don't be doing that." He turned his head, shaded his eyes with his hand, and peered toward the hills silhouetted against the distant horizon.

"B'ain't wise. Weather's right dicey up on yon moors this time o'year. Sunny for a bit, like now, but then t'clouds roll in and t'rain comes down in torrents. Blows in from yon North Sea, it does that."

"Thanks for telling me, Wilf," I murmured and hurried on down the path, thinking what an old fool he was, gormless, as Andrew had always said. It was as clear as a bell today; the sky was blue and without a single cloud.

But something about his words must have registered at the back of my mind, because in the end I avoided the moors. It was such a long, steep climb, anyway. Instead, I went for a more leisurely walk through the woods, and a half hour later I came back and circled the pond, before taking the wide stone path that cut through the lawns. I had been out long enough today. I already felt tired. Obviously I was out of shape and still quite weak.

As I approached the house, I saw Hilary coming toward me, waving and beckoning.

I increased my pace, and when we met in the middle of the stone path, she said, "There's a phone call for you, Mrs. Andrew. From New York. It's Mr. Nelson."

"Thanks, Hilary."

Together we went around the side of the house to the back door, and as we hurried in, I said to her, "Would you tell him I'll be there in a moment, please. I just want to get my Wellies off."

"Yes, Mrs. Andrew," she answered, disappearing down the back hallway.

A few seconds later I was picking up the phone on the long refectory table in the library. "Hello, David, how are you?"

"Good, Mal, and you?"

"I've finally recovered from the flu. There's nothing wrong, is there? My mother's all right, isn't she?"

"Yes, she is, and everything's fine. She worries about you, of course, and keeps talking about coming over to see you. She wants us to take a trip to England, if you're planning on staying in Yorkshire for a while."

"Why don't you come? Is that the reason you're calling, David?"

"No, it isn't. I have some news for you, Mal."

I caught the change in his voice, the tension. My chest tightened. I gripped the receiver harder as I said, "From DeMarco?"

"Yes. There's been a break in the case. He just called me about fifteen minutes ago. Luckily, I wasn't in court today."

"Have they caught the killer? The gunman?" I asked in a tight voice.

"No, but they will, and very soon, Mal. This is what happened. Twenty-four hours ago, Johnson and DeMarco arrested a small-time narcotics dealer who operates in that neighborhood. Those arches under the elevated train tracks are part of his territory. Anyway, he's trying to strike a deal, to plea-bargain. He says he knows who shot Andrew and the children. Four local youths who hang out together, one of whom has talked about it. He's given their names and addresses to DeMarco, and he and Johnson hope to take them into custody today, bring them into the Twenty-fifth Precinct for questioning immediately. DeMarco's got a strong feeling that those unidentified fingerprints found on Andrew's Mercedes will match up with theirs. He's banking on it."

My legs suddenly felt weak, and I sat down heavily on the cut-velvet chair. I could hardly speak, but finally I managed to say, "If the fingerprints do match, what happens then?"

"The perpetrators will be taken down to Central Booking in Police Plaza and booked on charges of murder in the second degree. And all four of them will be booked, Mal, you see—"

"I thought there was only one gunman?" I cut in.

"That's what DeMarco believes, yes. But a person doesn't have to pull the trigger to be booked or found guilty of murder. Just being there, just standing there when the crime is committed, is enough to convict," David explained. "It's called *acting in concert.* If there's enough evidence, within seventy-two hours they'll go in front of a grand jury in criminal court downtown. And if they're indicted in the grand jury hearing, they'll go on trial."

"When would that be?"

"I'm not sure. It could take several months. Not only to get on the docket, but the assistant district attorney will want to be sure he has every scrap of evidence he can get, that he has a watertight case. DeMarco and Johnson will have to work their butts off on this one, and they will, I've no doubt. The prosecutor wants a guilty verdict, not an acquittal, and so do they."

"And if the youths *are* found guilty?"

"There's no death penalty in New York State, Mal. They'll get twenty-five or thirty years to life. No parole."

"I see. Could they—" I paused, took a deep breath, and asked, "Could they get off?"

"No way. DeMarco and Johnson are convinced they've struck pay dirt with the drug dealer, that they'll turn up all the evidence they need for a conviction."

"I hope so."

"They will. It's a personal crusade with them, especially

DeMarco. Also, I know the judicial system inside out, and the judge will go for the maximum, trust me on this. The killers will never see daylight again; they'll never get out."

"Should I call DeMarco, David? What do you think?"

"You don't have to, Mal. He asked me to pass the news on to you. Anyway, I doubt that you'd get him right now. He's on the investigation full blast. Now that he's got this lead, he wants results fast. He wants to put these . . . animals away. He wants them under lock and key. Today."

"I understand. And thank you, David, for everything."

"I'm always here for you, Mal. Give Diana my best."

"I will. Oh, does Mom know about the break in the case?"

"Yes. I told her before I called you. She sends her love."

"Give her mine."

"I'll be in touch as soon as I have more information from DeMarco."

"When you speak to him, thank him for me."

"I will, honey. Bye."

"Bye, David."

After we hung up I sat with my hand resting on the phone, pondering everything David had told me. I felt nothing, only emptiness inside. Knowing the killers of my family were about to be arrested did not relieve my pain and grief. And it would not bring them back.

Gazing out of the mullioned window, I drifted with my thoughts for a while. But at one moment the sky darkened, and I lifted my eyes. The garden was still filled with sunlight, but on the moors the blue sky had turned, was curdled and gray. Ominous dark clouds were blowing in, and up there it had started to rain, just as old Wilf had predicted. Shivering involuntarily, feeling suddenly cold, I walked over to the fire and sat down on the sofa to get warm. And to wait for Diana.

I must have fallen asleep, for I woke up with a start when I heard her voice. She was coming into the library with Hilary in her wake carrying the tea tray.

"Hello, darling," Diana said, hurrying forward. "Are you feeling a bit better today?"

I would never feel better. But I nodded; it was the easiest thing to do.

She bent over me, kissed me on my cheek, and then went and stood with her back to the fire, as she often did, just as Andrew had done. Saying nothing, she surveyed me for a few moments. As soon as Hilary had put the tea tray down and departed, she said, "What is it, Mal? You look as if you have something to tell me."

"I do," I replied. "David called me a short while ago. There's been a break in the case at last."

"Tell me all about it!" she exclaimed. She came and sat down next to me on the sofa.

Her eyes did not leave my face as I recounted my entire conversation with David.

When I finished, her reaction was the same as mine had been. "Thank God," she said quietly. "But it won't bring my son and my grandchildren back to life . . . " Her voice wavered slightly, and she took a moment to regain her composure, then she added, "But at least we know that justice will be done, and that those responsible will be punished."

"It's small comfort," I murmured. "But it's better than knowing they are free."

"And that they might kill again," Diana said.

29

"I have to go to Paris on Wednesday," Diana said. "Why don't you come to London with me tomorrow? And then we'll go to Paris together. I think it would do you good, Mal."

Diana and I were sitting in the library on Sunday morning, reading the newspapers. Or rather, she was reading; I was merely glancing through them.

Looking up, I shook my head. "I don't think so. I'm still feeling a bit debilitated after the flu."

Diana stared at me for the longest moment, and then she said, "Nonsense, Mal, you're much better, and you have been for the last week. Your problem is your mental apathy."

Startled by her brisk, matter-of-fact tone as well as her words, I recoiled slightly, then said, "Maybe you're right."

"I know I am," she replied and put down her newspaper. Leaning forward, focusing every ounce of her attention on me, she continued, "Mal, you can't go on like this."

I returned her steady gaze, but I remained silent.

"What are you going to do? Sit on that sofa in this library for the rest of your life? Is that your plan?"

"I have no plans," I said.

"But you do have a *choice*. Actually, you have three choices. You can sit around forever, as you're doing now, letting your life drift away from you. You can kill yourself, which I know you've contemplated more than once, from the things you've said to me. Or you can pull yourself together, pick up the pieces and go on from here."

"Go where?" I muttered. "I just don't . . . don't know . . . what to do . . . what to do with myself," I began hesitantly, at a loss in more ways than one.

Diana sat studying me, her eyes full of love, her expression sympathetic, as it always was. Her voice was caring when she murmured softly, "I know only too well what you've lost—those you loved with all your heart, those most precious and dear to you. But as hard as it may seem, you must begin again. That is your *only* choice, Mal darling. Trust me, it is. God knows, you've nothing to lose, you've already lost it all, but you do have everything to gain."

"I do?"

"Yes. Your *life*, for one thing, a new life. You must try, darling, not only for yourself, but for me."

I sighed and looked away, and then I felt the tears rising to flood my eyes. "I can't," I whispered, fighting the tears, the pain, and the grief. "I'm weighted down. My sorrow is unendurable, Diana."

"I know, I know. I'm suffering too . . . " Diana could not finish her sentence. Her voice choked up, and she came and sat next to me on the sofa. Taking my hand in hers, she held on to it tightly and said finally, "Andrew wouldn't want to see you like this, Mal. He always said you were the strongest woman he'd ever known, other than me."

"I can't live without him. I don't want to live without him and the twins."

"You're going to have to," Diana said in a voice that was low, suddenly quite stern. "You've got to stop feeling sorry for yourself, right now. Do you think you're the only woman who has ever lost loved ones? Lost a family? What about me? I've lost my son, my only child, and my grandchildren, and before that I lost a husband when I was still a young woman. And what about your mother? She is as grief-stricken and heartbroken as we are."

Taking a deep breath, she added, "And what about the millions of other people in the world who have had to survive the loss of their families? You only have to think about the survivors of the Holocaust—those who lost husbands and wives and children and mothers and fathers in the death camps, to realize we are not alone. Loss of loved ones is part of life, I'm sorry to say. It's terrible, so difficult to accept—"

Diana could not continue speaking. Her emotions got the better of her, and she began to weep, but after only a moment or two she said through her tears, "There isn't a day goes by that I don't think about him, think about my Andrew, and about little Lissa and Jamie. And my heart never stops aching. But I know I can't give in, that I mustn't. And so I try to keep myself together, the best way I can. Mal, listen to me. You can't throw your life away. You have to try, just as I try."

The tears trickled down her cheeks, and she looked at me helplessly. I put my arms around her and held her close to me. And I wept with her.

Her words had found their mark, had touched the core of me, and I realized with a small shock how badly I had behaved; I had thought only of myself.

"I've been so selfish, Diana," I said at last. "Very selfish. You're right, I've only thought about my feelings, about *my* loss, *my* pain, not yours or Mom's."

"I didn't mean to sound harsh, darling," she murmured, extricating herself from me, sitting up on the sofa and drying her cheeks. "I was only trying to make you see . . . see things a little more clearly."

I didn't say anything for a few minutes, then glancing at Diana, I asked quietly, "What did you mean when you said I had everything to gain?"

"I told you, your *life*, primarily. But that also means your health, your well-being, your sanity. You're only thirty-three, Mal, still so very young, and I simply won't allow you to become a vegetable, a blob sitting around doing nothing except mourning and feeling sorry for yourself. It's vital that you mourn, yes. We must do that, we must get the grief out. But I can't, I *won't* permit you to throw your future away."

"Do I have a future, Diana?"

"Oh, yes, you do. Of course you do. That's another thing you have to gain. Your future. But you must reach out, grab life with both hands and start all over again. It will be the hardest thing you've ever had to do, the most painful, even, but it *will* be worth it, I promise you that."

"I don't know what to do. How would I begin again?" I asked, my mind starting to work in a more positive way for the first time since Andrew's death.

"First, I think you have to get yourself completely fit physically. You're far too thin, for one thing. You must start eating properly, and walking and exercising, so that you regain your strength, that vigor and energy of yours which I've always admired. And then you must think of the kind of job you'd like to find. You must work, not only because you need to earn money, but because you must keep yourself busy."

"I wouldn't know where to start." I bit my lip and shook my head. "I realize I have to begin to support myself, and very quickly. I can't let my mother and Dad go on helping me. But I don't have any idea what I could do. Or what I'm capable of doing, for that matter."

"You wrote advertising copy once," Diana reminded me.

"That was a long time ago, and I'm not sure how good I was, even if Andrew did say I was brilliant. Besides, I don't think I'd enjoy working in an office, and I know I can't live in New York. So we can forget Madison Avenue."

"You could live in London," she suggested, eyeing me intently. "I'd like that. You're all I have left, Mal, the only family I have."

I nodded. "I know, Diana, and you're very much a part of me, part of my life. It's a possibility, living in London, I mean. I suppose I could always sell Indian Meadows."

"What's happening with the apartment? You haven't said anything lately about Sarah's cousin and her plans."

"Vera wants to buy it, and she's agreed to the price my mother asked. But she hasn't gone before the board yet, the board of the cooperative. I think she's supposed to be interviewed by them this coming week. I'm not worried though, Diana; I know she'll pass."

"Getting back to a job for you, if you stay in London, you might consider working with me at the shop. You do love antiques, and you know a lot about them. I could certainly use your expertise. And your obvious talents as a decorator."

When I said nothing, Diana sat back, stared at me for a few seconds, and then reached out and took my hand in hers. "I'd like you to become my partner, Mal."

"Oh, that's so generous of you! Thank you, Diana. I'm not sure. Can I think about it?"

"Yes. Take your time." She half smiled and then reached out, touched my cheek. "You're like my daughter. No, you *are* my daughter. And I love you."

"I love you, too, Diana. You're very special to me."

"I started to say I could use your talents as an interior designer. You're awfully good at decorating, and I have a lot of clients who don't just want to buy antiques from me. They also want me to put together whole rooms for them. Whole houses, in fact."

"I do enjoy decorating, but I'm not sure I'd want to do it for other people," I said. "But it is a possibility, I guess."

"We could always have a trial run. We've nothing to lose."

"What do you mean?"

"There's no good reason why you shouldn't stay on in London for a few months. You could work at the shop, travel with me to France on buying trips, even make trips on your own. Then you could spend weekends up here with me. It's always lovely at Kilgram Chase in the summer months. At the end of the summer you could go back to Connecticut, if you wanted to, if that's what you decided was best for you."

"There's nobody like you, Diana, you're so kind, so loving." I leaned my head against the cushions and closed my eyes. A small sigh escaped me.

She said softly, "I won't press you anymore, but do think seriously about it, Mal. And remember, it would please me enormously to have you as my partner."

That night when I went to bed, I lay awake for a long time, watching the light from the fire flickering across the ceiling and the walls.

Here in this room that had once been his as a boy, Andrew was always close to me. And tonight I felt his presence more acutely than ever. It was as if he stood at the foot of the bed, keeping watch over me.

I talked to him, asked him what I should do, and it seemed to me that he was telling me to stay here with his mother at Kilgram Chase. If that was what he wanted me to do, then I would do it. Here in Yorkshire I was far away from New York and the terrible violence that had claimed my family. I felt safe here, just as I felt safe in London. Yes, perhaps it would be best to stay in England, best to start my new life here.

I turned this thought over and over in my mind until I finally fell asleep.

30

Diana had gone off to London en route to Paris, and I was alone at Kilgram Chase once more.

The library had become my sanctuary in the last few weeks, and now as I sat here on Monday morning, glancing at the newspapers and drinking a cup of coffee, I thought of the things Diana had said to me over the weekend.

She had been right, had spoken only truths.

I had acknowledged this to her and to myself. Self-delusion was not one of my faults. Nonetheless, I knew already that it was going to be hard for me to come to grips with my grief, that it would take me a long time to get it totally under control. The pain inside me was relentless, never seemed to diminish; my sorrow was overwhelming; my loneliness filled me with desolation.

The memory of the terrible violence that had taken my family from me and changed my life forever would always be there in my heart. That was a given. But I *would* try to make a new start. Somehow. I had promised Diana I would; I owed it to her and to myself. And that, at least, would be some sort of a beginning.

I still did not know what I was going to do with the rest of my life, where I was going to live or how I would earn a living. The first thing I had to do was pull myself up out of my despair, rise above it if I could. I was not sure how to do this.

Earlier this morning it had occurred to me that I ought to find something to focus on, if only for a short while, something to take my mind off my troubles, take me out of myself. Going back to my painting, as Sarah had suggested before I left Indian Meadows, did not particularly interest me now, and therefore, it was not a solution.

However, there *was* one thing that had fascinated me when I was here at Kilgram Chase last November, and that was the diary I had found in this very room. I realized, as I thought of it again, that the seventeenth-century Lettice Keswick still intrigued me. And I could not help wondering, as I had last year, whether or not there was another volume, perhaps even volumes of her writings somewhere in this house.

The diary had no monetary value as far as I knew, and certainly it had nothing to do with my earning a living. On the other hand, looking for another volume, a continuation of the first book, would give me something to focus on. And that in itself would be a step in the right direction.

I would do it. I would start a search. It would keep me busy until I had worked out some sort of plan for my future, bleak though this seemed at the moment.

The library steps were at the other side of the room, and I dragged them over to the fireplace, deciding to look at all the books in this area first. After all, Clarissa's copy and the original had been found on one of the shelves here.

I had just started to mount the steps when there was a tap on the door; Hilary came in for the coffee tray.

"Do you remember those diaries your father and I found last year, Hilary?" I asked, peering down at her.

"Yes, I do, Mrs. Andrew. Quite a find they were. Mrs. Keswick showed them to the vicar. Very impressed, he was."

I nodded. "I thought at the time that there might be more of them, but I never did get around to doing a search before I left. So I've decided to start one today."

"My father and I have already done that, Mrs. Andrew," Hilary explained quickly. "You see, Mrs. Keswick thought the same as you, that there might be another one knocking around, and anyway, she wanted all the books dusted, so we've been working the entire library section by section for some time."

"Oh," I said, feeling a small stab of disappointment. "And you found nothing?"

"No, I'm afraid we didn't. Not so far, anyway. We haven't done the two walls on either side of the fireplace yet, where you're standing. And not that one down there." She nodded in the direction of the end wall with its door leading out into the corridor.

"All right. I'll continue looking here, Hilary."

"And I'll come back and help you if you like, Mrs. Andrew," she said. "I'll just take the tray to the kitchen, I won't be a minute."

"Thanks, I'd really appreciate the help," I said, going higher on the library steps, peering at the leather-bound volumes in front of me. Once I'd read every title, I pulled a couple of books out and felt behind them, hoping for hidden treasures.

Within minutes Hilary returned with Joe, who was carrying the tall ladder he used for cleaning the chandeliers.

"It'll be right grand if we find another diary, Mrs. Andrew," Joe said as he propped the ladder against the end wall. "Mrs. Keswick'll be ever so chuffed if we do."

"So will I, Joe," I said, adding, "By the way, I'm not dusting any of these. Do you think perhaps I should?"

"Aye, no, don't worry about that!" Joe exclaimed. "Hilary can give the books a bit of a flick with the feather duster later. Hilary," he turned to his daughter and said, "Run back t'kitchen, like a good lass, and bring the small stepladder. That way you can follow on behind Mrs. Andrew and dust them there books once she's looked at them."

I was about to protest, but then I remembered how obstinate he could be and decided I'd better not interfere. I continued reading titles and poking around on the shelves, as did Joe and eventually Hilary in other parts of the library.

When Parky appeared at one point to announce that my lunch

was ready, I was completely taken aback. I glanced at my watch and saw to my astonishment that it was exactly one o'clock. How quickly the time had flown this morning.

We had a fruitless afternoon, came up empty-handed, and both Joe and Hilary had long faces. Their disappointment was quite evident. It struck me that for some unknown reason they had expected *me* to find something truly special, even if it wasn't another volume of Lettice's diaries.

"Never mind," I said, as we abandoned the search for the day. "Maybe we'll be luckier tomorrow. I fully intend to keep going, to investigate every shelf you two haven't already tackled."

"And we'll help you, Mrs. Andrew," Hilary said. "It's a challenge."

"Aye, it is that," Joe added over his shoulder, going out with the ladder.

That evening Diana called me from London, as she usually did, and I told her what I'd been doing all day.

"I was so intent on finding another Lettice diary, I forgot about the time," I said. "Not only that, I even met with Parky's favor today."

Diana chuckled softly at the other end of the phone. "Don't tell me. You actually *ate* something, is that why she was pleased?"

"Yes. I managed a small plate of cottage pie. Parky was flabbergasted. To tell you the truth, Diana, so was I."

"I'm glad you've started to eat again, however small the plate. It's a start, and you need to build yourself up. I'm relieved that you took my words to heart. I must admit, I worried driving back to London this morning, worried that I'd been too strong with you, but I needed to get through to you."

"Tough love," I replied.

"Is that what you call it?"

"Yes, and Mom says it's the best kind of love when somebody's in trouble and needs help."

"I'm here for you, Mal, with tough love and whatever else you need."

"I know, and I'm here for you. We have to support each other now, get each other through this—"

"We will, darling."

We chatted for a few minutes longer about other things; Diana told me she would be staying at the Crillon in Paris, then gave me the number. After saying good night, we hung up. But within minutes Diana called me back.

"I've just thought of something, another place for you to look for the diaries, or rather, a copy by the Victorian Clarissa, who was so intent on preserving things for the future."

"You mean a place other than the library?" I asked.

"The attics in the west wing," Diana explained. "There are several steamer trunks up there. They've got torn old labels on them, you know, labels from steamship lines, such as the P & O and Cunard. Anyway, in those trunks are all sorts of items from the Victorian era. My mother-in-law showed them to me years ago, just after Michael and I were married. She said they'd been packed up by one of the Keswick wives years before her time, at the turn of the century, in fact. Perhaps it was Clarissa who put those things in the trunks."

"And you think she might have included the diaries, if they exist, in amongst them?" I said.

"There's that possibility. In any case, it's worth looking, don't you think?"

"I certainly do," I said. "And thanks for calling back."

"Good night, Mal."

"Night, Diana."

"Look at this embroidery, it's exquisite, Mrs. Andrew," Hilary said, glancing up at me.

She was kneeling on the attic floor in front of one of the old trunks, and she handed me a claret-colored velvet cushion covered in beads. It was obviously Victorian.

I examined the work, surprised that the cushion and the beading were in such good condition after these many years. One entire side was covered with claret bugle beads, with gray, black, white, and silver beads used for the design. This was a combination of roses and leaves, bordered by delicate ferns around the edge. In the center of the cushion, white beads had been worked to form three words.

"*Amor vincit omnia*," I read out loud. "Latin. It's quite a well-known phrase. I think it means 'love conquers all.'" Staring at Hilary, I lifted a brow questioningly.

"Don't look at me like that, Mrs. Andrew," she exclaimed with a laugh. "I never studied Latin. Mrs. Keswick would know what it means, though, she took Latin at Oxford University. At least, I think she did."

"Yes, she did," I concurred.

Bending over the trunk, Hilary pulled out another cushion, this one larger and cut from olive-green velvet. Silver, gold, and bronze beads formed the background; white beads made a pattern of calla lilies, with green beads for the stems. Once again there was a Latin phrase at the bottom, worked in green beads.

I took the cushion from Hilary and read, "*Nunc scio quid sit Amor.* I'm afraid I don't know this phrase at all, but again, it has something to do with love."

"Yes," Hilary agreed, plunging her hands into the treasure trove. She pulled out two more cushions, both Victorian, heavily embroidered with beads and bearing Latin phrases.

As she showed them to me, I shook my head. "I can't tell you what they say, but let's take them downstairs. Mrs. Keswick will be interested in seeing them when she gets back from Paris."

"I can't believe she's forgotten how beautiful they are," Hilary murmured. "What I mean is, you told me she'd seen them years ago. You'd think she'd want to have them out. On the sofas and chairs, I mean."

"Yes. But then perhaps she *has* forgotten, Hilary, just as you said. After all, it was quite a long time ago when she was shown them. Forty years, as a matter of fact."

"Look at this, Mrs. Andrew!"

Hilary now passed me the most beautiful piece of black lace, cut in a large square, edged with jet beads, and encrusted with black bugle beads.

I held it up to look at it in the lamplight.

"What do you think it is?" Hilary asked me. "A mantilla? Like Spanish women used to wear?"

"I don't know. I don't think so, though, it's not quite long enough for a mantilla. But you're right, it's gorgeous. Is there much else in there?"

"Just old linens at the bottom of the trunk."

Hilary began to lift out this collection of items, which had been carefully folded years ago, and handed them to me one by one. Then she pushed herself up on her feet. "This trunk's empty now, Mrs. Andrew."

Together we examined the folded white linens, discovered several Victorian nightgowns made of cotton, half a dozen hand-embroidered pillowcases, and six matching, hand-embroidered sheets.

"Mrs. Keswick can probably make use of these antique linen sheets and pillowcases," Hilary announced. "In the two guest rooms. But I don't know what she'll do with the nightgowns. They're a bit old-fashioned." As she spoke Hilary held one of them against herself. "It smells of mothballs," she muttered and made a face.

For the remainder of the week, Hilary and I spent most of our afternoons poking about in the attics of Kilgram Chase.

There were quite a lot of them located in the four wings of the house, and we ventured into all of them. I had never been up in the eaves before, and I was fascinated by these vast spaces and all that they contained.

Aside from the Victorian steamer trunks in the west-wing attics, we found a variety of other trunks, huge cardboard boxes, and many wooden tea chests stored at the top of the house.

Inside them we discovered a wealth of lovely old things, from more beaded cushions, needlepoint samplers, and a big selection of old linens to china, glass, and all manner of Victoriana: tortoise-shell stud boxes, mother-of-pearl calling-card cases, papier mâché trays, decorative boxes, and tea caddies.

But no books. No diaries by Lettice Keswick. No copies by Andrew's Victorian ancestor, Clarissa.

On Friday afternoon, Hilary and I were in the northeast attic above the library when I stumbled on an old leather trunk. Not quite as large as the other ones we had come across, it was decorated with brass nailheads, now badly discolored, and looked very ancient.

"This might prove to be interesting," I said to Hilary. "But wouldn't you know, it's locked."

"I've got this kitchen knife with me," Hilary answered. "Let me try to prise it open." She came and knelt with me in front of the trunk. She worked away at the lock but was unable to get it to open.

"What about a hairpin?" I suggested. "That sometimes works."

"I don't have one. Do you, Mrs. Andrew?" she asked, looking at my pile of red hair upswept onto the top of my head.

"No, I'm using combs today," I explained. "But there are some pins in my bedroom, I'll rush down and get them."

"Wait a sec. I'll have a go with one of these old keys we found the other day," Hilary replied, pulling a diverse collection of small, very ancient keys out of her apron pocket.

Selecting one at random, she tried to push it into the lock; it did not fit. After trying a number of others, she finally found one that slid into the lock with ease.

"This just might work," she muttered to herself, twisting the key and jiggling it around. It took a few seconds, and then there was a distinct, if slight, click.

"I think I've done it!" she cried with a triumphant look at me.

"Go on, then, open it," I said.

She lifted the lid, and together we looked inside.

"Books!" I exclaimed, bending over the edge of the leather trunk.

"I'm not going to touch them, Mrs. Andrew; they might be very valuable. I wouldn't want to go and damage one."

"I know what you mean, Hilary." I began to nod to myself as I added, "Maybe we've struck gold."

And we had, as it happened.

The first book I put my hands on turned out to be a treasure indeed, although at first glance it looked like nothing of much importance. Bound in black leather, worn, and torn a bit on the spine, it had a frontispiece written in a hand I instantly recognized. There was no mistaking that elegant, feathery, seventeenth-century script.

Lettice Keswick Her Garden Book, the frontispiece said, and as I turned the pages, I caught my breath in surprise and delight.

Lettice had written a charming little book about the gardens at Kilgram Chase, *her gardens*: She told how she had planned and designed them, what she had planted, and why. But most important, the book was beautifully illustrated with watercolors and drawings by Lettice herself. In this it resembled the original diary we had come across last November, but there were many more illustrations in this particular book.

Hilary also exclaimed about its beauty when I showed it to her, and she went as far as to say it was better than the diary.

I did not agree. But there was no doubt that Lettice's illustrations of flowers, trees, shrubs, and plants were superb, as were her actual plans of the various gardens.

Investigating the trunk further, I pulled out four other old books, hoping against hope that they were all Lettice's work.

One was bound in purple leather, and it looked a little less scratched and used than the others. I discovered, on opening it, that it was a volume of Victorian recipes. All were written out in Clarissa's wonderful copperplate handwriting, which I had so admired before. There was no doubt in my mind that it was of her own compilation and that it reflected her own tastes in the culinary art.

There was also a cookbook by the prolific Lettice, and this contained all kinds of seventeenth-century recipes, along with household tips and advice on the use of herbs for medicines.

But it was the last two books which thrilled me the most. One was Lettice Keswick's diary for the year 1663; the other was Clarissa's careful copy of it, again written out painstakingly in her unmistakable copperplate. I could hardly wait to read it.

"It's been worth all the hard work this week, Hilary," I said, struggling to my feet and bending down to pick up the books. "These are very special."

"What will Mrs. Keswick do with them, do you think?" she asked, a quizzical expression settling on her face.

"I'm not sure. Probably nothing in the end, because I don't know what she could do, Hilary, to tell you the truth. But they're nice to have, aren't they?"

"Yes. Maybe she'll put them on display, you know, in a glass case, like they do with old books in libraries," Hilary murmured, sounding thoughtful all of a sudden. "Mrs. Keswick has the garden fête for the church every summer. Maybe people could pay something extra to come into the house and see the books. Proceeds to go to the church, of course."

"That's a good idea, Hilary. Clever of you."

Looking pleased at my compliment, she went on more confidently, "There're a lot of people around here would be interested to get a tour of this house, too, but Mrs. Keswick will never open it to the public."

I didn't say anything.

Hilary said, "Well, she wouldn't, would she?"

"I don't know. I'd have to ask her," I said.

After I had had my cup of tea, which Parky usually brought to me at about four-thirty, I went back and sat at the refectory table in front of the soaring, mullioned window. It was a clear, sunny afternoon, and anyway, the light was always good on this side of the library.

I had just begun to read Lettice's diary, which she had started in January of 1663, when the loud shrilling of the telephone made me jump slightly.

Automatically, I reached for it and picked up the receiver.

"Kilgram Chase," I said.

There was the sound of static, and then I heard David's voice saying, "Mal, is that you?"

"Yes, it is," I said and found myself clutching the phone all that much tighter. "Do you have news?"

"DeMarco's done it!" he exclaimed. "He and Johnson arrested the four youths over the weekend. I didn't call you earlier, because I was waiting for further developments, and—"

"Did they do it?" I cut in, my voice rising an octave.

"Yes. DeMarco and Johnson are positive the four of them are the perpetrators. Two sets of fingerprints from the car match those of two of the youths. Another was in possession of the gun, the nine-millimeter semiautomatic. It went to ballistics, and the report is conclusive: It is the gun that was used."

"So they'll go before a grand jury?"

"They have already. DeMarco and Johnson moved with great speed, on Monday. The hearing was yesterday, and the grand jury has voted to indict them on charges of murder in the second degree. They'll be going to trial."

"When will that be?" I asked.

"DeMarco's not sure. The prosecutor has to prepare the case, as I explained to you last week. Bail was denied, naturally. And all four currently are in jail. Which is where they'll spend the rest of their lives. They're not going to get off, I can assure you of that."

"Was it . . . " I stopped and took a deep breath. "Was it like Detective DeMarco said . . . was it an attempted carjacking, David?"

"Yes, it was. Gone wrong, of course."

"Did DeMarco tell you why . . . why Andrew and the twins were shot?" I asked, my voice so low it was barely audible.

"He told me that two of the youths were hopped up. Doped up, Mal, full of drugs. They'd apparently been smoking crack cocaine, and one of them just went wild for no reason at all. Just started to fire the gun wildly . . . "

"Oh, God, oh, God, David," I whispered. I could hardly speak.

"I know, I know, honey," he answered, his voice loving and as sympathetic as it always was. "Are you all right?"

I couldn't respond. I sat there in the library, gripping the phone, my knuckles white and my eyes staring blindly into space.

"Mal, are you there?"

I swallowed hard. "I'm here." I took another deep breath. "Thanks for calling, David. I'll be in touch."

"Take care of yourself, Mal. We'll phone you on Sunday. Bye."

I hung up without saying another word and went out of the library. Crossing the hall, my body hunched over and my arms wrapped around myself, I made it to the staircase without anyone seeing me.

Grabbing hold of the bannister, I dragged myself upstairs, slowly lifting one foot after the other. They felt as heavy as lead.

Once I was inside my bedroom, I fell onto the bed and pulled the comforter over me. I had begun to shake, and I couldn't stop. Reaching for a pillow, I buried my face in it, wanting to stifle the sound of my dry, wracking sobs.

My husband and my babies had died needlessly, for nothing, for no reason at all.

31

Yorkshire, May 1989

Up here on the wild, untenanted moors it was a truly pretty day. The sunlit air was soft, balmy, and the vast expanse of sky was cerulean blue, scattered with wispy white clouds.

The air was pure, and I breathed deeply as I walked along the path that had led me from the woods of Kilgram Chase, across the adjoining field, and up onto the lower reaches of the moors.

At one moment I looked up and caught my breath, as always awed by the high-flung fells that soared above me like giant cliffs. They dwarfed everything below, made the floor of the valley and the pastoral green dales seem so much gentler.

I would not go up to the fells today; distances were deceptive in these hills, and they were much farther away than they appeared. In any case, it was too difficult a trek.

But it did not take me long to reach my destination. This was the spot that Andrew had loved from his childhood, and where he had often brought me in the past. It was a stretch of moorland above Kilgram Chase, under the shadows of the great Ragland Fell, up near Dern Ghyll. It was a deep ravine, with an extraordinary waterfall cascading down over its sheer drops and rough-hewn stones.

I had discovered long ago that I was never very far away from the sound of running water on these moors. They were seamed with tinkling little becks and larger streams, and waterfalls that came effortlessly tumbling down over the rocks and crags in the most unexpected places.

Feeling quite warm after my walk, I took off my jacket, spread it on the ground, and sat down on it. I stared at the vast panorama stretching out before me; there was nothing but rolling moors sweeping down to the dales and the fields, for as far as the eye could see. No dwellings here. Except, of course, for Diana's house nestled against the trees directly below me.

After a short while, I lay down with my head on my jacket and closed my eyes. I enjoyed the peace up here; I was transported into another world.

There was no noise at all, except for the gentle sounds of nature. The faint buzzing of a bee, the scurry of rabbits rustling through the bilberry and bracken, the occasional bleat of a stray sheep, the trilling of the birds, and that ever-present rush of water dropping over the edge of Dern Ghyll close by.

Today was Thursday, the fourth of May.

My birthday.

I was thirty-four years old today.

I felt older, much older than my years, and scarred by the deaths of my children and my husband. Without them my life would never be the same, and sorrow was my constant companion.

But I no longer had the overwhelming urge to kill myself, and those terrible, debilitating depressions took hold of me less frequently these days. On the other hand, I had not solved the problem of earning a living or finding a job that I liked. I was at a loss, living in a kind of limbo.

I sighed and brushed a fly away from my cheek.

Lulled by the warmth and the sun on my face and bare arms, I felt suddenly drowsy. I drifted off, calmed by the peacefulness of this place.

Big drops of rain splashing on my face awakened me, and I sat up with a start, groaning out loud when I saw the darkening sky, the rain clouds gathering just above Ragland Fell.

In the distance there was the crack of thunder sounding off like cannon, and a sudden flash of bright white lightning lit up the sky. It ripped through the blackened clouds which had suddenly begun to burst.

A moment later I was already drenched by the most ferocious, slashing rain. Snatching up my jacket, I struggled into it and began to run down past Dern Ghyll, making for the winding path which would lead me back to Kilgram Chase.

In my haste I stumbled several times, and once I almost slipped, but somehow I managed to keep my balance. I went on running, pushing my wet hair away from my face, trying to keep up a steady pace. And I kept asking myself why I never heeded Wilf's warnings about the unpredictable weather up here.

Later, when Diana asked me what happened, I was unable to tell her because I had absolutely no idea how I came to fall. But fall I did. Without warning, I went sprawling at the top of an incline, and before I could check myself I was sliding and rolling down the side of the steep moorland.

I finally came to rest in a gully, and I lay there for a few minutes, gasping, catching my breath. I was winded and felt slightly battered after tumbling such a long way.

Struggling into a sitting position, I looped my wet hair behind my ears and tried to get up. Instantly, I felt the pain shooting from my ankle up my leg, and I sat down again. I realized I had either wrenched or sprained it; I didn't think it was broken. I slithered along the ground until I reached the rock formation at one side of the gully. Here I gripped a protruding rock, endeavoring to pull myself to my feet. I discovered I had difficulty standing, let alone walking.

Thunder and lightning had started raging again, and it seemed to me that the rain was much heavier than before. Uncertain what I ought to do, I decided it would be wisest to shelter here under the rocks until the storm abated. Only then would I try to make it back to Kilgram Chase.

The rocks offered me some protection because they formed an

overhang. By crouching down, I was able to shuffle myself under this, where it was reasonably dry. I attempted to wring out my hair with my hands, and then I squeezed the bottom of my trousers. My loafers were wet through and covered in mud, as were the rest of my clothes.

Much to my dismay, the rain continued to come down in great streams; the thunder and lightning were a constant barrage and seemed never-ending. Shivering with cold, my teeth chattering, I pushed myself against the back wall of the rocks, praying that the weather would calm down as quickly as it had erupted.

But it did not, and it grew darker by the minute. Hardly any blue sky was visible now as the thunderheads came scudding in, whipped along by the wind, which had started to blow quite fiercely. From this spot I could just make out the trees bending and swaying in the fields below me.

I sat under the rocks for over two hours, shaking with cold, trying to keep myself calm. The light had grown much dimmer, and I was afraid I was going to be stranded up here in the dark. Even when the rain stopped, I knew I would not get very far hopping or limping my way back to the house.

Growing more stiff and cramped and numb, I twisted my body, stretched out my legs, and lay lengthwise. This was a bit more comfortable, but not much.

From time to time the rumbling clouds parted and I saw a sliver of gray sky. Then it changed unexpectedly, and a peculiar white light began to shimmer on the edge of the horizon, suffusing the dark clouds with an aureole of radiance.

The sky was looking strange, almost eerie, but it was nevertheless quite beautiful. The light grew brighter, sharper, and I held my breath. Eerie or not, it was magnificent.

As I lay staring at that brilliant sky, trying to still my worry, I heard his voice. Andrew's voice. *Mal.*

It was clear, very close, so close I pushed myself up swiftly and changed my position under the rocks. Again I heard my name. *Mal.*

"I'm here," I answered, almost to myself.

Don't be afraid. You'll be all right. Listen to me now. You must be strong and brave. As long as you are alive you will carry the memory of me in your heart. I will live on in you. As Jamie and Lissa will live on in you. We are watching over you, Mal. But it's time for you to move on. Gather your strength. You must go on with your life. Go forward into the future.

"Andrew," I said, looking about me anxiously. "Are you there? Don't leave me, don't go away."

I am always with you, darling. Always. Remember that.

The thunder and lightning stopped.

I peered around again.

I was alone.

The rain ceased abruptly, without any warning. The bright light streaming out from behind the clouds was beginning to diminish and fade, and the stormy clouds were speeding away across the heavens. A fragment of blue appeared above me.

I closed my eyes, thinking.

Had Andrew spoken to me? Or was it all in my own head?

Was my imagination playing tricks again?

"She never paid me any mind, Mrs. Andrew didn't," Wilf grumbled. "I allus told her not to come up on these 'ere moors, Joe. I did that. Dangerous they are."

"Let's just try and find her," Joe said. "Stop yakking."

When I heard their voices nearby, I managed to push myself to my knees. "Help!" I shouted weakly. "Help! I'm down here! Joe! Wilf! Down in the hollow!"

"That's Mrs. Andrew calling us, Joe," Wilf cried excitedly. "She's tummeled in yon gully, I bet she has. Come on, Joe."

A fraction of a second later Wilf and Joe were peering down at me, relief spreading across their weather-beaten faces.

"Whatever's happened to you, Mrs. Andrew?" Joe cried, clambering down into the hollow.

"I fell, rolled down the moor, and ended up in here. I hurt my ankle," I explained, "I'm not sure how well I can walk, Joe. I think I can only hop or limp."

"Don't you worry, we'll have you back home in two shakes of a lamb's tail," Joe said. "Now, come along. Put this barbour on, it'll keep you warm. By gum, you're as white as a sheet, and you must be frozen. You're shaking like a leaf."

"I be warning you afore, Mrs. Andrew," Wilf said. "But you never paid me no mind."

"I'm sorry, Wilf, I should have listened. And you're right, the weather *is* unpredictable up here."

"It is, by gum. Many a poor soul's been lost on these moors, not found till it was too late. Dead as a doornail, they was," Wilf intoned in a dolorous voice.

"That's enough, Wilf," Joe said. "Now, Mrs. Andrew, just put one arm around my neck, and let's see if I can help you up out of this gully."

32

Joe and Wilf half walked me, half carried me back to the house.

We made slow progress because of my ankle; I felt ill, frozen through to my bones, and I had a raging headache. But at least it was no longer raining, and the wind had dropped considerably.

When we finally arrived at Kilgram Chase, Parky, Hilary, and her husband Ben were all waiting for us in the kitchen, their faces anxious.

"Oh, dear, Mrs. Andrew, what happened to you?" Parky cried. "Have you hurt yourself, then?"

"Sprained her ankle, she has," Joe answered.

"I'm all right, Parky," I reassured her, although I didn't feel it at this moment.

"Found her up near yon ghyll, we did, she'd tummeled in a gully," Wilf said. "And I—"

"It could have been worse," Hilary exclaimed, cutting him off sharply. Taking charge with sudden briskness, she went on, "There's no point standing around here nattering. Now, Mrs. Andrew, let's get you upstairs, get those wet clothes off you. A hot bath is what you need, and something hot inside you."

Hilary came to me, put her arm around my waist, and helped me across the kitchen.

"I'll ring up Dr. Gordon, ask him to come, shall I?" Ben said, looking at Hilary.

"Yes, you'd better," she replied.

"I'm okay, honestly I am," I interjected. "I'm just cold. Very cold. A bath will do the trick."

"I think the doctor had better look at your ankle. Best to be on the safe side," Joe said as we went out into the corridor.

I heard Parky say, "I'll put the kettle on."

And then Joe replying, "Nay, Mother, what yon lass needs is a shot of good scotch whiskey, not tea."

Hilary tightened her grip on me as we started up the stairs. "Can you make it all right?" she asked worriedly.

I nodded.

Once we were in my bedroom, she went to run me a bath.

I stripped off my muddy clothes, threw them on the floor, and put on a dressing gown. I limped into the bathroom.

Hilary looked around as I came in and said, "Shall I put some of these Epsom salts in the bath? They're good for aches and pains."

"Yes, that's a good idea," I answered, sitting down on the bathroom stool.

"I'll be back in a few minutes with the tea and the whiskey," Hilary said, walking over to the door. "I'll leave it in the bedroom for you. Oh, and I'll put a bottle of aspirin on the tray."

"Thanks, Hilary. Thanks for everything."

"You're welcome," she murmured and closed the door behind her.

I sat soaking in the hot tub for a long time, enjoying the heat of the water, feeling myself thawing out. The Epsom salts did help my bruised body and my ankle; and even though this was badly sprained, I was now certain it was not broken.

But it was quite obvious that I had had a lucky escape.

When I had gone for a walk earlier this afternoon, I hadn't told anyone where I was going, and it was only by chance that I had seen Wilf in the orchard as I had walked past. He had waved. I had waved back, and then I had gone on down the path into the woods. When the storm had started and I had not returned, he must have been the one to sound the alarm. I experienced a stab of guilt as I thought of the way Andrew and I had always characterized him as stupid—*gormless,* as Andrew said.

Andrew.

I closed my eyes, concentrating, picturing my husband in my mind's eye.

Had he really spoken to me this afternoon? Freezing cold, in pain from my ankle, frightened that I might not be found before nightfall, that I might easily be lost on the moors, might I not have simply imagined it? Might I not have conjured him up for comfort?

I did not know. Just as I did not know whether I had dreamed that Lissa had slept in my arms all those months ago at Indian Meadows.

Was there such a thing as an afterlife? Certainly religions have preached for thousands of years that there is. And if there is an afterlife, then there must be ghosts, spirits of the dead who come back to this physical plane for a reason. To comfort and calm those loved ones left behind grieving? To show themselves as guardian angels?

Suddenly I remembered a book I had seen the other day in the library. It was about angels and ghosts; I had leafed through it quickly. Later I would look at it again.

"You've been very lucky, Mrs. Keswick," Dr. Gordon said, putting his stethoscope away in his bag. "Very lucky indeed."

"I realize that," I responded. "I could have broken something, not just sprained my ankle."

"Very true. But what I meant is, you're fortunate you're not suffering from hypothermia. You were out in that wretched storm for over two hours, and one's body temperature drops very quickly with that kind of exposure to the elements. And when hypothermia does occur, a person can be in serious trouble."

"But Mrs. Andrew *is* all right, isn't she?" Hilary asked, her concern apparent.

"Yes, she's fine." He glanced from Hilary back to me. "Your temperature is normal, and you don't seem to have suffered too much damage. Even the sprain is not that serious. A couple of days, you'll be all right. But do be sure to keep that ankle of yours bandaged."

"I will, Doctor, and thank you for coming over."

"I was glad to pop in, and if you have any problems at all, please don't hesitate to ring me."

"I will. Thanks, Dr. Gordon."

"Good-bye, Mrs. Keswick."

"Bye."

Hilary jumped up.

"I'll see you out, Doctor," she said and hurried after him. Turning back to look at me from the doorway, she asked, "Do you need me for anything else, Mrs. Andrew? Shall I come back and help you get dressed?"

"Thanks, Hilary, that's sweet of you, but I can manage."

Left alone, I took off my robe, put on a pair of gray flannels, a russet-colored silk shirt, and a matching wool jacket. Sitting down on the bench at the bottom of the bed, I pulled on a pair of white wool socks and slipped my feet into a pair of suede moccasins.

Picking up the walking stick Parky had brought upstairs for me, I hobbled out of my bedroom, went along the hall and down the staircase, taking steps very carefully, walking sideways.

The library had become my favorite room at Kilgram Chase these past four months, and knowing this, Joe had turned on the lamps and started the fire earlier, whilst I had been with the doctor.

Even though it was May, the great stone house could be chilly at night, especially this room, with its high-flung ceiling and over-scaled proportions. The fire blazing up the chimney and the warm glow of the lamps gave it a cheerful ambience on this rainy evening.

Once I had found the book about angels and ghosts, I went over to the fireplace and sat down in the wing chair. I would look at it whilst I waited for Diana. She was driving up from London tonight instead of tomorrow, so that she could spend the evening with me; she did not want me to be alone for my birthday. She was due in about an hour, and I was glad she was coming.

A memory of my last birthday insinuated itself into my mind, and I couldn't help recalling how happy it had been. My mother had given an early dinner at her apartment, and Lissa and Jamie had come with me and Andrew and Sarah. There had been champagne first and a cake after dinner, and the twins had sung "Happy Birthday" to me. Andrew had given me mabe pearl earrings; the twins had painted their own special cards for me and saved up all year to buy me a pretty silk scarf.

My throat tightened, and I felt the tears sting my eyes as the memories came rushing back. I pushed them aside, took hold of myself, leaned back in the chair, and closed my eyes. Eventually the pain of yearning for them passed.

I began to leaf through the book about angels and ghosts, and I soon found the section I was looking for, the references I wanted.

I read that angels were considered to be messengers of the divine, that they only ever brought good news and aid to those in need of it. People who had seen them said they were filled with goodness and warmth and were surrounded by light, that frequently they were vividly and brilliantly colored, and that a special kind of radiance emanated from them.

Other people interviewed for the book said that when they had seen an angel, or several angels together, they had felt themselves filling with joy, bursting with happiness; some said they had filled with sudden laughter.

The section on ghosts came next, and I read that they were the spirits of the dead, and always took their own form when they materialized. The idea that ghosts did exist was apparently found in every country and culture, and that in general most people agreed on how they actually looked. They were misty, cloudy, transparent, and floating.

Usually, ghosts came to help their loved ones, according to the book. They brought messages of hope and love and frequently materialized in order to tell us that everything was all right. Seemingly, ghosts were attached to the physical world, our world, by their longing for those they had left behind.

The book said there were also bad ghosts, evil spirits who could do harm and who sometimes took demonic possession of a person. I began to read about the Roman Catholic church's attitude toward evil spirits, and the exorcisms which were performed by priests. I found this a bit frightening and closed the book. I did not want to know about evil spirits. I had experienced enough evil to last me a lifetime.

After returning the book to its place on the shelf, I went and sat in front of the mullioned window, staring out at the moors. They were a peculiar blue-black color at this twilight hour, rain-swept and formidable, and a shiver ran through me as I thought of being out on them in this weather tonight.

And yet, curiously, I had been close to Andrew up there this afternoon in the storm, closer than ever, and at one moment I had felt his presence most acutely.

Was this because he had always loved storms? Because he had wanted to go out in them when he was a boy, had wanted to become at one with his ancestors riding out to fight their enemies?

I smiled inwardly, thinking of him with such love. My heart was full of him. Unexpectedly, I experienced a feeling of great calmness. It was flowing through me, suffusing my entire being; it was the kind of calmness I had forgotten existed.

I sat there for a long time, looking out the window, thinking about Andrew's words to me today. My birthday. Had he spoken to me *because* it was my birthday?

I sighed to myself. I was still not sure what had happened out there this afternoon, whether his voice had been real or simply inside me, conjured up because of my yearning for him.

"Here's to you, darling," Diana said, touching her glass of white wine to mine. "I'm glad you're here. I'm glad we can spend your birthday together."

"So am I, Diana."

Placing her goblet on the coffee table, she picked up the small gift-wrapped package she had brought into the library with her a few minutes ago. Handing it to me with a smile, she said, "This is for you, and it comes with all of my love."

"Thank you," I answered, taking it from her and unwrapping it. The small black leather box I held in my hands was worn, a bit rubbed on one side, and when I opened it, I let out a little gasp. Lying on the black velvet was an antique cameo, one of the most exquisite I had ever seen. "It's beautiful, Diana, thank you so much."

Rising, I went over to the sofa and kissed her on the cheek, and then I pinned the cameo onto the lapel of my jacket.

"My mother-in-law gave it to me years ago, for one of *my* birthdays," Diana explained. "I thought it was a nice idea to pass it on to you, since it's a Keswick heirloom."

"You're always so thoughtful, so loving," I murmured, going back to the chair and sitting down. "You spoil me."

"There's something else I want to talk to you about," Diana went on. "And now is as good a time as any."

She sounded suddenly rather serious, and I looked at her questioningly. "Yes, of course."

"It's about this house, Mal."

"What do you mean?"

"You're my heir now . . ." She paused for a moment, and I saw the emotion crossing her face. But she recovered herself immediately. "My only heir, and I just wanted you to know that I have had my will redrawn. I've left Kilgram Chase to you, and everything else I own, actually."

"Oh, Diana, I don't know what to say . . . thank you, of course . . ." I was at a sudden loss and couldn't find the right words to express myself.

Diana said, "You're young, Mal, only thirty-four today, and much of your life is still ahead of you. And one day I'm sure you'll remarry, perhaps even have children again, and I like to think of you being here with them."

I gaped at her. I was aghast. "No!" I exclaimed. "I won't remarry—"

"You don't know what's going to happen," she said, interrupting me. "I know how you feel at this moment, and perhaps I was wrong to bring the subject up tonight. So I'm not going to continue this conversation. Certainly not now. However, I do want to say one thing, and it is this, Mal darling. You must go on. We must all go on. Life is for the living, you know."

I had a strange affinity with Lettice Keswick.

I felt curiously drawn to her, and yet she had been an ancestor not of mine, but of Andrew's. Nonetheless, I did feel oddly close to this seventeenth-century Yorkshirewoman, dead now for several hundred years though she had been.

I had grown to know Lettice through her writing—those two diaries covering two years of her life in Stuart England, her cookbook full of recipes for food and wine, and her enchanting, illustrated garden book.

As I sat in the library at Kilgram Chase this morning, leafing through those various books again, I could not help thinking that Lettice had been a lot like me, in many ways. A homemaker, a cook, a gardener, a painter, a woman interested in furnishings and all those things which made a home beautiful. And she had been a devoted mother and an adoring wife, just as I had.

Basically that was my problem. I had not known anything else after college; certainly a few months in an ad agency didn't count. And without my husband and my children, I had no focus, no purpose. Certainly I had nothing to do, and that was not good, not good at all, as Diana kept pointing out. A job was essential.

But what kind of job?

That old question came back to nag me, as it had for some months.

Sighing under my breath, feeling suddenly impatient with myself, even irritated, I pushed back my chair and went outside. I also felt the need for some air before lunch.

I found my steps were leading me toward the walled rose garden, always a favorite spot of mine. But perhaps more so of late, since I knew it had been designed almost three hundred years ago by Lettice. It was exactly the same today as it had been then.

Opening the oak door which led into the garden, I walked down the three steps and stood looking around for a moment or two. It was not a large garden, but it had a special kind of charm, due in no small measure to its ancient stone walls and paths covered with moss and chamomile, two sundials, and various wooden garden seats placed here and there.

Lettice's design was simplicity itself, but that was the reason it worked. There were hedges of shrub roses, ramblers climbing the ancient walls, rectangular beds of floribundas, and circular beds of hybrid tea roses. My favorites were the Old-Fashioned roses, a variety raised before the twentieth century; I liked to think these resembled the roses planted by Lettice so long ago.

It was late May, and since most of the roses currently planted bloomed in June, the garden was not as beautiful or as colorful as it would be then and through the rest of the summer. But because the walls gave the garden shelter and the sun shone on it in the afternoons, a few of the June roses were already starting to flower.

I sat down on one of the garden seats, my mind still focused on a job. I had no idea what I could do or what I wanted to do. I had decided weeks ago that I did not want to work in an office, and of course that limited my choices.

Last weekend, when my father and Gwenny had come to stay with us, he had been in favor of my going to work with Diana at her antique shop in London. And she herself was all for it, was waiting for an answer, in fact.

"You should be with people, Mallory," my father had said. "That's why a shop's ideal. And in this instance, it's the perfect shop for you, loving antiques and art the way you do." Gwenny and Diana had agreed, and all three of them had tried to talk me into the partnership she had so generously offered.

I thought about this idea one more time, assessing the pros

and cons. Perhaps they were right. I did care about antique furniture, objects of art and paintings, and I had quite a wide knowledge of them. Though I didn't want to decorate for people, I
wouldn't mind selling things to them. Actually, the thought of
being in a shop appealed to me.

Except . . .

Except what?

I wasn't sure exactly what it was that was making me balk.

Then it hit me. I had a moment of truth, of such extraordinary
clarity of vision I was momentarily stunned.

I didn't want to work in Diana's shop or become her partner
because I didn't want to stay in England.

I wanted to go home.

Home to Indian Meadows. My home. The place Andrew and I
had so lovingly made ours. I missed it. I was homesick. I needed to
be there in order to get on with my life.

Everybody had been telling me I must do that, but I hadn't
been able to make a move. I had been stationary, marking time
here, because England was the wrong place for me at this juncture
of my life. I loved it; I would always come back to Yorkshire. But
now I must move on. Immediately.

I must go home. Whatever my life was going to be, I suddenly
knew that I wanted to, no, *must* live it in Connecticut, in that old
house. I needed to be in its lovely cool rooms, to be close to my old
apple tree and my barns. I longed to see the horses in the long
meadow, the mallards on the pond. I wanted to be with Nora and
Eric and Anna.

Indian Meadows was mine. Andrew and I had created it
together, made it what it was. I felt *right* there, at ease. I had fled
Indian Meadows in January in search of Andrew. But I no longer
had to look for him here in his childhood home. He was with me
always, inside my heart, part of me, just as Jamie and Lissa were
part of me. And would be for as long as I lived, for all the days of
my life.

But if I were to keep my Connecticut homestead, I had to earn a living.

I could open my own shop. Right there at Indian Meadows.

This thought took me by surprise.

I pondered it, realized at once that it was not a bad idea at all. Except that there were innumerable antique shops in the area, stretching from New Milford and New Preston all the way up to Sharon.

But it didn't have to be an antique shop, did it?

No. What kind of shop, then?

A shop for women like me. Or rather, women who were married with children, the way I had been once. Homemakers. Mommies. Besotted wives. I could sell them all of the things I knew about, from the days when I was a wife and mother: kitchenware, cooking utensils, and baking tins; beautiful pottery for beautiful tables; herbs and spices, jams and jellies; potpourri, fancy soaps, and beeswax candles. All of these things women had loved since Lettice Keswick's time.

Lettice Keswick. Now there was a name to conjure with. I could call it Lettice Keswick's Kitchen. That had a nice ring to it. No, I preferred Indian Meadows. Why not keep *that* name? It had always meant a lot to us. It was the name of the house, but there was no reason why it shouldn't also be the name of the shop.

My shop.

My very own shop. Indian Meadows. A Country Experience.

That also had a nice ring to it. But why was it a country experience? It would only be a shop, after all. But it could be an experience if something special happened there. It could be a café as well. A small café in the center of the shop, serving coffee, tea, cold drinks, soups, small snacks, and quiche.

A country shop and café in an old red barn in the foothills of the Berkshires, the northwestern highlands of Connecticut. God's own country, Andrew and I had always called it.

Nora and Anna could help me run it. They'd enjoy it; certainly they'd enjoy making the extra money. And perhaps Eric could be a part of it; after all, things were not very good at the lumberyard, Nora had written to tell me. She had also said she missed cooking for me. Well, she could make jams and jellies, chutneys and spreads to her heart's content. There were enough recipes in Lettice's cookbook to keep her busy. That was it. Our own label. *Lettice Keswick's Kitchen.*

I experienced such a rush of excitement I could hardly contain myself. All kinds of ideas were rushing into my head, ideas for other labels, other lines of products. There might even be a catalogue one day.

A catalogue. My God, what a great idea that was.

I jumped to my feet and glanced around the rose garden.

Thank you, Lettice Keswick, I thought. Thank you. For there was no question in my mind that Lettice had had a hand in this.

PART SIX

INDIAN MEADOWS

33

Connecticut, June 1989

It was a warm Friday afternoon at the end of the month, and Sarah had driven up to stay with me for the weekend.

Even before she had changed from her chic city clothes into her country-bumpkin togs, as she called them, she had wanted to see the barns, to review the progress I had made in her absence.

And so here we stood in the middle of the biggest of my four barns, surveying the work which had been done by my building contractor, Tom Williams, whilst she had been away on business.

"I can't believe it, Mal!" she exclaimed excitedly, her dark eyes roaming around, taking everything in. "Tom *has* moved with great speed, you're right."

"And Eric's been just as fast," I pointed out. "He's already painted the second floor, and tomorrow he'll start down here."

"It was such a good idea of yours, extending the old hayloft. Now you've got a second floor, but without losing the feeling of spaciousness."

As she spoke Sarah looked up toward the new loft at the far end of the barn.

"The café will be under the loft," I said, "if you remember the architect's plans. And I think it's kind of cozy to have it there. Tom's suggested putting in a big potbellied stove for the winter months, and I think it's a terrific idea, don't you?"

"Yes, and you might want to consider one of those gorgeous porcelain stoves from Austria. They're awfully attractive, Mal."

"And expensive, I've no doubt. I've got to keep an eye on the budget, Sash. But come on, let's walk down there, and I'll tell you a bit more about the café."

Taking hold of her arm, I drew her to the other end of the barn. "Now, here, Sarah, in the very center of this space, I'm going to have little tables for four. Green metal tables and chairs, the kind you find in sidewalk cafés in Paris. I've already ordered ten from one of the showrooms you sent me to last week, and that means I'll be able to seat forty."

"So many!" she exclaimed. "Can you handle that number of customers? Serve them, I mean?"

"Yes, I could if I had to. But I honestly don't think there will ever be forty people crowding into the café all at the same time. They'll drift in and out, since they'll mainly have come to shop. At least I hope that's why they'll be here."

Drawing her farther into the café area, I continued, "The counter and cash register will be down near the back wall, just in front of those doors Tom has already put in. They lead outside to the kitchen addition."

"When's he going to start that?" Sarah asked, walking over, opening a door, and peering out.

"Next week."

"I thought Philip Miller's plans for the kitchen were really on target, Mal, didn't you?"

"At first the kitchen seemed a bit too big to me. But when I really thought it through, I realized he had taken growth into consideration. Not that we can grow that much."

Sarah said, "Better to err on the side of largeness, rather than building a kitchen you discover too late is too small."

"I took Philip's advice. And when I saw him last Friday, I also listened to him when it came to the appliances. I've ordered two restaurant-size freezers and two restaurant-size refrigerators, as well as two heavy-duty cooking stoves. Oh, and two microwave ovens for reheating and warming food."

"Are you planning to serve a lot of hot dishes now? Has the menu changed, Mal?"

I shook my head. "It's still the same one we discussed. Various soups, quiche lorraine, maybe cottage pie, but that's it. The rest will be sandwiches and cakes, plus beverages. However, don't forget that Nora will be making our own line of jams, jellies, lemon curd, mincemeat, and chutneys."

"Lettice Keswick's Kitchen," Sarah said, a smile crossing her face. "I love it, and it's a great name for a label."

Turning slowly in the center of the floor, Sarah waved an arm around and continued, "And the walls here in the café will be lined with floor-to-ceiling shelves displaying cooking utensils, pots, pans, cookware, and pottery."

"And the Lettice products as well," I reminded her.

"It's going to be great, Mal! A fabulous success. I can just smell it," Sarah enthused.

"From your mouth to God's ear, as my mother would say."

"My money's on you, Mal, it really is. Oh, Tom's already put in your new staircase. Can we go upstairs to the loft?"

"Yes, but just be careful," I warned. "As you can see, there's no bannister yet."

I led the way up into the old hayloft, now totally remodeled and revamped. Tom had, in effect, created a gallery which floated out into the middle of the barn. It had a high railing at the edge, instead of a wall, and because of this it was airy and light-filled.

Sarah prowled around, nodding to herself as she did. "Up here you're going to sell china, pottery, ceramics, glass, cutlery, linen, tabletop items for dining, that's right, isn't it?"

"It's what you and I decided before you went away. You said it was better to keep the food items downstairs."

She nodded. "The whole idea of the shop-café was inspired. Having the café makes it just that little bit different, and yes, the food should be downstairs. Have you decided what you're going to do with the other barns, if anything?"

"One of them will have to be an office. Mine in the house simply won't be big enough. But it can also double as a place for storing products and—"

"I thought you were going to use the basement of the house for that?" Sarah cut in. "That's what you said the last time I was here."

"I *am* going to use the basement, yes. But to store the bottled food stuff, the nonperishable things, mainly the Lettice Keswick line. It's cool and roomy, and Eric's cleaned it out and given it a fresh coat of white paint. Tom's got two of his crew putting up shelves down there, but what I need is a storage place for inventory, for my stock."

"You're right, you *will* need plenty of space," Sarah agreed, and then she began to laugh. "I can see that my lessons in retailing over the past few weeks have served you well. But then you always were a fast learner, Mal."

"And you're a good teacher. Anyway, to continue, I thought I'd make the third barn into a little boutique called Indian Meadows, and the fourth into a gallery, which I'm naming Kilgram Chase."

"Catchy," Sarah said, and then grinning at me, she teased, "expanding before you've even opened, eh?"

"That's thanks to you again. You did tell me two weeks ago that I ought to have more than one private label, in order to give the shop a certain kind of cachet. So I did a bit of creative thinking and came up with the idea of the Kilgram Chase label and a gallery, and an Indian Meadows label for the boutique."

"What are the products?" she probed.

"Let's go over there, and I'll tell you on the way," I answered.

Within seconds we were outside, heading in the direction of the other barns on my property. These were clustered together on one side of Anna's cottage and the stables.

"That big barn at the back, the one closest to Anna's place, will be the administration office and the storage barn," I explained.

"The two smaller ones I'll turn into the gallery and the boutique."

"Tell me what you're going to sell, Mally. You know I'm a born retailer, and I'm riddled with curiosity."

Pushing open the door of the barn I had chosen to become the gallery, I went in first, saying over my shoulder, "Everything in here will be English in feeling or made in England, Sash. I've found a crafts and embroidery company up here, and they're going to make small needlepoint pillows for me. What will make my pillows different is their design. They'll be copies of those Victorian beaded cushions I found in the attics of Kilgram Chase. The designs will be exactly the same, and so will the Latin mottoes. What do you think?"

"Clever idea, but what about quantity? Can this company make plenty for you? As many as you want?"

"I don't plan to have more than about a dozen at a time, and I'll take special orders," I told her. "I'm going to sell English watercolors, botanicals, and vegetable prints, already framed. And Diana's going to seek out bits and pieces in London, you know, small antique items such as stud boxes, snuffboxes, tea caddies, and candlesticks. She says it's easy for her, a snip, and she'll just ship them over or bring them when she comes. I'm also going to feature English soaps and scents, beeswax candles, and potpourri. Oh, and Ken Turner perfumed candles, as well as some of his smaller dried-flower arrangements. Again, I'm getting those through Diana."

"I think such items will move very well. People do like things that are different, even if they are slightly more expensive. And you've got a good market for them up here. But tell me about the Indian Meadows boutique."

"Come on, let's go over to the barn where I plan to house it," I said.

Once we were inside, Sarah strolled around and asked, "Are you going to sell clothes? You *are* calling it a boutique."

"Yes, I am, but I'm also going to have other things as well. Everything will be American, from my own watercolors, which you tell me are good enough to sell, to Early American and Colonial-style quilts and cushions, soft toys, all handmade, and some really beautiful American Indian blankets from the Southwest."

"And the clothes?"

"They'll be made by Pony Traders, the company Anna knows up near Lake Wononpakook. But I need your help with them."

"I'll do anything to get this project off the ground, you know that, Mally, what do you need me to do to help you with Pony Traders?" A dark brow lifted quizzically.

"You know every aspect of fashion and retailing, you're the fashion director of Bergman's, for heaven's sake. I'd like you to talk to the two women who own the company. Maybe you could persuade them to give me some items on an exclusive basis, and then there's the pricing. If I'm buying a large quantity of their stuff, shouldn't I get some sort of special deal? A discount?"

"It depends," Sarah replied thoughtfully. "But of course I'll come with you, and I'll do what I can. Anyway, now that you're going to sell clothes, I'll come up with some other vendors for you. I guess it's a sort of ethnic look you're after? American Indian?"

"Not necessarily, but certainly casual, comfortable, country-style clothing. Thanks, Sashy. Your help's going to be invaluable."

"I'm just so thrilled about this project of yours, and as I just said a few minutes ago, I feel really good about it in my bones. I just know it's going to take off. And it's going to give you a whole new lease on life. It already has, actually."

Linking her arm through mine, Sarah guided me out of the barn, and we walked back up to the house together.

"Andrew would be so proud of you—" Sarah stopped with that awful suddenness she had adopted lately whenever she mentioned him. She glanced at me swiftly, looking chagrined.

"I know he would be *very* proud of me," I said calmly. "And you don't have to avoid mentioning him, Sashy darling, or stop midsentence when you do. As I told Mom yesterday, Andrew

Keswick lived, he existed, he was my husband for ten years, the father of my children. He was on this planet for forty-one years, Sarah, and he made a big difference to a lot of people, not only his mother and me and the children. He loved me. I loved him. He was my lover, my best friend, my true soul mate, and my dearest companion. He meant everything to me, he was my whole life, you know that. So I don't want you to stop yourself every time his name crops up in conversation."

"I won't, I promise, Mal. And I understand, I really do. You're right, we risk negating him by never speaking about him."

"It's the same with Jamie and Lissa. I want you to talk about them to me, remember them, discuss them whenever you feel like it. You will, won't you?"

"Of course."

"It's comforting, you know," I went on softly. "And it helps to keep them alive."

"I'm so glad you've told me. I *was* being scrupulously careful."

"I know . . . " I let my sentence trail off. We walked on up to the house in silence for a few seconds. Then I said, "They were so special, weren't they, Sash? Your godchildren."

"Yes, they were. Your Botticelli angels, your small miracles, and mine, too. How I loved them. And Andrew."

"They loved you, Sarah, and he loved you, just as I do. I'm so glad you're my friend."

"I am, too. We're very lucky to have each other."

"I was thinking the other day . . . about Andrew," I said, looking at her. "Do you remember when you first met him, Sash?"

"I certainly do. I was bowled over, and jealous to death of you!"

"You called him Dreamboat. Do you remember that?"

"Yes, I remember," she murmured, returning my long look. Her lovely dark eyes grew suddenly moist, and I saw her swallow hard. "I remember everything," she said in a whisper.

"Don't cry," I said softly. "Don't cry, Sashy."

She could only nod.

34

As we entered the house, Sarah said, "I'll go and change out of these clothes. I'll be down in a few minutes."

"There's no hurry, Sash," I answered. "I'm going to be in my office. When you're ready, join me there. I want to show you the sign for the main gate, the labels for the different products, all the things I've designed this past week."

"Give me ten minutes, Mal," she murmured with a faint smile as we walked down the back hall together.

"No problem, Sashy."

I stood outside my office, my eyes following her as she ran upstairs. She had been quite upset a few moments ago; I realized she wanted to be alone for a while, to compose herself.

Turning, I stepped into my little office and sat down at the desk, where I spread out the various labels. Leaning forward, I studied them for a few moments. "Keep it simple," Sarah had said to me before she left for California. "Remember what Mies van der Rohe said—'Less is more,' and he was right."

I was glad to have Sarah's advice. There was always the temptation to add some sort of decorative element to a label, along with the name. But I resisted, used only the words *Indian Meadows* and *Kilgram Chase*, concentrating on a distinctive type of lettering.

I had also kept simple the drawing for the sign for the main gate into Indian Meadows, using the name and the slogan I had dreamed up in Lettice's rose garden at Kilgram Chase a few weeks ago: *A Country Experience*. I hadn't even added anything about a café or shops. I wanted to keep the sign uncluttered, and people would soon know what we were about.

The phone rang, and I reached for it. "Hello?"

"Mal, it's me. How are you?"

"Hi, Mom, I'm okay. Sarah's here. She arrived a short while ago, and I've been showing her around. She's impressed, excited about everything."

"So am I, darling, and I can't wait to see how it's progressed in the last couple of weeks. You're still expecting us on Sunday for lunch, aren't you?"

"Yes, of course I am."

"What time?"

"I thought about eleven-thirty, twelve. You can take a stroll around, and then we can have lunch at about one. How does that sound?"

"Wonderful, darling. We'll be there. Here's David, he wants a word with you."

"Bye, Mom." I frowned to myself, wondering what David had to tell me. Had he heard from DeMarco? Most probably. I felt myself automatically stiffen and gripped the phone that much tighter.

"Hello, Mal," David said. "I'm looking forward to seeing you on Sunday."

"Hi, David. You've heard from DeMarco, haven't you?"

"Yes, this afternoon. He wanted me to know that the date for the trial has been set, and—"

"When is it going to be?"

"Next month. The end of the month."

"Will it be in criminal court downtown? Like you said?"

"Yes, it will."

"I want to go. I can, can't I?"

"Yes, you can, but I don't think you should."

"David, I have to be there!" I cried, my voice rising.

"Mal, listen to me. I don't think you should expose yourself to something like this. You've never been to a criminal trial, you don't know what it's like. But I do. I'm in criminal court almost every day of my life. You're going to be very upset again—"

"I'll be all right," I interrupted quickly, "Honestly, I will."

"No, you won't. Please take my word for it. Mal, I understand *why* you think you want to be there, but you mustn't go, not under any circumstances. I don't want you exposed to that . . . filth, and neither does your mother."

"My family was exposed to it; they're dead because of those animals."

"I know, honey. Listen to me, I want you to think very carefully about the trial and going to it, and we'll discuss it when I come out on Sunday."

"We don't have to, David. I've made up my mind."

"Don't do that. Keep an *open* mind. I'll explain things to you, tell you what the trial's going to be like, and then you can make a decision."

Knowing it was useless to argue with him, I said, "All right, David. We'll talk about it on Sunday."

"Good. See you then."

We said our good-byes and hung up.

I sat staring into the middle of the room, thinking about the impending trial and those who had been responsible for killing my family, and I began to tremble. The calmness I had acquired of late instantly disappeared; I was suddenly filled with agitation and anxiety.

I heard Sarah's footsteps on the staircase, and I glanced toward the door as she came into the room.

"What's wrong?" she asked, staring at me.

"I just spoke to David. DeMarco called him today. The trial's set for late July."

"Oh," she said, walking across the little office and sitting down in the chair near the fireplace. "I've been wondering when it was going to be."

"I want to go to it, Sash, but David doesn't think I should."

"I tend to agree with him."

"I have to go!" I exclaimed.

"If you really feel you must, then I'll go with you, Mal. I'd never let you face that alone. I don't suppose your mother would either."

"How can you come with me? There's your job."

"I'll take some of my vacation time."

"But you were going to spend your vacation out here with me, getting Indian Meadows ready," I reminded her.

"I know, and I'd much prefer to do that. On the other hand, I couldn't stand it, knowing you were in court without me, even if your mother were with you. Anyway, what did David say?"

I told her quickly, then continued, "I feel funny about not being there, Sarah. Those youths are going to be on trial for the cold-blooded murder of Andrew and Lissa and Jamie, and I ought to be in that courtroom."

Sarah did not speak for a moment or two. She sat thinking; eventually she said slowly, "I know you, Mal, and I know how your mind works, so I know you feel you should be present to see justice done. I'm right, aren't I?"

"Yes," I admitted. "I want justice."

"But whether you're there or not won't affect the verdict. The evidence against those guys is conclusive and overwhelming, Mal. According to everything DeMarco has said, forensics has a make on the fingerprints found on the car, and ballistics on the gun. And then there's the confession of one of the youths. You know they're going to be found guilty and sentenced to life. There's no way out for them. So, if I'm truthful with you, I agree with David. I don't think you should go. You can't contribute anything, and it would be painful for you to bear."

I said nothing, simply sat there looking at her, biting my lip worriedly.

Sarah went on, after a moment's reflection, "Why put yourself through it all over again?"

"I feel uneasy about *not* going . . . "

"You've been so much calmer since you came back from Yorkshire, and made such progress. I think it's important to forge ahead, to think about the project here, to get on with it. And listen, there's another thing . . . the press. Can you honestly cope with another media circus?"

I shook my head. "No, I couldn't."

Sarah got up and walked to a window, then stood looking out. She was silent. I stared at her for a moment, noticing that she held herself rigidly; her shoulder blades protruded slightly under her thin cotton shirt. She was tense, worried; I knew her so well, as she knew me.

Leaning back in my chair, I closed my eyes, turning the whole thing over in my mind. Eventually I sat up and said quietly, "I just feel Andrew would want me to be in court."

Swinging around to face me, Sarah exclaimed vehemently, "No, he wouldn't! That'd be the last thing he'd want! He would want you to take care of yourself, look to the future, do exactly what you *are* doing now. He'd hate you to cause yourself unnecessary heartache, Mal, he really would. Please believe me, there is nothing to be gained by going to that trial."

"But you'd go with me, wouldn't you?"

"How could I let you go alone? But honestly, David knows what he's talking about. He's been a criminal lawyer all his life, he knows how horrendous these kinds of trials are; and then again, he cares about you, wants the best for you. I'd listen to him, if I were you."

I nodded slowly and reached for the phone. I dialed my mother's apartment.

David answered. "Hello?"

"It's me," I said in a subdued voice. "Sarah's here, David, and she agrees with you about the trial. I've made a decision, but I just wanted to ask you again . . . do you really think I shouldn't be there?"

"I do, Mal."

"I've decided not to go."

I caught a note of relief in his voice as he said, "Thank God. But there's something I should point out to you, something you may not know. You can be present for the sentencing, to make a statement to the judge, if you so wish, stating your feelings about the kind of sentence you think should be imposed on the criminals."

"I didn't know that."

"How could you? In any case, Mal, you may very well want to go to court at that time. And naturally I would come with you, and so would your mother. Think about it."

"I will, David."

"You made the right decision. I'll tell your mother, I know she's going to be pleased. Good night, honey."

"Good night, David."

I told Sarah what he had just said; she listened carefully as she always did, and then she went and sat down in the chair. Finally, she said, "Maybe you *should* go to the sentencing, Mal. Somehow that makes sense. Sitting through a trial, no. It would make you ill. But saying your piece to the judge, expressing your loss, your pain, well, that's a whole different thing, isn't it?"

"It is. Maybe I'll do it," I said. Then I got up and walked to the door. "Come on, Sash, I'll buy you a drink. I don't know about you, but I could really use one."

35

Connecticut, July 1989

Once I had made up my mind not to be present at the trial, I managed to push it to the back of my mind.

There was no point dwelling on it, since that served no good purpose and only tended to deflect me from my goal. This was forging ahead with the shops and the café at Indian Meadows.

Every day there was something new to keep me busy, yet another decision to be made, plans to be approved, additional merchandise to be ordered, labels to be manufactured, and countless other jobs.

There were times when I would stop in the middle of doing something and wonder at myself and all that had happened in two months.

I had come back from Yorkshire with the idea of opening a shop and a café, and everything had taken shape immediately. I had formed a company, applied to the town of Sharon for commercial zoning permits, borrowed money from my mother, my father, David, and Diana, and opened a business bank account.

They had all wanted to give me the money, to become my partners, but I had refused. I did not wish to have any partners, not even Sarah, who had also volunteered to be an investor.

I told them I would repay their money with interest, as soon as I could, and I had every intention of doing so.

Armed with my newly printed business cards and my check-book, I had gone to the product showrooms in New York. Two were housed in a building on Fifth Avenue and another in one on Madison Avenue, and it was there that I found everything I needed for the kitchen shop. It was Sarah who had told me about these showrooms, pointing me in the right direction, explaining that I didn't have to travel to foreign countries to buy the merchandise for my different lines.

"You'll find the best of everything right there in Manhattan," she had explained. "I talked to various buyers on the home floors at Bergman's, and they recommend these particular showrooms." She had handed me the list and gone on, "You'll see from the nota-tions next to each showroom that you can get French, Italian, Portuguese, and Spanish pottery, porcelains, and cookware, all that kind of stuff, and table linens as well. Everything you want for the tabletop, in fact."

She had also told me that the International Gift Show was held twice a year in New York at the Jacob Javits Convention Center. "And there are other gift shows, held on the piers at the passenger-ship terminal on the Hudson. There's a wealth of American prod-ucts as well as merchandise from all over the world."

I felt as if I had walked across the world, the first day I went on a buying trip to Manhattan.

I covered every one of the showrooms on Sarah's long list, and I thought I had lost my feet by the end of the day.

In fact, I was so exhausted by four o'clock that I took a cab up to my mother's apartment, where I promptly collapsed. Even after a rest and dinner with her and David, I hadn't had the strength to drive to Sharon. Since I no longer had an apartment in New York, I spent the night in my old room.

I drove back to Indian Meadows the following morning, feel-ing that I had accomplished miracles on my first buying trip.

Eric stood poised in the doorway of my studio. "Am I inter-rupting you, Mal?" he asked.

"No, it's okay, come on in," I replied, putting down the water-color I was holding. "I'm just trying to sort through these paint-ings. Sarah's going to take them to that good frame shop in New Preston this afternoon, and I was just trying to select twenty of the best ones to begin with."

He came and stood looking over my shoulder at the watercol-ors, which I had spread out on the table. After a moment studying them, he said, "They're all beautiful, Mal, it's hard to choose."

"They're not bad, are they?" I said, glancing at him. "But you look as if you're bursting to tell me something, so come on, what is it?"

"They all want to come and work for us, Mal!" Eric exclaimed, grinning broadly. "Billy Judd, Agnes Fairfield, and Joanna Smith. So I thought I'd hire 'em, if that's all right with you."

"Of course it is, Eric. We're going to need three people at the very least. We may even have to take on another two helpers later."

"Billy wants to work with me, serving in the café and the food shop. Joanna Smith is in love with the idea of selling beautiful things for beautiful dining, so she could run the shop upstairs in the new loft. Agnes had wanted to be in the boutique, but I told her that was Anna's territory, and so she's agreed to handle the Kilgram Chase Gallery. It's worked out well, hasn't it?"

"It has indeed, thanks to you. I assume they agreed to the money we're paying."

Eric nodded. "Oh, yes, no problem, and they're all prepared to stay in their current jobs, starting with us in October."

"Good. That gives us six months to get everything ready for the opening in Spring of 1990. There's a lot to do, though. What do you think, Eric? Can we manage to unpack all of the products, get price tags on everything, and put the merchandise on display in that amount of time?"

"I think so."

"I'll discuss it with Sarah later, just to be sure. But originally she did tell me to set aside three months just to deal with the mer-chandise."

"It's not putting the price tags on that's the problem," Eric volunteered. "It's making attractive displays of everything. Sarah says that's very important."

"Crucial," I agreed. "But she has promised to come out here and supervise us, you know."

He grinned at me.

I handed him a collection of watercolors. "Do you mind helping me with these, Eric?"

"My pleasure, Mal."

I picked up a second pile of my paintings, and together we left the studio.

It was a boiling-hot July morning, and as we left the air-conditioned studio, a blast of warm air almost knocked me over. "It's terribly hot today," I muttered, glancing up at the hazy sky and the brilliant sun already breaking through the clouds.

"It's going to be a real scorcher by noon," Eric commented.

"The sign for the gate is going to be ready tomorrow," I told him as we walked toward the house. "One of Tom's carpenters has made it, and he's bringing it over. Then I can paint the background and our name on it: *Indian Meadows: A Country Experience.* In the meantime, let's go and find Sarah."

"She's in the kitchen, sticking her nose into all of Nora's bubbling pots. She doesn't know which jam to try first. And every time Nora gives her a new one to taste, she declares it's her favorite."

Eric had spoken the truth.

I found Sarah with Nora in front of the stove, taking small samplings of her jams and putting them on a plate.

"What do you aim to do with all of that?" I asked as I walked through the kitchen, heading for my little office at the back of the house.

"Eat it, of course," Sarah said. "On these two slices of home-made bread, also courtesy of dear Nora here. And I know, before you say it, Mal, I'll regret it later. And yes, my diet's gone to hell."

36

New York, August 1989

What I was about to do today would be difficult. But I knew it must be done, no matter what.

In a few hours I was going to stand up in a court of law and speak to the judge in the case brought by the district attorney against those who had killed my family.

I was going to tell the judge, the Honorable Elizabeth P. Donan, about Andrew and Jamie and Lissa and the pain their deaths had caused me. I was going to bare my soul to her and to everyone else who would be seated in that courtroom this morning.

And I was going to ask the judge to mete out the maximum penalty under the law. As David had said: This was my *right* as the victims' next of kin.

The four defendants had been found guilty of murder in the second degree after a trial which had lasted less than a week. There was obviously no doubt in the jurors' minds about their culpability. They had returned the guilty verdict within a couple of hours of going into deliberation.

Soon it would be my turn to say my piece, as David called it. He was going to be with me in criminal court in downtown Manhattan. So were my mother, my father, Diana, and Sarah.

Diana had flown in from London two days ago, after Detective

DeMarco had given David the date the sentencing would be held; my father had arrived early yesterday evening from Mexico, where he was currently conducting a special archaeological project for the University of California.

Everyone wished to give me moral support; they also wanted to see justice done, as I did.

"Of course I'm going to be with you," Diana had said when she had spoken to me on the phone from London over a week ago now. "It would be unthinkable for me not to be there. I lost my son and my grandchildren; I must be present. And your father feels the same way. I discussed it at length with him some time ago. This is about family, Mal, about a family standing together in a time of crisis, pain, and grief."

I had driven in from Sharon yesterday afternoon so that I could spend the evening with my family, which included Sarah, of course. Now I finished dressing in my old room at my mother's apartment. Then I went over to the mirror and stood looking at myself for a moment, seeing myself objectively for the first time in a long while. How thin my body was; I looked like a scarecrow. My face was so pale my freckles stood out markedly.

I was gaunt, almost stern in my appearance.

I was wearing a black linen suit totally unrelieved by any other color, except for my red hair, of course, which was as fiery as it always was. I wore it pulled back into a ponytail, held in place by a black silk bow. The only jewelry I had on were small pearl earrings, my gold wedding ring, and my watch.

Stepping into a pair of plain black leather pumps, I picked up my handbag and left the room.

My mother and Sarah were waiting for me in the small den with Diana, who was staying with us. The three of them were dressed in black, and like me, they looked severe, almost grim.

A moment later David walked into the room and said, "Edward should be here any minute."

My mother nodded, glanced at me, and murmured, "Your father is always very punctual."

Before I could comment, the intercom from downstairs rang. I knew it was my father.

The press was present in full force, not only outside the criminal court building on Centre Street but in the courtroom as well.

This was already packed with people when we arrived, and David hurried me down to the front row of seats. I sat between him and Sarah; in the row behind us were my mother, my father, and Diana.

I recognized the chief prosecutor from newspaper photographs and television. He was talking intently to Detective DeMarco, who inclined his head in our direction when he saw David and me. I nodded in return.

Looking around the courtroom, I suddenly stiffened; my hackles rose, prickling the back of my neck.

My eyes had come to rest on the four defendants. I stared at them.

They were seated with their attorneys, and this was the first time I had seen them in the flesh. They were neatly dressed, spruced up for this procedure, I had no doubt. I held myself very still.

Three youths and a man.

Roland Jellicoe. White. Twenty-four years old.

Pablo Rodriguez. Hispanic. Sixteen years old.

Alvin Charles. Black. Eighteen years old.

Benji Callis. Black. Fourteen years old. The gunman.

I would never forget their names.

Their names and their faces were engraved on my memory for all time.

They were the fiends who had killed my babies and my husband, and my little Trixy.

My eyes were riveted on them.

They stared back at me impassively, indifferently, as if they had done nothing wrong.

I felt as though I couldn't breathe. My heart was beating very fast. Then something erupted inside me. All of the anger I had been suppressing for months, ever since last December, spiraled up into the most overpowering rage.

My hatred took hold of me, almost brought me to my feet. I wanted to jump up, rush at them, hurt them. I wanted to destroy them as they had destroyed mine, destroyed those I loved. If I'd had a gun, I would have used it on them, I know that I would have.

This thought brought the blood rushing to my head, and I began to shake all over. Gripping my hands together, I gazed down at them, endeavoring to steady myself.

I knew I dare not look at the defendants again, not until I had done what I had come here to do today.

The court clerk was saying something about rising, and I felt David's hand under my elbow, helping me to my feet.

The judge entered and took her seat on the bench.

We all sat down.

I looked at her with curiosity. She was about fifty-five, I guessed, and she had a strong, kind face. She was quite young-looking but had prematurely silver hair.

She banged her gavel.

I fumbled around in my handbag looking for the statement I had written, peering at my words, blinded by my rage and pain, oblivious to what was going on around me.

The words I had written on the sheet of paper started to run together, and I suddenly realized my eyes were wet. I blinked and pushed back the tears. Now was not the time for tears.

A terrible pain filled my chest, and that feeling of suffocation swept over me again. I tried to breathe deeply in order to steady myself, to keep myself as calm as possible.

Then I became aware of David touching my arm, and I glanced at him. "The judge is waiting, Mal, you must go over to the podium and read your statement," he said.

All I could do was nod.

Sarah whispered, "You'll be all right," and squeezed my hand.

I rose a bit unsteadily and walked slowly to the podium which had been set up in front of the bench. I spread the paper out on the podium and stood silently before the judge. And I discovered I was quite unable to speak.

Raising my face, I looked up into hers.

She returned my gaze with one that was extremely steady; I saw the sympathy reflected in her eyes. It gave me courage.

Taking a deep breath, I began.

"Your Honor," I said, "I am here today because my husband, Andrew, my two children, Lissa and Jamie, and my little dog were all brutally killed by the defendants in this courtroom. My husband was a good man, a devoted and loving husband, father, and son. He never did harm to anyone, and he gave a great deal of himself to all those who knew him and worked with him. I know that everyone benefited from their relationships with Andrew. He made a difference in this world. But now he's dead. He was only forty-one. And my children are dead. Two harmless little innocents, six years old. Their lives have been snuffed out before they had begun. I won't see Jamie and Lissa grow up, go to college, and have careers, fulfilled lives. I will never attend their graduations or their marriages, and I will never have grandchildren. And why? Because a senseless act of violence has torn my life apart. It will never be the same again. I am facing the prolonged anguish of living without Andrew, Lissa, and Jamie. My future has been taken away from me, just as their futures were so cruelly taken away from them."

I paused and took a deep breath. "The murderers of my family have been found guilty by the jury. I ask this court to punish them for their crimes to the fullest extent of the law, Your Honor. I want justice. My mother-in-law wants justice. My parents want justice. That is all I am asking for, Your Honor. Just justice. Thank you."

I stood staring at Judge Donan.

She stared back at me. "Thank you, Mrs. Keswick," she said.

I nodded. Then I picked up the piece of paper, which I had ignored. I folded it in half and walked back to my seat.

The courtroom was totally silent. No one seemed to breathe. The only sound was the faint hum of the air-conditioning.

After a few moments staring at the papers on her desk, Judge Elizabeth P. Donan started to speak.

I closed my eyes, barely listening to her. I felt exhausted by my effort and emotionally drained. Also, the fury still raged inside me; it had taken over my whole being.

Vaguely, I heard the judge speaking of the heinous crime that had been committed, the defendants' lack of remorse for the murders of an innocent man and two children, the great loss I had suffered and my family had suffered, the senselessness of it all. I kept my eyes closed, blocking everything out for the next few minutes, trying to still that rage fulminating inside of me.

David touched my arm.

I opened my eyes and looked at him.

"The judge is about to pass sentence," he whispered.

I felt Sarah reaching for my hand, taking it in hers.

Sitting up straighter, I stared at Judge Donan, all of my senses suddenly alert.

The defendants were told to rise.

Focusing on the youngest, the gunman, the judge said: "Benji Callis, you have been tried as an adult and found guilty on three counts of murder in the second degree. I hereby sentence you to twenty-five years to life on each count of murder, each sentence to run consecutively."

She gave the other three defendants the same sentence: seventy-five years.

Judge Donan had seen to it that they received the maximum punishment under New York State law. It was exactly as Detective DeMarco and David had predicted it would be.

But for me it was somehow not enough.

In a way, I felt my family had not been properly avenged. Certainly I felt no satisfaction, only emptiness inside, and my smoldering rage.

Once the proceedings were over and the courtroom began to clear, David took me over to Detectives DeMarco and Johnson, and I thanked them for everything they had done.

Outside the criminal court building there was a barrage of newspaper photographers, television cameras, and reporters. Somehow David and my father managed to get me through the mêlée and into the waiting car.

From criminal court we sped uptown to my mother's apartment on Park Avenue for lunch. Everybody seemed as exhausted as I was, and slightly dazed. Conversation was desultory at best.

My father was coming to stay with me at Indian Meadows for a few days, before returning to Mexico City. As soon as coffee was finished, he took charge.

"I think we'd better get going, Mal," he said, rising and heading for the door of the library.

I pushed myself to my feet and followed him.

Diana also got up and put her arm around me. "You were wonderful in court, darling. You spoke so eloquently. I know it was hard for you, but I think the judge was touched by your words."

I merely nodded, hugged her, and said, "Thanks for coming, Diana, you gave me courage. Have a safe flight back to London tomorrow."

David came out into the hall. I turned and watched him walking across to me, thinking how well he looked today. Fresh-complexioned, with silver hair and light gray eyes, he was a handsome man, always well dressed. In his circles they called him the Silver Fox, because of not only his appearance but his ability, and it was deserved.

Embracing him affectionately, grateful for everything he had done for me, I said, "Thank you, David. I couldn't have gotten through this without you."

"I didn't do anything," he said with a faint smile.

"You dealt with DeMarco and Johnson, and that was a big help," I answered.

My mother came to me, kissed me, and held me longer than usual. "I'm proud of you, Mal, and Diana's right, you *were* wonderful today."

37

Connecticut, August 1989

"I thought I'd feel better after the sentencing, but I don't, I really don't, Daddy."

My father was silent for a moment, and then he said, "I know what you mean. It's a bit of a letdown in a way, anticlimactic."

"I wanted the death of my family avenged, but even consecutive twenty-five year sentences don't seem to be enough, not to me!" I exclaimed. "They might be incarcerated, but they still can see the sunlight. Andrew, Lissa, and Jamie are dead, and those bastards ought to be dead too. The Bible got it right."

"An eye for an eye, a tooth for a tooth," my father murmured quietly.

"Yes," I said.

"There's no death penalty under New York State law, Mal," my father pointed out.

"Oh, I know that, Dad, I've always known it. It's just that . . . well . . . " Leaving my sentence unfinished, I jumped up, walked to the edge of the terrace, and stood staring out across the lawns. Agitation was suddenly gripping me again, and I tried to clamp down on the feeling, to demolish it completely.

I stood very still, breathing in the beauty of the landscape. It was a lovely August evening, not too hot, with a soft breeze rustling through the trees. In the distance the foothills of the

Berkshires loomed up, lush and green against the fading sky. It was dusk. Twilight was descending, and behind the dark hills the sun had sunk low. Now burnt orange bleeding into lilac and mauve, it slowly disappeared below the horizon.

"I'd like a drink, Dad, would you?" I asked, turning around to face him.

"Yes, I would. I'll go and fix them. What would you like, Mal?"

"A vodka and tonic, please. Thanks."

Pushing himself to his feet, he nodded, then went into the sunroom heading for the kitchen.

I sat down on one of the chairs under the big white market umbrella, waiting for him to come back. I was glad that he was with me, that we had this opportunity to spend the weekend together before he went back to his project in Mexico.

My father returned within minutes, carrying a tray with the drinks on it. He sat down opposite me at the table, lifted his glass, and touched it to mine. "Chin-chin," he murmured.

"Cheers," I answered, then took a long swallow.

We sat quietly together for a few minutes, and finally I said, "I have this terrible rage bubbling inside me, Dad. It erupted yesterday in the courtroom. When I saw the defendants, I thought I would go out of my mind. I wanted to do physical damage to them, even kill them. The hatred just overwhelmed me."

"I experienced something very similar myself," my father confided. "I think we all did. After all, we were just a few feet away from the men who attacked and murdered Andrew, Lissa, and Jamie in cold blood. Wanting to strike back is a natural impulse. But, of course, we can't go around killing people. That would bring us down to their level, make animals of us all."

"I know . . . " I stopped and shook my head, frowning worriedly. "But the rage won't go away, Dad."

My father reached out, covered my hand with his. It was comforting. He said quietly, "The only way it will dissipate is if you let go of it, darling."

I stared at him, saying nothing.

After a moment, my father went on slowly, "But that's not easy. I know exactly what you're going through. You're very like me when it comes to your emotions. Sometimes you have a tendency to mask your feelings, as do I. Certainly you've been suppressing your anger for months, but it had to come out eventually."

"Yes," I agreed. "It did."

My father looked at me for a long moment, his eyes thoughtful. "And it *is* all right for you to be angry, Mal, it really is. You'd be abnormal if you weren't. However, if you allow it to, it will eat you up, destroy you. So . . . just let it go, darling, just let it go."

"How, Dad? Tell me how."

He paused, then he leaned forward and stared into my eyes. "Well, there is one thing you could do."

"There is?"

He nodded. "When we were at Kilgram Chase in May, I asked you where you had scattered the ashes, and you told me you hadn't done so. You confided that you had bought a safe and locked the ashes inside it. 'To keep them safe,' you said to me, and you added, 'Nothing can ever hurt them again.' I'm sure you remember that conversation, don't you?"

"Of course I do," I said. "You're the only person I ever told about the safe, Dad. Why I wanted it."

"And are their ashes still in the safe here? Still upstairs?"

I nodded.

"I think it's time to put your family to rest, Mal, I really do. Maybe if they're at peace, you might be able to find a little yourself. Anyway, it would be a beginning . . . "

The following morning I got up at dawn.

I had taken my father's words of the night before to heart, and in the early hours, unable to sleep, I had come to a decision.

I would do as he had suggested.

I would put my family's ashes in their final resting place. It was fitting to do so now.

I dressed quickly in a pair of cotton pants and a T-shirt, and then I went downstairs, heading for the basement. Only last week I had purchased a large metal cash box for the shops, and it was ideal for what I had in mind.

Carrying the box, I returned to my little sitting room upstairs. Putting it down on the sofa, I went into my walk-in closet. The key to the safe was in a hatbox on the top shelf; climbing up on the small stepladder, I retrieved the key, got down, and opened the safe.

First I took out Andrew's ashes and Trixy's; then I went back for the small containers that held Jamie's and Lissa's. I placed the four cans in the metal box, closed it, and took it downstairs with me.

I had always known in my heart of hearts that if I ever buried their ashes, I would put them under the ancient maple tree near my studio.

The tree was huge, with a wide, gnarled trunk and great spreading branches, and it must have been three or four hundred years old. It grew on the far side of my studio and sheltered the building from the fierce heat of the sun in the summer months, yet without blocking the light.

The tree had always been a favorite of Andrew's, as had this shady corner of the property, where we had often had picnics. The twins had loved to play near the tree; it was cool there under its leafy green canopy on those scorching hot, airless days.

I dug a deep hole under the tree.

When I had finished, I straightened, stuck the spade in the earth, and went to get the box.

Kneeling down at the edge of the grave, I placed the box in it, then paused for a moment, letting my hand rest on top of the box. I closed my eyes and pictured them all in my mind's eye.

You'll be at peace here, I said to them silently. *You're forever in my heart, my darlings, always with me. Always.*

Standing up, reaching for the spade, I began to shovel the earth on top of the box, and I did not stop until the grave was filled.

I stood there for a few moments, then I picked up the spade and went back to the house.

Later that morning I told my father what I had done.

Then I took him down to the maple tree to show him where I had buried their ashes.

"If you remember, we used to have picnics under the tree sometimes, and the twins often played here, especially when I was in the studio painting."

My father put his arm around my shoulder and held me close to him. He was visibly moved and could not speak for a few moments.

At last he said, "And there shall be in that rich earth a richer dust concealed."

I looked up at him, my eyes filling. "That's lovely . . . "

He held me tighter against his body. "Rupert Brooke."

"What's the rest of it? Do you know the whole poem, Dad?"

My father nodded. "But it doesn't really apply."

"Why not?"

"Because it's to do with a soldier's death. An English soldier's death. Rupert Brooke wrote it before he died en route to the Dardanelles in the First World War."

"But Andrew was English, and the twins were half English, Daddy. So it is appropriate. Please, I'd love to hear you recite it, the way you used to read to me."

"Well, if you really want me to."

"Please."

My father began to speak slowly, softly, and I leaned into him and closed my eyes, listening.

> *If I should die, think only this of me:*
> *That there's some corner of a foreign field*
> *That is for ever England. There shall be*
> *In that rich earth a richer dust concealed;*
> *A dust whom England bore, shaped, made aware,*

Gave, once, her flowers to love, her ways to roam,
A body of England's, breathing English air,
Washed by the rivers, blest by the suns of home.
And think, this heart, all evil shed away,
A pulse in the eternal mind, no less
Gives somewhere back the thoughts by England given;
Her sights and sounds; dreams happy as her day;
And laughter, learnt of friends; and gentleness,
In hearts at peace, under an English heaven.

38

Connecticut, August 1990

"What a stunning success you've got on your hands!" Diana exclaimed, turning to me and smiling broadly. "It's just wonderful, Mal, what you've accomplished in the first four months of being in business."

"I know, even I've been a bit surprised," I admitted. "And I couldn't have done it without your support and Mom's. And Sarah's help and advice. You've all been terrific."

"That's nice of you to say, but it's actually all due to your own hard work and inspired ideas, and let's face it, your extraordinary business acumen," Diana replied with a laugh, looking pleased. "Who'd have thought you'd turn out to be another Emma Harte?"

"Not quite, not yet," I said. "I've a long way to go."

Diana laughed again. "I like to think of you as a woman of substance for the nineties."

"Let's hope so. I'll tell you this, Diana, I do love retailing. Every aspect of it, in fact. Getting the shops here running properly has been tough, but doing it *and* getting it right has given me a lot of satisfaction."

"Meeting a challenge usually does," Diana answered. "And in my opinion there's nothing quite like hard work. It helps to take our minds off things, and certainly it gives us a great outlet for our energies. I know at the end of the day I'm ready for bed, and I fall asleep immediately, I'm so exhausted."

"I'm the same way," I said.

Diana fell silent, studied me for a moment, and then asked in a careful voice, "How are you really, darling?"

I sighed, "Well, there's not a day goes by that I don't think of them, of course, and the sadness and the grief are there, deep inside me. But I've forced myself to keep going, to function. And as we both know, being so incredibly busy works wonders."

"I learned that myself a long time ago," Diana murmured. "It was the antique shop and my business that saved my life, after Michael died. Work is a great cure-all for anyone with problems."

"Talking of work, I'd like to show you something," I said, getting up and walking across the administration office I'd created in a corner of the big red barn.

Opening one of the filing cabinets, I took out a couple of manila folders; then I returned to the seating arrangement in front of the window, where Diana and I had been having coffee.

Sitting down opposite her, I went on, "Last May at Kilgram Chase, when I had the idea of opening the shop-café, it also occurred to me that I could start a catalogue, that this would be a natural outgrowth of the shops."

"You didn't mention it," Diana said, settling back against the quilted throw pillows and crossing her legs.

"No, I didn't, because I thought you'd think I'd gone totally mad, that I was being too ambitious."

"Nobody can be too ambitious, as far as I'm concerned."

"That's true," I agreed. "Anyway, the shops have been so successful, such good money earners in such a short period of time, I've decided to go ahead with the catalogue. I've already designed it, created the mock-up. Sarah and I have done it together, and she's putting up some of her own money. We're going to be partners in this venture."

"I'm delighted to hear it, Mal. You're so close, and who better to have as a partner than your best friend? Besides which, I'm sure her input will be invaluable."

"It has been already, and she's helped tremendously with the shops as well. I thought it only fair to ask if she wanted to participate. I suggested it months ago, when I'd already started to create the catalogue, and she jumped at the opportunity."

"Is she going to leave Bergman's?"

"No. The catalogue will be a sideline for her." I joined Diana on the sofa and showed her the catalogue.

She took out her glasses, drew closer to me, then looked at the cover. This featured the red barn where the kitchen shop and the café were housed, and underneath the picture, a painting I had done especially for the catalogue. It said: *Indian Meadows,* and on the next line: *A Country Experience.* The third line read: *Spring 1991.*

"So you're not going to bring it out until next year?" Diana asked, raising a brow.

"No, it wouldn't work before then. I've got to stockpile a lot of merchandise to begin with, and then I've got to do a mailing. We've already purchased several mailing lists for key areas across the country, and Eric and Anna have compiled a local list. We'll mail out the catalogue early in January for the spring. There's a lot of planning involved when it comes to a catalogue, you know."

"I can well imagine."

I flipped open the catalogue to reveal the inside cover. "Here's a more detailed painting of the little compound of barns, the pastures, and the stables, and on the page facing is my letter telling them about Indian Meadows," I explained, and handed Diana the dummy of the catalogue, continuing, "It's divided into three comprehensive sections, as you'll see. The first is Lettice Keswick's Kitchen, featuring the jams and jellies and bottled items, as well as a good selection of products from the kitchen shop. All of the things we sell there, such as cookware, pottery, porcelain. The middle section is called Indian Meadows Boutique and offers clothing, accessories, and American quilts, that kind of thing. The last part is Kilgram Chase Gallery, presenting decorative items with an English flavor."

Diana opened the catalogue and began to look through it, exclaiming about the clever way we had presented everything. When she had perused it carefully for a few minutes, she gave it back to me and said, "I'm very impressed, Mal, very impressed indeed."

"Thank you. Mom and David thought it was pretty good, too. Very inviting, with appealing merchandise. My mother said she could buy half of the things without batting an eyelid. But come on, I want to show you two places you haven't seen yet."

"More surprises! How wonderful," Diana exclaimed, as always enthusiastic about everything I was doing.

I led her across the barn. "As you know, I divided this floor of the barn into separate areas. There's the office, where we just were, and this is the packing room," I explained, opening the door and taking her inside.

"The helpers pack everything which has to be mailed out in here, on these trestle tables. Then the packages are stacked up over there, ready for UPS, who already pick up every day."

"Do you still get a lot of orders that people want sent?"

"Yes. As you know, we've always had a good number of mail orders, ever since we opened in the spring. They have steadily increased, and that's what made me believe a catalogue would work very well."

I guided Diana next door, into one of our storage rooms. "This is where the kitchen merchandise is stored."

"And all of the Lettice jams and jellies are in the basement of the house, that I do remember," Diana added.

I nodded. "On the floor above this, which I had built last summer, we store clothing, soft toys, table linen, that kind of thing."

We strolled back to the administration office and sat down. Diana said, "You seem to have covered everything. And let me say it again, Mal. You've worked miracles here."

"Thanks, but I will need some extra storage space soon. That's my only real problem left to solve. In fact, when she arrives tomorrow, Sarah is going to talk to my neighbor, Peter Anderson."

"The stage director?"

"Yes. He owns the big pasture opposite the entrance to Indian Meadows, on the other side of the road, where there are two big barns. He doesn't use them. Sarah's hoping we can buy the land and the barns from him, but I don't think he'll sell."

"Perhaps he'll rent to you."

"We're hoping so, and if anybody can persuade a person to do something they don't want to do, it's Sarah."

An affectionate expression slid onto Diana's face. "She can charm the birds out of the trees, that's true, and I *am* fond of her; she's such a special woman."

"The best, and I don't know what I would have done without her. She's been a rock for me."

"Has she met anyone nice lately?" Diana asked.

I shook my head. "I'm afraid she hasn't. Travel the world though she does, an attractive man has remained elusive."

"I know what you mean," Diana responded, giving me a rueful little smile.

I stared at her, and before I could stop myself, I said, "Whatever happened to the man you told me about years ago, the one you thought was special? You said he was separated but not divorced, and was therefore verboten to you."

"He's still in the same situation."

"So you don't see him?"

"I do occasionally, yes. But only for business."

"Why doesn't he get a divorce, Diana?" I asked, riddled with curiosity, as I had always been about the situation.

"Religion."

"Oh, you mean he's a Roman Catholic?"

"Good God, no, not my Calvinistic Scotsman! It's his wife who's a Catholic and won't divorce him."

"Oh," I said, and fell silent, not wanting to probe any further.

Diana was also silent. She stared out the window for a second or two, her face pensive, her eyes sad. Then, rousing herself, she swung her face around to me and said quickly, "You've met him, you know."

"I have!"

"Yes, of course."

"Where?"

"In the shop, when you were in London with Andrew. In November of 1988. Robin McAllister."

"That tall, very good-looking man?" I asked, staring at her.

Diana nodded. "I was showing him some tapestries, if you recall."

"I remember him very well. He's the sort of man who leaves an impression."

"True." Diana glanced at her watch and stood up. "It's one o'clock. Shall we go and have lunch in the café? I'm feeling a bit hungry."

"Let's go!" I exclaimed, also jumping up, realizing she wanted to change the subject.

"Won't you need a lot of extra help to fulfill your catalogue orders?" Diana asked, taking a sip of her iced tea.

"Not at first, since we're doing our initial mailing in January, for the spring," I replied. "When I started the shops this year, my busy days were Friday, Saturday, and Sunday, so that leaves Monday, Tuesday, Wednesday, and Thursday for the staff to pack and wrap orders. That is, in the early spring. Everybody'll pitch in at first, and then I'll just take it from there. The summer months are obviously more difficult, and we'll have to adjust things. I'm going to play it by ear."

Glancing around, I added, "It's only Wednesday, and look, the café is already very busy."

"And you had quite a lot of people in the Kilgram Chase Gallery earlier, I noticed," Diana said. "But take it one step at a time, one day at a time, Mal, that's always been my motto."

"The thing that's surprised me is the success of the café," I said.

"It's been a hit ever since it opened. We're doing a lot of business, and people actually call up to make reservations."

"It's a charming place, with these little green tables, the fresh flowers, and all the plants scattered around. And the products on display make a statement. It reminds me of a big country kitchen," Diana remarked. "And it does smell delicious."

"The food's delicious too. You'll see in a minute."

"And Nora's doing all the cooking?" Diana asked.

"Her niece comes to help her on weekends, when it's really busy, otherwise she's alone except for Billy and Eric. Guess what is her most popular hot dish?"

"Cottage pie, recipe courtesy of Parky," Diana said, winking at me.

"Yes. And the rest of the things on the menu are quiche, soups, and sandwiches. However, she now wants to do a few salads, and I think she's right, in view of the popularity of this place. And speaking of Nora, here she comes."

Nora glided over, drew to a standstill at our table, and thrust out her hand. "Nice to see you, Mrs. Keswick."

Diana shook her hand and said, "And it's wonderful to see you, too, Nora. Quite a success you've got here. Well done, Nora, well done."

"It's all Mal," she answered quickly. "She's the brains." But nonetheless, she looked pleased. She gave Diana one of her rare smiles. "I hope you'll stop by and see my kitchen later. Now, what can I get you?" she asked, handing Diana a menu.

I said, "I'm going to have one of your pita-bread concoctions, Nora, please."

"Don't tell me. You want sliced avocado and tomato."

"However did you guess?"

Nora shook her head. "Oh, Mal, there's not a lot of nourishment in that. Let me put chicken in it as well."

"Okay," I agreed, knowing it would please her. "And I'll have another iced tea, please."

"And I'd like to have the avocado and shrimp on pita bread," Diana said. "And another iced tea, too, please, Nora."

"Back in a minute," Nora said and hurried away.

Diana asked, "Is she waiting on the tables as well, Mal?"

"No, she just wants to serve *you*. She's sort of proprietary at times, possessive, especially with the family."

Diana smiled. "She's always been very devoted. And who's Iris, the young woman who looks after the house now? She seems awfully pleasant. She couldn't do enough for me this morning."

"That's Nora's other niece. Iris's sister, Rose, is the one who helps out in the kitchen on weekends. I had—" I broke off as Eric came hurrying toward the table, carrying the tray of iced teas.

"Here we are, Mal, Mrs. Keswick," he said, giving us each a glass.

We both thanked him.

He half turned to go back to the cash register, which he had made his station, but hesitated.

"What is it, Eric?" I asked, looking up at him.

"Sorry to trouble you now, Mal, when you're at lunch. But I've just had a call from one of our customers, a Mrs. Henley. She wants to know whether or not we do private parties."

I frowned. "Do you mean catering?"

"No. She wants to have a private party here. In the café. A sweet-sixteen party for her daughter and the daughter's young friends."

"When?"

"In September. On a Friday night."

"Oh, I don't know, I don't think so, Eric, that's bound to be a busy time, people will want to come in for cold drinks—"

"Don't say no quite so quickly," Diana interrupted, putting her hand on my arm. "It could be quite profitable to have private parties, and it helps to get the place better known than it is already."

Eric bestowed a huge smile on Diana. "I agree with you, Mrs. Keswick."

"All right, Eric, tell the lady yes, but that you'll have to get back to her about the cost."

"I will, Mal," he said, giving me a little salute, which was a new habit of his, before he disappeared.

"I do like him," Diana said to me. "He's the salt of the earth."

"Just like Joe, Wilf, and Ben," I said.

After we had eaten our pita-bread sandwiches, I sat back in the chair, regarding Diana for a moment. Finally, I said, "I have a proposition for you."

"You do! How wonderful!" she exclaimed, then paused and viewed me intently. "I thought you didn't want any partners."

"I don't, in the shops. But this is something else."

"Well, it can't be the catalogue. Sarah's your partner in that."

"It's an idea I had months ago, but I've only just managed to think it through properly," I explained. "I want to start a small publishing company, and I'd like you to become my partner in it."

Leaning back in her chair, her head on one side, my mother-in-law studied me for a moment or two, then asked, "Isn't publishing rather dicey?"

"I think it can be, yes. But I'm talking about a small country press, publishing only a few specialty books, for sale only through my catalogue and here in the shops."

"It sounds interesting, Mal, but don't you think you have enough on your plate at the moment?"

"I am doing a lot, that's true, Diana. But I'm not thinking of starting the publishing company until next year, and I'm not asking you to put up any money."

"Oh, I see. But you *did* say you had a proposition for me."

"I do. I'd like you to become my partner, as I said, publishing only four books to begin with, in fact, we might never publish anymore, after that."

"Which books?" she asked, giving me a speculative look.

"Your books, Diana. The two Lettice Keswick diaries, her cookbook, and her garden book. Later we might do Clarissa's Victorian cookbook, but I'm not sure. If we went ahead, I would publish the Lettice diaries first, then her cookbook, and finally her garden book. It would be a special series, and therein lies its appeal, in my opinion. Eventually, once they'd all been published, the series could become a boxed set, a gift item. I really think it'll work."

"Where *will* you get the money? You say you don't want it from me."

"Only because I don't think I'll need very much," I pointed out. "Look, you own the books, and you're going to give me the rights. I can type up her text and do copies of her drawings. My only cost will be the printer and the bindery."

"I'm willing to give it to you."

"Thanks, Diana, but by the time I do it next year, I may well be able to finance the publishing project myself."

"Whatever you want. But in any case, I think the idea is brilliant, Mal! Just brilliant! I'd love to be involved. In any way you want."

I reached out and squeezed her hand. "Thanks. By the way, I'm going to call it Kilgram Chase Press. Is that all right with you?"

"I love it! How clever you are, darling." She stared at me for a moment, and then she began to shake her head wonderingly. "What I said earlier is perfectly true, Mal. You *are* going to be a woman of substance for the nineties."

39

Connecticut, May 1992

I lay in bed, staring at the clock in the dim light of the room. I could see that it was only four-thirty.

I had awakened sooner than I usually did. Although I was an early riser, and always had been, I generally slept until six. Lingering in bed for a while, I let myself drift with my thoughts. Then I remembered what day it was: Monday, the fourth of May. My thirty-seventh birthday. *Thirty-seven.* That didn't seem possible, but it was true.

Sliding out of bed, I went to a window, opened a blind, and stood peering out. It was still dark. But far off, beyond the trees and the wetlands, the horizon was tinged with a green luminescence, and wisps of pale light were trickling up into the sky. Soon it would be dawn.

Walking into my little sitting room next door, I sat down and stared at my painting of Lissa and Jamie, then my eyes automatically swung to Andrew's portrait above the fireplace.

Though my grief was held in check, my sorrow contained, my longing for them had not lessened. There was an aching void inside and, at times, moments of genuine despair. And busy though I was with Indian Meadows, loneliness was a familiar companion.

Last year I had finally found the courage to sort through

Jamie's and Lissa's clothes and toys. I had given everything away—to Nora's family, Anna's friend, and the church. But I had been unable to part with my children's two favorite possessions, Oliver, Lissa's teddy bear, and Derry, Jamie's dinosaur.

Going to the bookshelves, I took down these well-cuddled toys and buried my face in their softness. Memories of my children momentarily overwhelmed me. My throat suddenly ached, and I felt the rush of tears. Blinking them away, I took firm hold of myself, placed the toys in their places, and went into the adjoining bathroom.

After pinning up my hair under a cap, I took a quick shower. A few minutes later, as I toweled myself dry, I found myself glancing at the corner of the bathtub near the taps, as I frequently did. I had never found my art knife, after it had vanished the night I planned to kill myself. What had happened to it? It was a mystery, just as the empty tub and the open kitchen door were also mysteries.

Recently I had confided in Sarah, who had listened to me attentively.

When I had finished my tale, she had been silent for a moment or two, and then she had said, "I'm sure there's a logical explanation for these things, but I like to think it was something inexplicable, like a special kind of intervention, or perhaps the house itself looking after you."

Sarah and I had long agreed that there was an especially wonderful atmosphere in the house these days. It seemed to us that it was more benign and loving than it had ever been, and there was an extraordinary sense of peacefulness within its old walls.

"It's a house full of loving, friendly ghosts, just as Andrew once said," Sarah had murmured to me only last weekend. We had stared at each other knowingly then, as we realized we were thinking the same thing: Andrew, Jamie, and Lissa were present in the house, for it was alive with our memories of them.

Once I had dressed in my usual working clothes of jeans, a T-shirt, jacket, and penny loafers, I went downstairs.

After putting on the coffee, I drank a glass of water, picked up the bunch of keys for the shops, and went outside. I stood looking around, breathing the air. It was fresh, redolent of dew-laden grass and green growing things; the scent of lilac planted around the house wafted to me on the light breeze.

It was going to be a pretty day, I could tell that. The sky was clear, unblemished by clouds, and it was already pleasantly mild.

As I struck out toward the ridge, a bevy of small brown birds flew up into the sky, wheeling and turning into the haze of blueness soaring above me. I heard their twittering and chirping as I walked, and in the distance there was the *honk-honk* of Canada geese.

Since I had plenty of time this morning before opening up the shops, I sat down on the wrought-iron seat under the apple tree. Like the lilacs, this too was beginning to bloom, bursting with green leaves and delicate little white buds. Soon it would be in full flower.

Mommy's Place. That was what Andrew had always called this spot. I settled back against the seat and closed my eyes, and I heard their voices clear and resonant, saw their images so vividly in my head. They were here with me, as always. Safe in my heart.

This was the fourth birthday I had spent without Andrew and the twins. I knew from past experience that it would be a sad day for me, just as their birthdays and special holidays were always tinged with sorrow, hard for me to bear without them.

And yet despite my pain and loneliness, I had managed to go on living. One day I had finally come to understand that no one could really help me or do it for me. I had to find my courage myself.

To do this I had reached deep inside myself, gone to the very core of my being, the center of my psyche, and there I had found hidden resources, a strength I had never known existed in me. And it was this strength of character, and a determination to start anew, to make some sort of life for myself, that had propelled me forward, brought me to where I stood today.

Perhaps it was not the best place, but given the circumstances of my life, it was a good place to be. I was healthy mentally and physically; I had managed to open a business, become self-supporting, pay off my debts, and keep the house I loved. I had even been able to reduce the loans from my parents, Diana, and David. By the end of the summer I would retire the loans in full, I was certain of that.

You're making it, Mal, I said under my breath. You're not doing badly at all.

I got to my feet and went down the hill toward the compound of barns. As I drew closer, I noticed that the pond was alive with wildlife this morning, mostly the mallard ducks and a few geese. Later in the summer the blue heron would come and pay us a visit, as it usually did. We had all grown attached to it, awaited its arrival eagerly. And brief though its stay was, we loved having it with us. It had become a sort of mascot, and I was thinking of using the name Blue Heron for another label, a line of locally crafted baby clothes.

Unlocking the door of Lettice Keswick's Kitchen, the café-shop, I went inside and was instantly greeted by the delicious smells of apples and cinnamon.

Switching on the light, I stood in the doorway for a second, admiring the café. Painted white, with dark beams floating above, it had a new floor of terra-cotta tile, so much easier to keep clean, we had discovered, and bright red-and-white checked curtains at the few small windows. It was fresh, cheerful, and inviting, with many green plants everywhere and metal shelving filled with our specialties.

Walking forward, I let my eyes roam over some of the shelves stocked to the hilt with jars and bottles of the Lettice items. Marvelous jams and jellies—apple and ginger, rhubarb and orange, plum and apple, apricot, blackberry and apple, pear and raspberry. There were jars of mincemeat, lemon curd, chutneys, pickled onions, red cabbage, beets, and walnuts, and Piccalilli, a mustard pickle which was a favorite of mine and which originally hailed from Yorkshire.

Also, we carried a small selection of pastas, wild rice, and cous-cous, imported English biscuits, and French chocolates. And Nora's pasta sauces, recent additions.

She had turned out to be something of a miracle in the kitchen, and had found her true vocation. Aside from the pasta sauces, mostly with a tomato base, she made all of the other Lettice products in our own café kitchen. I was very proud of her and of her cooking.

The Lettice Keswick line had caught on quickly, become a huge success here in the shop and in the catalogue. The latter, which Sarah and I had started seventeen months ago, had been another big hit, so much so we were both still reeling.

Only last week I had had to hire three new employees to work in the packing and dispatching department; Eric had taken on two new waiters for the café, since I had just promoted him. He had become the manager of the shops and the café and was now in charge of the twelve other people who worked at Indian Meadows.

Pushing open the kitchen door, I glanced inside. Everything shone brightly in the early-morning sunlight; I nodded to myself, went on upstairs, gave the cookware and tabletop shop a cursory glance, and headed back to the main floor.

Once outside again, I paid a visit to the Indian Meadows Boutique, unlocked the door, looked inside quickly, and then progressed to the Kilgram Chase Gallery.

Although I loved all of my shops and all of my products, in a funny sort of way this little gallery was my favorite. Perhaps this was because it was reminiscent of Yorkshire and Andrew's child-hood home. In any case, it had been well patronized so far, and it was hard for me to keep the merchandise in stock. Everything was sold before I could turn around to order more.

The gallery's biggest hit, though, had been and still was *Lettice Keswick's Journal,* published under my Kilgram Chase Press imprint last summer. In the year it had been out, it had sold almost thirty-five thousand copies in the gallery and through the catalogue. Sarah told me that her friends in publishing in New

York were quite astounded, although they were admiring of the book and found it fascinating. Apparently so did everyone else.

Once more, I gave the gallery only a cursory glance and, closing the door behind me, made my way back to the house. Things down here were in good order; at seven Anna would be floating around, at nine Eric and Nora would arrive, and by nine-thirty the rest of the workers would be here.

As I walked up the hill, I told myself yet again how lucky I had been with the business. Every different project had worked well here. Each of the shops was a success; all of our products were popular; the catalogue just grew and grew; and the café was a runaway success with locals and strangers alike. Whenever I mentioned the word *lucky* to Sarah, she would guffaw loudly. "If you call working twelve to fourteen hours a day, seven days a week for over two years *lucky,* then yes, you have been," she would exclaim. "Mal, you've made Indian Meadows the success it is because you've worked nonstop around the clock, and because you have tremendous business sense. You're one of the smartest retailers I've ever met."

Of course she was right in certain ways. I had poured all of my energy and drive into Indian Meadows, and I had been highly focused. Tunnel vision had turned out to be a handy asset to have.

But despite all of the hard work, not only on my part, but on the part of the entire staff, I still believed in the element of luck. Everyone needed a bit of it, whatever the business or artistic venture.

When I got back to the house, I stopped at one of the white lilac trees and broke off a small branch. I carried it into the kitchen. I filled an old jam jar with water, tore off stems of the lilac, and arranged them in the jar, then I carried the jar outside.

I made for the huge maple tree near my studio, where I had buried my family's ashes on August 19, 1989. Kneeling down, I removed the jar of drooping flowers from within the small circle of stones I had arranged three years ago and replaced it with the jar of lilacs.

I knelt there for a moment, staring down at the flat paving stone made of granite, which I had placed there in October of that same year.

Engraved upon its dark surface were their names.

Andrew, Lissa, and Jamie Keswick. And Trixy Keswick, their beloved pet. And underneath was the date of their murders, *December 11, 1988,* and below the date were those beautiful words of Rupert Brooke's, which my father had recited to me the morning I had laid them to rest:

"*There shall be in that rich earth a richer dust concealed.*"

"Happy birthday, Mal," Nora said, coming into the kitchen.

"Thanks, Nora," I answered, swinging around.

She came forward, gave me a quick hug, and then stepped away.

Eric, who was behind her, said, "Happy birthday, Mal," and thrust a big bunch of flowers at me. "We thought you'd like these, your favorites."

"Thank you so much, it's so sweet of you both." I took them from him, hugged him, and lowered my face to smell the white lilac, tulips, narcissi, and daffodils wrapped in cellophane paper and tied with a big yellow bow. "They're beautiful. I'll put them in water."

"No, I'll do that!" Nora exclaimed, taking them from me before I could protest and marching over to the sink.

Turning to Eric, I said, "Would you like a cup of coffee?"

He shook his head. "No, thanks, though. I should get down to the café, I'm running a bit late this morning."

"Yes, you'd better do that," I shot back. "Otherwise the boss might be mad at you."

He grinned, saluted, and hurried out.

Nora stood at the sink, arranging the flowers.

I sat down at the kitchen table and took a sip of my second cup of coffee.

Nora said, "I see you mother's car is out front. Did she stay over last night?"

"Yes, she did. She wanted to be here for my birthday today. Sarah took Mr. Nelson back to the city."

"I'm glad they were all here yesterday for lunch . . . it was nice, wasn't it?"

"Yes, thanks to you and all the lovely things you made."

"Oh, I didn't do much, Mal," she murmured. "Anyway, it was my pleasure."

"I thought I'd bring my mother down to the café at about twelve-thirty today, Nora. After lunch she's got to drive back to New York."

"Can I make you something special?"

I shook my head. "My mother loves your Cobb salad, and so do I. Why don't we have that?"

"No problem." She pushed the last spray of lilac into the vase she had found on the draining board, swung her head, and asked, "Where do you want me to put these?"

"In the sunroom, I think, since I spend so much time there."

She carried the vase of the flowers away, came back to the kitchen, poured herself a cup of coffee, and stood drinking it near the sink. After a moment she said, "I liked that woman your father brought by yesterday. Miss Reece-Jones. Is he going to marry her?"

I shrugged. "Don't ask me, Nora, I've no idea."

"Pity, if he doesn't. They seem well suited."

"I think they are." I studied her over the rim of my mug. Nora had always had a way of zeroing in on people, making quick and accurate assessments of them. She was rarely wrong.

After rinsing out the mug, she said, "Got to get down to the café kitchen. See you later, Mal."

"Thanks again for the flowers, Nora. It was so thoughtful of you and Eric."

She nodded. "Try and have a nice day," she said quietly, then hurried out.

*   *   *

Over lunch at the café, I said to my mother, "Do you think Dad will marry Gwenny?"

My mother stared at me for the longest moment before answering. Finally, she said, "No, I don't think he will. But I wish he would. She's very nice."

"Yes, she is, everyone seems to like her. But why do you think he won't get married?"

My mother bit her lip, looked reflective for a moment, then she said slowly, choosing her words with care, "Because your father's a bachelor at heart."

"Oh, so it's nothing to do with Gwenny, you just think he prefers to be single?"

"Put succinctly, yes."

"But he was married to you."

"True, but he was never there—" She cut off her sentence and gave me an odd look.

"Dad wants his cake, and he wants to eat it too, is that what you're trying to say, Mom?"

"No, I'm not, actually. I don't mean to imply that your father is a womanizer, or that he's promiscuous, because he's neither. He's just . . . a bachelor at heart, as I told you a minute ago. He prefers to be on his own, free to roam the world, digging about in ancient ruins, doing as he pleases. He's a bit of a loner, you know. If some woman comes along, and he likes her, well, then, I suppose he gets involved. But basically, he doesn't want to be tied down. I think that sums it up."

"I see. Well, I guess *you* should know," I murmured, pushing my fork into the Cobb salad.

My mother watched me for a moment or two and then said, "Yes, I really *do* know all about your father, Mallory, and perhaps now is the time to discuss my marriage to him. I know it's bothered you for years, I mean, the fact that we separated when we did."

"No, not that, Mom, not that at all! I don't understand why

Dad was always away when I was a child growing up. Or why we didn't go with him."

A small sigh escaped her. "Because he didn't really want us to go along on his digs, and anyway, as you got older you had to go to school. Here in the States. He insisted you were educated here, and so did I, to be truthful."

"So he went away on these extended trips for his work, and came back when he felt like it. How could you put up with that, Mom?"

"I loved him. And actually, Edward loved me, and he loved you, Mal, he really did. You were the apple of his eye. Look, I strove very hard to hold our marriage together, and for a very long time."

"You say he went off on his digs, and I understand. After all, that's his work. But there were other women when I was little, weren't there?"

"Eventually," she admitted.

I confided in her then. I told her about my memories of that Fourth of July weekend so long ago, when I had been a little girl of five; told her how that awful scene in the kitchen and their terrible quarrel had stayed with me all these years. Buried for so long because it was so painful and only recently resurrected, jolted into my consciousness four years ago.

She listened and made no comment when I finished.

My mother simply sat there silently, looking numb and far away, gazing past me into space.

At last she said, in a low, saddened voice, "A friend, I should say a so-called friend, told me Edward was having an affair with Mercedes Sorrell, the actress. I'm ashamed to admit that I believed her. I was young, vulnerable. Poor excuses. But anyway, I became accusatory, vile, really, and verbally abusive to your father. You remember that only too well, it seems. It was jealousy, of course. Later I discovered that it wasn't true. It had been a lie."

"But there *were* other women, Mom," I persisted. "You said that yourself."

"I suppose there were sometimes, when he was away on a dig for six months or longer. But it was me he loved."

"And that's why you stayed with him all those years?"

She nodded. "Anyway, your father fought hard against the separation, resisted it for a long time, Mal."

"He did?" I said, my eyes opening wider. I stared at her.

My mother stared back.

"Don't sound so surprised," she said after a second's pause. "And yes, he did resist the separation; what's more, he never wanted a divorce. Not only that, we continued to have a relationship for a long time after we separated."

"Do you mean *sexual?*" I asked, pinning her with my eyes.

She nodded, looked suddenly slightly embarrassed.

"Mother, you didn't!"

"I'm afraid so. In fact, your father and I remained involved with each other, off and on, until I met David."

"Good God!"

"Mal, I *still* love your father, in a certain way. But I knew years ago that he and I could never be happily married."

"Why not? Obviously you continued to sleep with him for years after you split up. You could have fooled me; you always behaved as if he didn't exist."

"I know. A defense mechanism, I'm sure. Why couldn't I be happily married to him? Possibly because I don't want to be with a man who has to wander the earth. Endlessly."

"You could have wandered with him, after I'd grown up."

"It wouldn't have worked, not in the long run."

"But you did have a strong sexual bond—"

"We did. But sex doesn't necessarily make a successful marriage, Mallory. There are so many other factors involved. Your father and I couldn't have made it work, take my word for it."

"Oh, I do, Mom," I said, and I reached out and squeezed her hand. "I've wanted to say this for a long time. Mother, thanks for always being there for me. I know Dad never was."

"In his own way, he was, Mallory. Believe that."

"If you say so, I do, and I love him, Mom, and I love you too, and lately I've come to understand, that I'm quite separate from your marriage. What I mean is, I'm outside your personal relationship with him. What went on between you and Dad never had anything to do with me."

"That's right. It was just between us."

"When I look back on my childhood, I realize that we were a dysfunctional family . . . " My voice trailed away; I looked down at my plate, then at her.

My mother sat there waiting, as if she expected me to say more.

I shifted slightly in my chair, cleared my throat, then took a sip of iced tea. I felt slightly uncomfortable.

Eventually, I said, "I hope you don't mind me saying this, Mom."

"No, I guess not. Actually, if I'm honest, I have to admit it's the truth."

"We *were* a dysfunctional family, and let's face it, I *did* have an odd childhood. I think that's why I wanted to have the perfect family when I got married. I wanted to be the perfect wife to Andrew, the perfect mother to Jamie and Lissa. I wanted it all to be . . . to be . . . *right* . . . "

"It was, Mal, it really was. You were the best wife, the best mother."

I looked at her intently. "I did make them happy, didn't I, Mom?"

Her fingers tightened on mine, "Oh, yes, Mal, you did."

40

It was a cold Saturday morning at the beginning of the month. The first snap of frost was in the air, after a mild October of Indian-summer weather. But nonetheless, it was a sparkling day, sunny, with a bright blue sky.

We were always busy at Indian Meadows on the weekends, but this glorious day had brought out more people than usual.

All of the shops were busy, and I was glad we had plenty of merchandise in stock. In the summer I had done a lot of heavy buying, anticipating brisk business over the holiday season. Thankfully, I had been right. If today was any kind of yardstick, then at Thanksgiving and Christmas we would be setting records.

I walked across from the Kilgram Chase Gallery to the café, and when I pushed open the door, I was startled. The place was already full, and it was only midmorning. I hovered in the doorway, looking for Eric. When I caught his eye, he hurried over.

"What a morning," he said. "We're busier than ever in here. Am I relieved we made that second parking lot down by the front gate. It's come in handy today." He grinned at me. "You were right, as usual."

"It didn't cost much, and I do believe we're here to stay, Eric."

"Have you ever had any doubts, Mal?"

I shook my head. "Have you heard from Sarah?"

"No. Why, is there a problem?"

"Probably not, but she hasn't arrived. When she phoned me from the city last night, she said she'd be leaving at six-thirty this morning, that way she'd miss the traffic and be here by nine." I checked my watch. "It's almost eleven."

"She may have been late leaving New York," he responded.

"Perhaps."

"Try not to worry, Mal."

I nodded. "I will. I'll be in the office if you need me," I said. I went out and walked over to the other red barn.

Ever since my family had been killed, I worried excessively if someone close to me was overdue. I just couldn't help it. And in any case, we lived in a dangerous world these days, one more dangerous than it had ever been, in my opinion. Carjacking was a common occurrence, guns had proliferated on the streets to such an extent it was mind-boggling, and the murder of innocent people had become the norm. Every time I picked up a newspaper or turned on the television there was some new horror that chilled me to the bone.

"Mal! Mal!"

I pivoted, saw Anna hurrying toward me.

"Can you spare me a few minutes?" she asked as she drew to a standstill.

"Sure, let's go into the office," I answered, pushing open the door to lead the way.

After we had shed our coats, we headed for the seating arrangement near the window. "Do you have some sort of problem, Anna?" I asked, sitting down on the sofa.

"No, I don't, Mal, but Sandy Farnsworth called me last night," she explained, seating herself opposite me. "She wants to sell Pony Traders. She asked me to ask you if you'd be interested in buying the company."

"No, I wouldn't," I said without hesitation. "I've expected this coming for a while now, Anna. Sandy's sort of hinted at it before. But I don't want to become a manufacturer, which is basically what they are, even if some of their items are handmade." I shook my head. "No way, Anna, too many headaches. I'm afraid I have to pass."

"I more or less indicated to Sandy that you wouldn't be interested," Anna replied. "I happen to agree with you, and I'm sure Sarah will too. But I promised to pass it by you."

"I understand. Has Sandy indicated what she's going to do? I mean, if she can't sell it? Will she continue the business?"

"I suppose she'll have to, or find herself a new partner. Lois Geery is moving back to Chicago, and that's what this is all about. I guess she wants to pull her money out of the company."

"If Pony Traders goes out of business, we're going to have to find a replacement, another manufacturer who makes their kind of casual country clothes," I pointed out. "I know we have Billie Girl and Lassoo, but we'll need a third."

Anna smiled at me. "I've already thought about that, Mal, and I've started to research it. I'll have a couple of new vendors for us by next week."

The door flew open, and Sarah came bounding in, much to my relief. She was looking harried and windswept.

"What a morning!" she exclaimed. "I'm sorry I'm so late, Mal. I hope you haven't been too worried."

"A little," I admitted. "And what happened to you, Sash? You look a bit disheveled, and you have a smudge on your face."

"I do? I wonder if it was there before? Oh, well, never mind. And what happened is that I had a flat."

"Oh, God, how awful for you, Sarah," Anna said as she got up. "I'd better get back to the boutique, Mal. See you both later."

"I'll be over soon," I answered.

Sarah smiled at her and said to me, "I could really use a cup of coffee, Mal. Shall we go to the café?"

"It's very busy, but Eric will find us a spot. Come on."

We hurried out after Anna.

*   *   *

"How did you manage to change your tire?" I asked as we sipped our coffee a few minutes later, tucked away in a corner of the café near the kitchen.

"I had help, thank God."

"Oh." I looked at her curiously. "Where were you when your tire blew?"

"On Route 41. Just down the road," Sarah explained, grinning at me.

"What's so amusing?" I asked.

"The encounter I had."

"When you blew the tire?"

"Yes, you see it occurred outside a house. Fortuitously for me, as it turned out, otherwise I'd still be sitting there with a flat. It was a small Cape Cod behind a white picket fence, and I went and knocked on the door. I asked the man who opened it if he would mind helping me, and he said he would be glad to. We changed the tire together. Mind you, Mal, he did most of the work. Anyway, while we were working, I managed to find out quite a lot about him. Including his telephone number."

"So he was attractive, Sash?"

"Not bad, not bad at all." Sarah paused, gave me an odd look, and added, "I asked him to dinner."

"You didn't!"

"Yes, I did."

"When?"

"Tonight."

"Sash!"

"Don't say *Sash* in that tone of voice, Mal. And I think it was a great idea."

"But Sash, *tonight*."

"What's wrong with tonight? You can't say we don't have any food, because this place is stuffed with it."

"That's true."

"Listen, why not have him over? He lives close by, and we don't have many attractive men for neighbors, in fact, none at all, at least none who are available."

"There's Peter Anderson," I reminded her.

"Mr. Lousy Big Shot!" she exclaimed. "He's a pain in the ass. He's strung me along for over two years about those damned barns of his, and now he's finally said no. He doesn't want to sell after all, he says. Not nice, Mal."

"He's a funny bird, I must admit. Eric told me he's had all kinds of tragedies in the last few years. In any case, we're managing all right, and we can always put up another ready-made barn down near the new parking lot, should we need it."

"I suppose so. But Peter's really disappointed me. He seemed so pleasant at first."

"What's his name? The man who's coming to dinner."

"Richard Markson."

I sat back, frowning, and took a sip of my coffee. "It's strange, Sash, but his name sounds familiar. I wonder if I've met him?"

She shook her head vehemently. "No, you haven't. I asked him. He's quite a well-known journalist, and he does a lot of television, so that's probably why you know his name."

"What kind of journalism?" I asked, always wary.

"Political stuff, mainly."

"What time is he coming?"

"I said eight, but I can make it later if you prefer, Mal. I said I'd call to confirm the time."

"Eight is fine. Now, about dinner. We can take one of Nora's cottage pies up to the house, and a container of her chicken bouillon with vegetables. We can make a green salad, there's a Brie cheese and fruit. How does that sound?"

"Great, Mal. The only thing you've forgotten is a loaf of Nora's homemade bread."

I must admit, I liked Richard Markson the moment he walked into the house.

He was a tall man, well built but by no means heavy, with dark brown eyes, dark wavy hair, and a pleasant face.

Almost immediately his presence seemed to fill the house. He was obviously self-possessed and at ease anywhere. Yet he had a quiet demeanor, and his reserved manner appealed to me.

"This is Richard Markson, Mal," Sarah said, bringing him into the kitchen where I was filling a bucket with ice. "Richard, meet my very best friend, Mallory Keswick."

"Thanks for having me on such short notice," he said as we shook hands. "And it's very nice to meet you, Mrs. Keswick."

"Please call me Mal, and I'm happy to meet you, and to welcome you to my home."

He smiled, glancing around. "It looks like a lovely place, and I must say, I'm very partial to these old colonials, they have such charm, as do the old farmhouses in Connecticut."

"Yes, they do. What would you like to drink, Mr. Markson?"

"A glass of white wine, thank you, and I hope you're going to call me Richard."

I nodded and carried the bucket of ice to the hutch, which generally served as a bar. "What about you, Sash? What are you going to have?"

"Me? Oh, I don't know. White wine, I guess. Is there a bottle in the fridge?"

"Yes," I said over my shoulder and took out three wine glasses.

"Let me do that," Richard said to Sarah when he saw her struggling with the corkscrew, and a split second later he brought the bottle of wine to me. "Here you are, Mal."

"Thanks," I said, then filled the glasses. "Let's go to the small den. It's cozy there. Sarah lit a fire a while ago, since it's turned so chilly tonight."

Once we were settled in front of the blazing fire, Richard lifted his glass and toasted the two of us.

"Cheers," Sarah and I said in unison, and then we all settled back in our chairs and fell silent.

It was Richard who spoke first. Later I came to realize that he was very good at breaking the ice, making people feel comfortable. Perhaps that was part of his great success as a journalist.

Looking at me, he said, "What a fantastic success you've made of Indian Meadows. It's great for us all, none of us knows how we could manage without it now."

"Oh, so you do use the shops, do you?" Sarah said, a brow lifting.

"Certainly do. I bought all of my Christmas gifts here last year, and I fully intend to do the same again. I'm frequently over here browsing around."

"Funny, we've never seen you," Sarah murmured.

I said, "It's nice to meet a satisfied customer. You are, aren't you?"

"Very much so," Richard assured me, smiling. He took a swallow of wine and went on, "And I love Nora and her cooking. To tell you the truth, I don't know what I'd do without her. I buy most of my meals from the café take-out—her soups, her salads, and that delicious cottage pie."

Sarah and I exchanged dismayed glances, and before I could say a word, she exclaimed, "It's a good thing you *do* like it, because that's what you're getting for dinner tonight. Nora's chicken soup and cottage pie."

"Oh," he said. "Oh, that's great. *Great.* As I said, I am her biggest fan."

"I could make something else, spaghetti primavera, if you like!" I suggested swiftly, feeling embarrassed.

"No, don't be silly. The cottage pie's wonderful."

"Bet you had that last night?" Sarah said, making it sound like a question."

"No, I didn't!" Richard protested, and then he broke off. His mouth twitched and he started to laugh. Glancing at me he shrugged. "But honestly, I don't mind eating it again."

The expression on his face was so comical I found myself laughing with him. Between chuckles, I said to Sarah, "We're going to have to start cooking again. We don't have much choice."

"You're right, Mally," she replied, gazing at me for the longest moment.

Richard asked me more questions about Indian Meadows, how I had come to start the shops, and I told him.

He mentioned the Lettice diary and confided how fascinating he had found it.

Sarah listened to us talking, occasionally joined in, went and got the bottle of wine from the kitchen, and kept filling our glasses.

At one moment she came back from the kitchen and said, "I've put the cottage pie in the oven," and pulled a funny face. We all laughed.

Later, when I went into the kitchen myself to check on things, Sarah followed me. "I can do it, really I can," I said. "Go and keep Richard company."

"He's all right, he's looking at the books on the bookshelves. Listen, I want to tell you something."

She sounded so peculiar, I turned around to face her. "What is it?"

"It's lovely to hear you laugh again, Mal. I haven't heard you laugh in years. That's all I wanted to say."

I stood there returning her loving gaze, and I realized that she had spoken the truth.

As it turned out, laughter was the keynote of the evening.

Richard Markson had a quick wit and a good sense of humor, as did Sarah, and their repartee was fast and furious. At one moment they were so amusing I found myself chortling yet again, and so much so I had to stop serving the cottage pie for fear of spilling it.

I sat down at the table for a second, letting my laughter subside, and I looked from one to the other, thinking how well matched they seemed. It struck me that he was the nicest man Sarah had brought around in a long time, and it was quite apparent that he liked her a lot. And why wouldn't he? My Sashy was beautiful and smart, kind and loving, and quite irresistible at times, like tonight. She was inimitable.

Rising, I went back to the oven and brought out the cottage pie again.

Sarah said, "Why don't you put the dish in the middle of table, Mal? We'll help ourselves."

"Good idea," Richard agreed.

I did as Sarah suggested and sat down.

After taking a sip of wine, I watched as Richard served himself, then stuck his fork into the pie on his plate. How awful that Sash and I hadn't been more inventive with the dinner. But how could we have known that he was a regular customer of the take-out kitchen? I began to eat, and a bit later, when I glanced at him out of the corner of my eye, I noticed that he was relishing the pie.

It was over the Brie cheese and green salad that Sarah zeroed in on him. Leaning back in her chair, she asked in an offhand way, "How long have you had a weekend place up here, Richard?"

"Just over a year."

"Your Cape Cod looks very charming from the outside. Do you own it?"

He shook his head. "No, it's a rental. Kathy Sands found it for me, and she's—"

"Kathy was our real estate broker for Indian Meadows," I cut in. "She's a terrific woman, don't you think?"

He smiled. "Yes, she is, and I started to say that she's been looking for a house for me to buy, but the houses are all far too big for me."

"Oh, so you live alone then, do you?" Sarah asked, throwing him a quizzical look.

"I'm single," he said. "And I certainly don't want a large house to roam around in alone."

"That's understandable," Sarah murmured. "I'd feel the same. But of course I come here every weekend to be with Mal." There was a little pause before she said, "I've never been married, have you?"

"No, I haven't," he said. "I've roamed the world as a journalist, been a foreign correspondent until recently, and I guess I was always too involved with my job to think of settling down. I came back to the States three years ago and took a job with *Newsweek*." He pursed his lips, gave a half shrug. "I decided I'd had enough of foreign places. I wanted to come back home to little old New York."

"Are you a New Yorker?" I asked.

"Born and bred. You are too, aren't you, Mal? And you, Sarah?"

"Yes," I answered. "We are."

"We've been friends since we were babies," Sarah informed him, laughing. "Actually, you could say we've been inseparable since our prams. Anyway, what brought you up to this neck of the woods for weekends?"

"I was a boarder at the Kent School before I went to Yale, and I've always loved it up here. To my way of thinking, the northwestern highlands of Connecticut are God's own country."

41

Connecticut, January 1993

The night I met Richard I was quite certain it was Sarah he was interested in, not me. But within a few weeks of knowing him, he had made it absolutely clear he was drawn to me. He liked Sarah as a person, he said, found her delightful, in fact, but that was as far as it went.

I was so taken aback, I found myself stuttering that she was going to be hurt and upset. Richard assured me otherwise; he pointed out that she had no interest in him either.

This, too, had amazed me; after all, she was my oldest and dearest friend. I knew her intimately, as well as I knew myself. I was quite convinced he was wrong in his reading of her.

But he was right.

When I asked Sarah about Richard, she admitted he was not her type. "A nice man, too nice, Mal," were her words. "I've got a horrible feeling I always fall for the rats like Tommy Preston."

Once I recovered from my surprise, I found myself agreeing to go on seeing him. But I did so cautiously. I realized it would take a long time for me to allow him into my life. I had been alone for four years now, and I saw no reason to change the situation.

But as Sarah said, Richard was a nice man, warm, kind, and thoughtful, and he did make me laugh. That dry humor of his constantly brought a smile to my face, and I discovered I looked forward to seeing him on Friday or Saturday, or sometimes Sunday, when he came up for weekends. And yet, for all that, I did withhold part of myself.

I think he knew it, of course. He was too astute not to understand that I was afraid of a relationship, in many ways.

He knew all about me and what had happened to my family. He had never come out and said so, had merely alluded to it. But he was a newspaperman, and a very good one, and he had been living in London in December of 1988. The murders of my husband and children had made headlines there, as well as here.

One of the things I liked about Richard was his sensitivity. On a Saturday evening in January, when I had known him for about three months, I came across him in the sunroom, looking at a framed photograph of Jamie and Lissa.

He held it in both of his hands and was gazing at it intently; there was such a tender look on his face I was touched.

I came in on him unawares, and he looked startled and embarrassed when he saw me. Swiftly he put the photograph back on the table, and still looking uncomfortable, he gave me a small, almost shy smile. He seemed about to say something, then he stopped.

"Say it," I said, walking over to him. "It's all right, really. Say what you're thinking, Richard."

"How beautiful they were . . . "

"Yes, they were. I used to call them my little Botticelli angels, and they were just that. They were adorable, mischievous, naturally, at times, but very bright and funny and . . . just great. They were *great*, Richard."

He reached out, put a hand on my arm gently. "It must have been . . . hard for you, heartbreaking . . . I'm sure it still is."

"Excruciating at times, and I suppose it always will be. But I've learned to go on living somehow."

A troubled expression flickered in his eyes as he said, "Look, I'm sorry, Mal, sorry you caught me staring at their picture. The last thing I want to do is cause you pain by making you talk about them."

"Oh, but it doesn't cause me pain," I said quickly. "I love to talk about them. Actually, most people think like you do, and they avoid mentioning Jamie and Lissa. But I want to reminisce about them, because by doing so it helps to keep them both alive. My children were born, they existed on this planet for six years. And they were such joyous little beings, gave me so much love and pleasure, I want to keep on remembering them, sharing my memories with my family and friends. I know I always will."

"I understand, and I'm glad you've confided in me, Mal," he said, "that you've shared this. It's important to me. I want to get to know you better."

"I've been very damaged," I murmured and went and sat on the sofa.

He took the chair facing me and said, "You're very brave."

"I'm very fragile. There are parts of me that are breakable, Richard."

"I know that, Mal. I'll be careful . . . I'll handle with care, I promise."

It seemed to me that after this discussion we drew a bit closer, but not that much, because *I* would not permit it. Deep down I was afraid of getting involved with him on an emotional level, if indeed I was capable of such a thing. I wasn't sure that I was.

But as the weeks passed and we continued to see each other when he came up on the weekends, the relationship did develop, and we kept discovering new things we had in common.

He had seen the grave under the old maple tree down by my studio, although I had never shown it to him. Perhaps Sarah had. In any case, one lovely April day he brought me a bunch of violets and asked me to put them on the grave. "For Andrew and the children," he said.

This was yet another thoughtful gesture on his part, and it moved me enormously.

After this I began to relax a little, to trust him even more, at least on a certain level. But the barriers I had erected were hard to scale, even harder to break down. As I found myself more and more drawn to him physically, I discovered I was still unable to open up my heart to him.

It was Sarah who pointed out to me how involved with me Richard was, but I pooh-poohed the idea.

"We like each other, we find each other attractive, we enjoy being together. In lots of ways. "But that's all there is to it, Sash. We're just good friends."

She gave me a skeptical look and changed the subject, drew me into a discussion about the catalogue and some of the new items we were including.

Much later on that particular April Saturday, as I got ready for bed, I thought about her words again. And I was convinced she was wrong about him, that she was exaggerating. Loving me as she did, Sarah wanted me to be happy, and in her opinion Richard Markson was part of the answer to that. But she was off track. He *was* a lovely man, I was the first to say so, but I know I could never care for him in the way he deserved. It just wasn't possible.

In May Richard came to see me on the morning of my thirty-eighth birthday, and I was very surprised to see him. It fell on a Tuesday this year, and he was the last person I expected to see strolling over to join me on the wrought-iron seat under the apple tree at eight o'clock in the morning.

"Why aren't you in New York? At work?" I exclaimed as he came and sat down next to me.

"Because I've taken the week off to prepare an outline for a book."

"You're going to write the Great American Novel?"

"No, a nonfiction book." He smiled at me. "Anyway, Mal, this is for you. Happy birthday." He leaned closer and kissed me. "I hope you like it."

"I'm sure I will." I looked at him and smiled, and opened my gift. "Oh, Richard how lovely of you to think of this!" I exclaimed. "Thank you so much." I sat staring at the dark red leather binding of *Collected Poems* by Rupert Brooke. Opening it, I looked inside, slowly turning the pages. "What a beautiful volume. Where on earth did you find it?"

"At an antiquarian bookshop in New York. It's quite old, as you can see. May I have it for a moment, please, Mal?"

"Of course." I handed it to him.

He leafed through the book, found the page he wanted, and said, "This is one of my favorites, Mal. Can I read a few lines to you?"

"Yes, please do."

> *In your arms was still delight,*
> *Quiet as a street at night;*
> *And thoughts of you, I do remember,*
> *Were green leaves in a darkened chamber,*
> *Were dark clouds in a moonless sky. . . .*

Richard stopped, and no words came for a moment.

I said quietly, "How lovely . . . "

"And here are just a few more lines from the same poem, Mal, and again I think they are very fitting." He touched my cheek and smiled that shy smile of his, then read from the book again.

> *Wisdom slept within your hair,*
> *And long suffering was there,*
> *And, in the flowing of your dress,*
> *Undiscerning tenderness.*

I didn't speak for a moment; I just sat there quietly, and then I said, "Thank you, Richard, not only for my birthday present, but for sharing with me."

"Can I take you out to supper tonight?" he asked, leaning back against the seat. "We could go to the West Street Grill in Litchfield."

"Thank you, I'd love that."

"See you later, then," he answered, looking pleased. "I'll pick you up about seven," he added, pushed himself to his feet and walked off briskly.

I watched him go, and then I looked down at the book in my hands and began to turn the pages, reading fragments of poems.

Later that week, on Friday morning, the boxes of books arrived from my printer, and I immediately called Richard. "The second volume of Lettice Keswick's diary has just arrived. Hundreds of them," I told him. "And since you're a fan of her writing, I'd like you to have one of the first copies."

"Thanks, Mal, that's great," he said. "When shall I come over for it?"

"Right now, if you like. I'll give you a cup of coffee."

"See you in half an hour," he replied and hung up.

When he arrived I led him into the sunroom. "I have coffee waiting, and the book for you. I hope you like it. I think they've done a good job, but I'm curious to have your opinion."

It took Richard only a few minutes to peruse the diary and tell me I had another success on my hands. "The layout is beautifully designed, for one thing, and the couple of pages I've read hold up. I suppose the entire diary is of the same high standard?"

"Very much so. It's such a marvelous record of everyday life in England in the seventeenth century. They were very like us, had the same hopes and dreams, troubles and worries."

"People haven't changed much over the centuries," he remarked, putting the book down on the table. "And you certainly stumbled on something very special when you found these."

"There are two more books," I confided.

"Diaries?" he said, looking slightly startled. "Don't tell me you have more of these treasures?"

I shook my head. "No, I don't, unfortunately, because the diaries are the best things she wrote. But I have her garden book and her cookbook, and I plan to publish those next."

"I think Kilgram Chase Press is going to be in business for quite a while," Richard said, smiling at me.

I shrugged. "I hope."

After drinking his coffee, Richard asked, "What's the garden book like?"

"Interesting, because her plans for the gardens at Kilgram Chase are very detailed, as are her lists of the plants, flowers, and trees. But I don't think it will have the same appeal."

"It might. People are very much into gardens these days, Mal. Look at the success of the Russell Page book on his gardens, and Gertrude Jekyll and her writings."

"Maybe you're right."

"Are there many illustrations?"

"Yes, I'll have to start copying them soon."

He laughed. "*Lettice Keswick's Garden Book* might turn out to be just as big a hit as the first diary. And this—" He tapped it and continued, "I'd like to give this to our book editor at the magazine, if you don't mind."

"No, that's fine. I'll get you another copy before you leave," I said.

We sat drinking our coffee and chatting for a few minutes, mostly about Kilgram Chase Press and books in general. I surprised myself when I said, "I once did a book, Richard."

A look of interest flashed across his face. "Was it published?" he asked.

I shook my head. "It's a special kind of book."

"Do you have it here, Mal?"

"Yes. Would you like to see it?"

"I'd love to. I must admit, I'm very intrigued."

I nodded and hurried out of the sunroom.

I was back within a few minutes. "Actually there are two books," I said. "I wrote and illustrated them for Jamie and Lissa. I was going to put them in their Christmas stockings, but of course they were dead by then."

"Oh, Mal," he said, and his dark eyes looked stricken.

"One is called *The Friends Who Live in the Wall,* and the other is *The Friends Who Live in the Wall Have a Tea Party*. Well, here have a look," I said, handing them both to him.

Richard sat for a long time poring over the books. Finally, when he put the second book down, he had the strangest expression on his face.

"What is it? What's wrong? I asked, staring hard at him.

He shook his head. "Nothing. But Mal, these books are extraordinary, just beautiful. They're enchanting, so imaginative, and your paintings are superb. You *are* going to publish them, surely?"

"Oh, no, I couldn't! I could never do that! I wrote them for my children. They're ... they're sort of *sacred*. The books were for Jamie and Lissa, and that's the way I want to keep it."

"Oh, Mal, you can't. Not something like these little . . . masterpieces. Small children will love them, and think of the joy and pleasure they'll give."

"No!" I exclaimed. "I can't, I won't publish them, Richard. Don't you understand?" I repeated shrilly, staring at him. "They're sacred."

"What a pity you feel that way," he said quietly.

"Maybe one day," I murmured, suddenly wanting to mollify him.

"I hope so," he said.

I lifted the books from the coffee table and wrapped my arms around them possessively. "I'll just put them away, I'll be back in a moment." I hurried upstairs.

As I laid the books away in the cupboard and locked the door, I suddenly wondered why I had shown them to Richard Markson. Only Andrew and Sarah had ever seen them. I had kept them hidden away for over four years. I hadn't even taken them out for Diana or my mother.

Why did I show him something so personal, so intimate, so meaningful? I asked myself as I went back downstairs to the sunroom. I had no answers for myself. In fact, I was quite baffled.

42

When he left for Bosnia, Richard had said he would be gone for
ten days.

But in fact he had been away for almost the entire month. He
had been scrupulous about calling me, and in a way I had been
grateful to hear from him, to know that he was all right. But at the
same time I felt I was being put on the spot.

Whenever he phoned me from Sarajevo, I became self-conscious,
almost tongue-tied, certain that he was expecting an answer to the
proposal he had made before he left.

I cannot give him one.

I was still ambivalent about my feelings for him. I liked him,
cared for him, in fact. After all, he was a good man, and in the ten
months I had known him he had proved to me that he was a good
friend. Then again, we were compatible, had common interests
and enjoyed being together. Yet to me that was not enough for
marriage, or even a trial marriage, as he suggested.

I am afraid—afraid of commitment, attachment, bonding,
intimacy on a daily basis. And ultimately I'm afraid of love. What
if I fell in love with Richard, and then he left me? Or died? Or was
killed doing his job? Where would I be then? I couldn't bear to suffer the loss of a man again.

And if I did marry him, as he wanted me to, and did so without loving him, there was still the possibility, no, the probability, of children. How could I ever have other children? Lissa and Jamie had been so . . . perfect.

This was how my mind was turning this morning, as I walked toward the ridge carrying a mug of black coffee. I lifted my eyes and looked up at the sky as I usually did.

It was a murky morning, overcast, and rain threatened up in the hills. Yet the sky was a curious color, etiolated, so bleached-out it looked almost white. No thunderheads rumbled above; nonetheless, the air was heavy and thick, and I sensed that the weather was going to break after a blistering August. Anyway, we needed the rain.

Sitting down under the old apple tree, I sipped my coffee and let my eyes roam around. They rested briefly on the cluster of red barns, now my compound of little shops, and I felt a small swell of pride as I thought of their great success. Then my gaze moved on to scrutinize the long meadow, finally settling on the pond. Mallard ducks and Canada geese clustered around the edge; and on the far bank the blue heron stood there proudly on its tall legs, a most elegant bird. My heart missed a beat. It was a welcome sight.

I smiled to myself. We had waited all summer long for the blue heron to pay us a visit. It had been sadly absent, but here it was this morning, looking as if it had never been away.

After finishing my coffee, I sat back, closed my eyes, and let myself sink down into my thoughts. Hardly a few minutes had passed when I knew what I must do, knew what my answer to Richard must be.

No.

I would tell him no and send him away.

Besides, what use to him was a woman who could not love again? A woman in love with her dead husband?

"Life is for the living," I heard Diana's voice saying, somewhere in the back of my mind.

I pushed that voice to one side, trampled on the thought. I

would send Richard Markson away, as I had always known I would.

But perhaps he had already gone away of his own accord. I had not heard a word from him for well over a week now. In fact, he had stopped calling me on a regular basis once he'd quit Bosnia.

He had stayed in that war-torn country for ten days, as he had always intended to do. And then he had moved on, had flown to Paris. It was his favorite city, he had told me when he had phoned. He had worked there once, as Paris correspondent for *The New York Times*, and he had loved every minute of his four-year stay in France. Four years was a long time. He undoubtedly had many friends there.

Maybe Bosnia and Paris had cured him of me.

Maybe I wouldn't have to reject him after all.

That would certainly be a relief, if I didn't have to tell him no to his face, if he just stayed away and never came back, or if he let our relationship peter out.

Maybe he had picked up with an old flame. That would be a relief, too. Wouldn't it?

"Hello, Mal."

I sat up with a jerk, so startled I dropped the coffee mug I was holding. It rolled across the grass and disappeared over the edge of the hill.

Speechlessly I gaped at him.

"I'm sorry if I took you by surprise," Richard said, towering over me.

"You made me jump, scared me!" I exclaimed. Taking a deep breath, I asked, "And where did you spring from?"

"My car. I parked over by the house."

"No, I meant when did you get back from Paris?"

"Last night. I drove straight up here from Kennedy. I was going to call you, but it was late. So I decided to come and see you in person this morning." He paused, looked at me closely. "How are you, Mal?"

"I'm fine," I replied. "And you?"

"Great," he said. "But I could use a cup of coffee. Shall we go to the café?"

I dangled the bunch of keys in front of his nose. "Not open yet. It's only eight-thirty. I was just on my way to unlock the doors."

"Oh, God, I'm on Paris time . . . for me it's already the afternoon."

"Come on," I said, "Walk me to the shops. I'll open up, and then we can come back to the house for that cup of coffee."

"It's a deal," he said, and stretched out his hand.

I took it, and he pulled me to my feet.

We walked down the hill in silence. Once we were at the bottom, I opened up the café, the Indian Meadows Boutique, and the Kilgram Chase Gallery, and pocketed the keys.

"That's it," I said. "Let's head for the kitchen. I'll make you some breakfast, if you like. How do scrambled eggs and English muffins sound?"

"Terrific!"

I smiled at him and then moved away from the cluster of barns, heading for the house.

"Mal."

I stopped and turned around.

Richard was still standing near the gallery door.

"What's the matter?" I asked.

Shaking his head, he hurried over to me. "Nothing's the matter. I just wondered . . . " He stopped. "Do you have an answer for me, Mal?"

I didn't say anything at first, having no wish to hurt him. Then I murmured slowly, quietly, "No, Richard, I don't."

He stood staring at me.

"That's not true. I do," I corrected myself. "I can't marry you, Richard. I can't. I'm sorry."

"And you won't live with me? Try that?"

I shook my head, biting my lip. He looked so crestfallen I could hardly bear it.

Richard said, "You know, Mal, I fell in love with you the first moment I saw you. And I don't mean the night ten months ago when I came to dinner, that day I helped Sarah change her tire. I mean when I *first* saw you, the *first* time I came to Indian Meadows. You were unaware of me; we never met. You just bowled me over. I wanted to be introduced to you, but one of my friends in Sharon said you were . . . off limits."

"Oh," I said, surprised.

"Finally meeting you, getting to know you, being with you all these months has been the best thing that's ever happened to me. I love you, Mal."

I stood there looking at him. I was silent.

"Don't you care for me at all?" he asked in a low voice.

"Of course I care about you, Richard, and I worried about you when you were in Bosnia. I worried about stray bullets and air raids and bombs and you getting killed."

"Then why won't you take a chance with me?"

"I . . . just . . . can't. I'm sorry." I turned away. "Let's go up to the house and have coffee," I mumbled.

He made no response. He just walked along by the side of me, saying not one word.

We went up the hill slowly.

I looked at him out of the corner of my eye, saw the tight set of his clenched jaw, the muscle beating on his temple, and something inside me crumbled. My resistance to him fell away. My heart went out to him in his misery. I felt his pain as acutely as if it were my own. And I knew then that I did truly care for him. I had missed him. I had worried about him. I was relieved he was here, unhurt and in one piece. Yes, I cared.

"Andrew wouldn't want me to be alone," I muttered, thinking out loud.

Richard made no comment.

We walked on.

Again I spoke. I said, "Andrew wouldn't want me to be alone, would he?"

"No, I don't think he would," Richard said.

I took a deep breath. "I'm not sure about marriage, not yet. It scares me. But, well ... maybe we could try living together." I slipped my hand into his. "Here at Indian Meadows."

He stopped dead in his tracks. And so did I.

Taking hold of my shoulders, he turned me to face him. "Mal, do you really mean it?"

"Yes," I said in a voice so low it was almost inaudible. Then more firmly, "Yes, I do. But you'll have to be patient with me, give me time."

"I've got all the time in the world for you, Mal, all the time you want."

He leaned into me, kissed me lightly on the lips. Then he said, "I know you're very fragile, that pieces of you are breakable. I promise to be careful."

I nodded.

"And there's something else," he began and stopped.

"Yes?"

"I understand that you've had a terrible loss. But you have everything to gain with me—"

"I know that," I said, and remembering Diana's words, I added, "My life. The future—if I have the courage to take it."

"You're the bravest person I know, Mal."

We went on walking up the hill, passed the old apple tree and the wrought-iron bench, heading for the front door. Richard put his arm around my shoulders as we crossed the wide green lawn.

I looked up at him.

He returned my gaze with one equally as steady and smiled at me.

As we went into the house together he drew me closer to him, his hand firm on my shoulder.

For the first time since Andrew's death I felt safe. And I knew that everything was going to be all right.